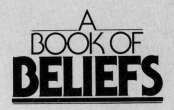

A BOOK OF BELIEFS

A BOOK OF BELIEFS

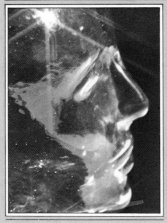

JOHN ALLAN
JOHN BUTTERWORTH
MYRTLE LANGLEY

A LION BOOK

Originally published in three volumes
A Book of Beliefs: Religions
A Book of Beliefs: Cults and New Faiths
A Book of Beliefs: Mysteries
Copyright © 1981 Lion Publishing

Published by
Lion Publishing plc
Icknield Way, Tring, Herts, England
ISBN 0 85648 504 7
Albatross Books Pty Ltd
PO Box 320, Sutherland, NSW 2232, Australia
ISBN 0 86760 264 3

First edition 1981
This one-volume paperback edition 1983
Reprinted 1984
Reprinted 1985

Printed by New Interlitho SPA, Italy

ACKNOWLEDGEMENTS

The photographs in this book are reproduced by permission of the following photographers and organizations:

Religions

Australian News and Information Bureau 11(right below)
Barnaby's Picture Library 16, 24(left), 26–27(centre), 31(above centre), 32–33(above), 34–35(above right, below), 43(right), 44–45(both), 54–55(centre)
J. Allan Cash 26(below), 38–39(background)
Church Missionary Society 60(below)
Douglas Dickins 12–13(above), 20(below left)
Mary Evans Picture Library 24(above left)
Fritz Fankhauser 8–9(centre), 18–19, 21(below right), 40–41(below), 48, 51(above)
Werner Forman Archive 6–7, 11(right above)
Sonia Halliday Photographs 50–51(left)
Hamlyn Group Picture Library 33(below), 42(left)
Michael Holford 24(right), 27(right)
Alan Hutchison Library 10–11(background), 12(below), 14(above), 17(above), 20–21(centre), 23(below), 30–31(background), 31(above left), 36–37(background), 52–53(both), 54(below), 56–57(both)
Lion Publishing: Jon Willcocks, title page, 4–5
Tony Cambio 46–47(below)
Macquitty International Collection 28–29(centre)
Mansell Collection 15(above), 49
Wulf Metz 20(below right)
Ann and Bury Peerless 17(below), 32(below), 36(left), 38–39(centre)
Picturepoint 47(above)
Axel Poignant 8(left)
Popperfoto 29(right), 38–39(below)
TEAR Fund 51(below)
John Topham Picture Library 12(above left), 15(below), 22–23(left and centre), 25, 31(above right), 42(right), 55(right), 60–61(background)
Victoria and Albert Museum 14(below)

Cults and New Faiths

Associated Press 94–95(both)
Barnaby's Picture Library 87, 88–89
Bisonte Archive 121(right)
Camera Press 68–69, 74–75, 102–103
E. J. Cardell 110–111(above all)
Mary Evans Picture Library 80, 81, 112–113(all)
Philip Hainsworth 108–109(all), 110–111(below)
Keystone Press 76–77(below), 83, 84–85, 102(left), 118(left), 120–121, 124–125
Peter Langford 90(picture in brooch)
Lion Publishing: Jon Willcocks, title page, 66–67, 72(below), 73(above), 78–79, 90–91, 104–105, 114–115, 122–123
Mansell Collection 72(above), 96–97(below)
Polydor Records 91, 99(right)
Popperfoto 70–71, 96(centre), 100, 101
Radio Times Hulton Picture Library 73(below), 98–99
David Redfern 118–119
Syndication International 76(above), 86
John Topham Picture Library 82

Mysteries

Barnaby's Picture Library 169(right), 183, 186–187(below)
Camera Press 146–147, 162–163(centre)
John H. Cutten 150–151(above), 153(right)
Daily Telegraph Picture Library 143(right)
Barry Kirk 144–145
Mary Evans Picture Library 151(above), 158–159(below), 172–173(centre); Harry Price Collection (University of London) 162(left), 176(left), 187(above); Society for Psychical Research 154–155
Fortean Picture Library 134(left), 135(right), 136–137(both), 176–177(right), 178–179
Alan Hutchison Library 164–165
Keystone Press 152–153(centre), 174–175(both), 185
Frank Lane Picture Library 134–135(centre)
Lion Publishing: Jon Willcocks, title page, 130–131, 132–133, 138–139, 166–167, 170–171(both)
Mansell Collection 140–141, 172(left), 184
Linda Mindel 156–157
Popperfoto 148–149(centre), 163(right), 188–189
Science Photo Library 142–143(below and centre)
Souvenir Press 182(left)
Syndication International 168–169(centre)
The Times Picture Library 160–161
John Topham Picture Library 147(right), 149(below), 158(above), 161(right), 180–181, 182(right)

INTRODUCTION

Suddenly, it seems, our age of science and technology has become an age of new religions. There is worldwide interest in every sort of cult, folk religion and superstition, as well as new study of old religions.

Is this a re-discovery of old magic and ancient values, a new spirituality? Are the cults and religions true – true to life as it is, true to life as it ought to be? Or are they dangerous delusions, a flight from reason into fantasy and unreality?

It is urgent that we understand what the claims of the new beliefs really are. This book aims to help. It gives an over-view of a wide range of beliefs, some mainstream, some freaky. The aim of the pictures is to get across something of their appeal and emotional impact. The text describes the key features of the faith or phenomenon, asking questions where necessary.

It is hoped that the book will serve, not just as a 'consumer's guide', but a valuable source of advice, help and objective description.

CONTENTS

MYSTERIES

RELIGIONS

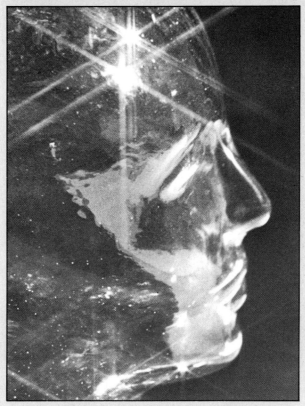

MYRTLE LANGLEY

INTRODUCING RELIGION

This is a brief illustrated introduction to the world's great religions. I have tried to present the essence of a large and complex subject, as interestingly, as simply, and as concisely as possible. The task has been both fascinating and rewarding.

For those of you who want some idea of what religion is and how I approach the subject, there is a short introductory chapter. It may well not be of interest to everyone. You may want to skim quickly and return to it later. For those who want to know what I believe and why, there is a short epilogue. I am unashamedly a follower of Jesus Christ, finding him to be without equal and beyond compare.

Having said this, I must add that I deeply respect the longings and aspirations of the founders and followers of the world's great religions. I seek to treat each religion fairly and with sympathy, letting each speak for itself and making no attempt either to interpret or to compare.

MYRTLE S. LANGLEY

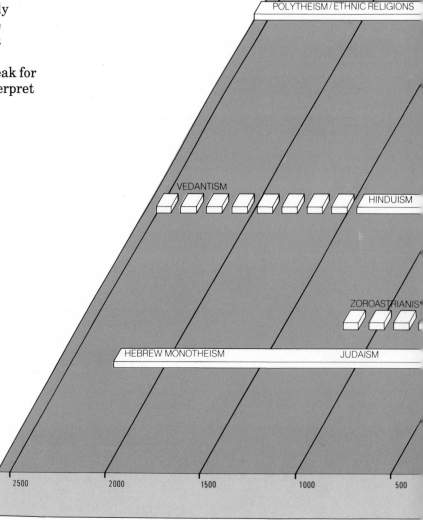

TWO TRADITIONS

This study of religions makes no attempt to draw comparisons. But there is one distinction which it is helpful to point out. The world's religions divide into two very different groups: the Western prophetic tradition and the Eastern salvationist or mystical tradition.

The Western tradition

Springs from a parent Semitic group.

Includes Judaism, Christianity, Islam and their offshoots.

Prophetic, emphasizing the revelation of God to men from outside the human spirit.

'World-affirming', accepting the essential goodness of the material, and seeking the redemption or transformation of this sinful world.

The Eastern tradition

Springs from a parent Indian root.

Includes Hinduism, Buddhism and their offshoots.

Mystical, emphasizing the finding of God by men from within the human spirit.

'World-denying', accepting the essentially spiritual nature of reality, and seeking release for the soul from the endless round of rebirth or reincarnation to which it is subjected in this world.

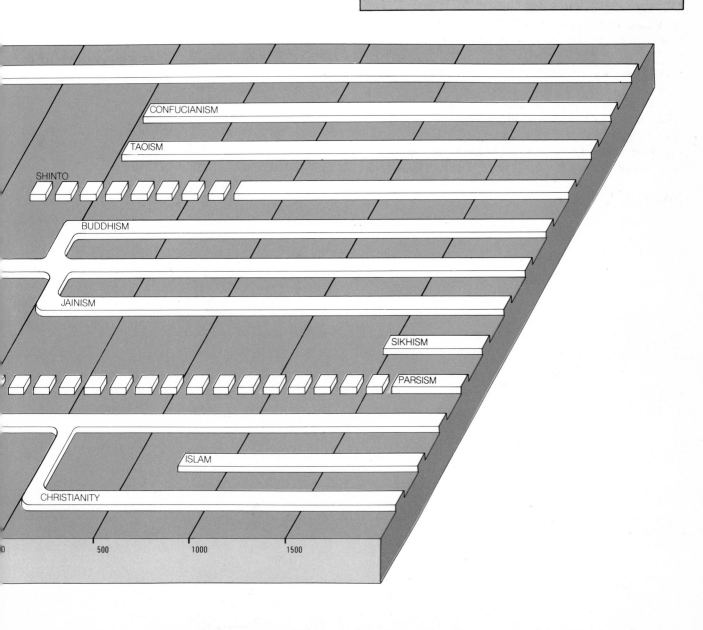

INTRODUCING RELIGION

Studying religion

No definition of religion can be entirely adequate. The Latin *religio*, from which our English word comes, originally meant reverence for the gods, or simply superstition. But it certainly means much more than that. It is helpful to look at any religion in terms of several aspects or 'dimensions', which concern the beliefs of the religion, its practices, and the way it affects the individual and society.

Religion has at least six dimensions. Which dimension we place first depends on whether we see religion primarily as what people believe or as what they do. Westerners tend to emphasize beliefs. But, a 'religious person' is still thought of as someone who practises his religion.

"RELIGION IS..."

Religion is
'the flight of the alone to the Alone'.
Plotinus

Religion is
'what a man does with his solitariness'.
A. N. Whitehead

'Men create the gods in their own image.'
Xenophanes

'One religion is as true as another.'
Robert Burton

'We must have religion for religion's sake ...
Victor Cousin

'You have created us for Yourself, and our heart is restless until it comes to rest in You.'
St Augustine of Hippo (354–430), the great leader of the early African Church

SIX DIMENSIONS

Religion has been looked at in at least six dimensions.

Doctrine A belief system which gives a total explanation of reality.

Myth Stories about God and the gods, creation and salvation, and events of historical significance. (Myth is not fiction.)

Ethics Values and codes of behaviour.

Ritual Worship, festivals, 'rites of passage' and initiations, and customs regulating food and dress.

Experience The individual's experience of the awe-inspiring and the transcendent, or a sense of belonging and commitment to something greater than the self.

Social The institutional organization of people to practise their religion.

'Religion is the sigh of the oppressed creature, the feeling of a heartless world, and the soul of soulless circumstances. It is the opium of the people.

'The abolition of religion as the illusory happiness of the people is the demand for their real happiness. The demand to give up the illusions about their condition is a demand to give up a condition that requires illusion.'

Karl Marx (1818–1883)

'Religion would then be the universal obsessional neurosis of humanity; like the obsessional neurosis of children . . . If this view is right, it is to be supposed that a turning-away from religion is bound to occur with the fatal inevitability of a process of growth . . .'

Sigmund Freud (1856–1939), founder of psycho-analysis

'If religion has given birth to all that is essential to society, it is because society is the soul of religion.'

Emile Durkheim (1858–1917), founder of modern sociology

Religion has 'its own independent roots in the hidden depths of the spirit itself'.

Rudolf Otto (1869–1937)

What is religion?

'Religion' is the response of human beings to the human condition. Faced with the difficulties of living in this world, we develop an understanding of our universe and our existence, so that life takes on purpose and significance.

To some people, religion is 'true' simply in terms of its usefulness. Emile Durkheim, the founder of modern sociology, considered that religion performed an essential function in society. Others, looking at religion in terms of its origins, say that it is nothing more than an escape-fantasy. Freud called it 'an illusion'. Karl Marx called it 'a sigh of oppression'.

To others again, religion is seen as man's best argument for the existence of God. Augustine saw this in what he called our 'restlessness of heart'. Rudolf Otto saw it in the 'sense of the awe-inspiring', the 'numinous'.

ETHNIC RELIGIONS

For the people of the world's small-scale ethnic societies, there is no distinction between religion and the rest of life.

In Africa, the Americas and Australasia live some 250 million people who belong to 'traditional', 'pre-literate', 'small-scale' or 'tribal' societies. For them 'religion' is almost the same thing as 'culture', or, as one African author has put it, 'all of life is religious'.

Religion has been defined as the unique attempt of each society to express the meaning of its existence. Often, people's environment is hostile: cyclones blow, thunderstorms rage and volcanoes erupt; nations go to war; and famine and disease, poverty and oppression disturb the balance of living. So their religion provides people with a framework within which to come to terms with their environment and to give their experience meaning.

Ethnic religions are the religions of small-scale pre-literate societies. They have no religious writings or scriptures. Instead, beliefs are handed down by word of mouth from one generation to another. Many of these societies have resisted for centuries the advancing world religions of Hinduism, Buddhism, Christianity and Islam. Others have accepted the new religions at one level and at another, deeper level, have persisted in the ways of their forefathers. This has led to mixed religions (syncretism), such as the Christianity of Mexico, the Hinduism of Bali, the Islam of Malaysia, the spirit-possession cults of South America and the Caribbean, some of the independent and spirit churches of Africa, and the cargo cults of Melanesia. ☞

Small-scale societies include the islanders of Papua New Guinea and Indonesia, the tribal hill peoples of India, China and South-east Asia, the remaining pockets of Amerindians in North America, the Eskimos, the Indians of the river valleys, forests and plateaux of South and Central America and, above all, more than 800 ethnic groups on the African continent.

AN AFRICAN PRAYER

O God, you are great,
You are the one who created me,
    I have no other.
God, you are in the heavens,
    You are the only One:
Now my child is sick,
    And you will grant me my desire.

Bali, in the Indonesian archipelago, is a small volcanic island of extraordinary beauty. The Balinese live on the slopes of active volcanoes, and their main temple, Besakih, lies half-way up the 9,000 ft/275 m high Gunung Agung. The Balinese believe that this is the dwelling-place of Shiva, the Hindu god of destruction. In 1963 the volcano erupted during a major festival. The people tried to appease the wrath of their god by kneeling down and praying in the path of the lava flow.

ETHNIC RELIGIONS

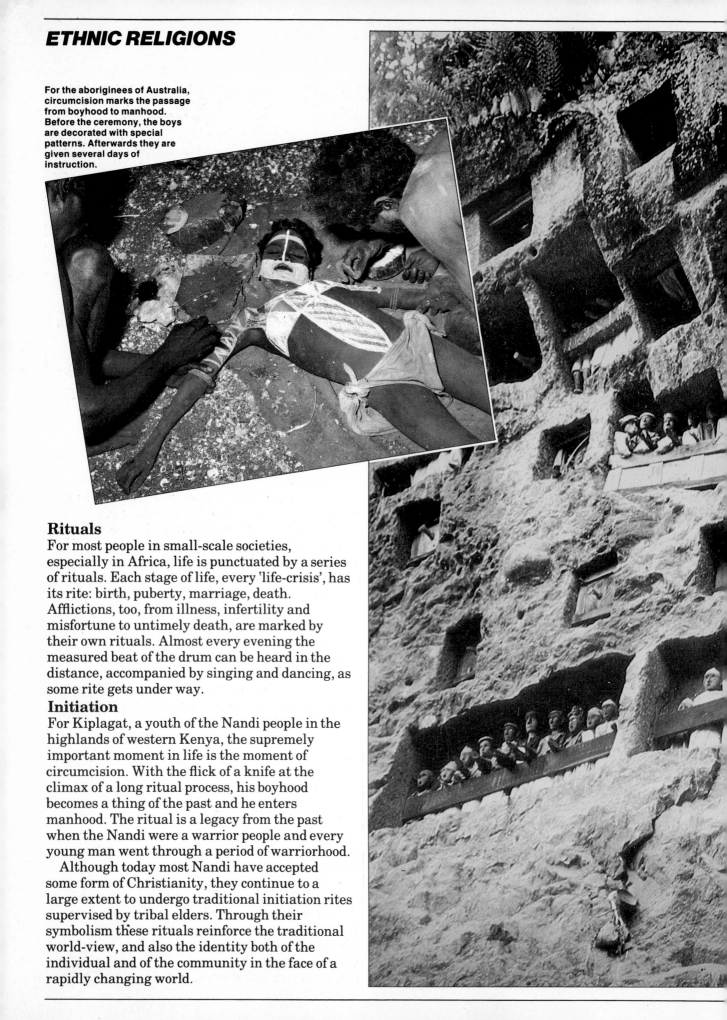

For the aboriginees of Australia, circumcision marks the passage from boyhood to manhood. Before the ceremony, the boys are decorated with special patterns. Afterwards they are given several days of instruction.

Rituals

For most people in small-scale societies, especially in Africa, life is punctuated by a series of rituals. Each stage of life, every 'life-crisis', has its rite: birth, puberty, marriage, death. Afflictions, too, from illness, infertility and misfortune to untimely death, are marked by their own rituals. Almost every evening the measured beat of the drum can be heard in the distance, accompanied by singing and dancing, as some rite gets under way.

Initiation

For Kiplagat, a youth of the Nandi people in the highlands of western Kenya, the supremely important moment in life is the moment of circumcision. With the flick of a knife at the climax of a long ritual process, his boyhood becomes a thing of the past and he enters manhood. The ritual is a legacy from the past when the Nandi were a warrior people and every young man went through a period of warriorhood.

Although today most Nandi have accepted some form of Christianity, they continue to a large extent to undergo traditional initiation rites supervised by tribal elders. Through their symbolism these rituals reinforce the traditional world-view, and also the identity both of the individual and of the community in the face of a rapidly changing world.

KEY PEOPLE

Medicine men Also called 'herbalists' or 'traditional doctors' (misnamed 'witch-doctors' by outsiders); purveyors of herbal remedies, formally or informally trained, and respected by the community.

Mediums Their task is to communicate with the spirits and the living dead (ancestors).

Diviners Concerned with divination, using mediums, oracles, possession and divination objects such as collections of oddly-shaped bones and roots, gourds, cowrie shells and pebbles; they often employ 'good magic' to counter witchcraft and sorcery.

Shamans They may be prophets or seers in some societies. They exercise control over the spirits.

Ritual experts Rainmakers, circumcision elders, and the like, who perform special duties.

Priests They are set aside for divine service and represent man to God and God to man. Strictly, priests are associated with temples and shrines, but in African situations the word also applies to those who perform religious duties in sacred groves and elsewhere.

Witches and sorcerers They employ evil magic against people. Witches use their innate and often involuntary possession of 'witchcraft' and sorcerers use a variety of devices.

In all cultures the transition from life to death has been surrounded by ritual. Amongst the Torajo people of Indonesia, the funeral of a high-ranking family is likely to last three weeks. A special village is set up to house the 10,000 guests who take part in the procession and watch the buffalo-fighting and dancing.

The burial place itself contains life-sized wooden models of the dead.

Affliction

For Metson, a depressed housewife in the fishing village of Tawang in Kelantan, Malaysia, a significant event is taking place. She is in trance and her 'possessing spirit' is being interrogated by a Malay *shaman*. Her malady is sickness or loss of soul, believed to be caused by malevolent spirits entering and upsetting the delicate 'humoral balance' of her body.

The aim of the seance is to exorcize the spirit, and so to restore her soul. To achieve this, the shaman has to go into trance and through his 'familiar spirit' to interrogate Metson's spirit. Then, once he has determined the nature of the spirit and the cause of possession he must send it back to its home.

Metson will not remain passive. She must actively desire the departure of the spirit. When the shaman has sent her into trance the spirit can come out into the open and be effectively admonished. In this way there is a public demonstration of the cause of illness and a public treatment. The following evening Metson will take part in a comedy to mark the successful expulsion of the spirit.

Metson lives in an Islamic society in which women have little religious or social status and divorce is often imminent. The seance gives much-needed psychotherapy, especially in cases of illness caused by social stress. It provides a theatre in which she can act out her emotions and come to terms with her role in society.

ETHNIC RELIGIONS

Beliefs

The religious beliefs of small-scale societies are obviously very varied. Much depends on the environment. But though details differ from group to group, there are certain aspects which recur worldwide, in particular belief in the closeness of spirits and in the living dead. Looking at a number of African tribes will give an idea of how these beliefs work out.

In Ankole, Uganda, the Nkore people believe in Ruhanga the Creator who made all things at once. Ruhanga is personal yet distant. He is the principle of order and is therefore good, but he is reluctant to intervene directly in the affairs of men. This belief recurs in African religions as the following myth from West Africa shows.

'There was once a woman who had a very long pestle, and when she pounded her corn the wooden pole hit against God who lived just above the sky. One day she gave a great bang, hitting God in the eye, and in anger he went away into the distance never to return.'

The 'lineage spirits' and the spirits of the living dead are much closer to the Nkore than Ruhanga. The guardian spirits of each tribal lineage group are said to be descended from a legendary ruling dynasty and ultimately from Ruhanga himself.

At least one member of each lineage group must be specially initiated, to become, in effect, the priest of the group, responsible for making offerings and for initiating future members into the cult of the lineage spirits. One of the most important results of the cult is that it enables members of the lineage group to co-operate in ensuring successful seedtime and harvest. Otherwise it attracts little attention unless the lineage spirits cause trouble.

It is the spirits of the living dead, the ancestors, who need and receive more attention. They are likely to be malevolent, punishing bad actions and not rewarding good ones. So care must be taken in the burial of relatives and even of strangers within the household. Neglect brings revenge. As among many peoples, the living dead become the custodians of the moral order.

In other East African societies, such as the Maasai and Nandi, attention is focussed on the Supreme Being rather than on the spirits. Among these peoples, God is seen to be more involved, and so he is invoked, often daily, for protection. He is the beneficent creator, the sustainer of life, the arbiter of justice. In other West African societies the Supreme Being is often attended by a host of divinities as well as spirits of men and nature.

KEY CONCEPTS

Magic Worldwide, magic denotes the attempt to control the course of nature by special powers or actions. It is found in all types of culture, even to some extent in modern scientific society.

Mana The Pacific term for what is known in Africa as 'dynamism', or 'vital force'. It springs from the belief that there is power (or powers) which can be tapped for man's benefit.

Totem Any object towards which members of a group have a special mystical relationship. It may be an animal, a place, or something inanimate. Totem animals cannot be killed or eaten except under very special circumstances.

Taboo This term applies to any person or thing which is regarded as 'holy' or forbidden and not to be touched.

A family shrine and altar in Nigeria

In Kikuyu mythology the first ancestor, Gikuyu, was taken to Mt Kenya by the Creator, shown all the land round about and then directed to his future wife, Mumbi. The Creator lives in the sky but he has temporary homes on earth and from time to time he comes to rest on Mt Kenya and four other sacred mountains.

The phenomenon of death caused by witchcraft and sorcery or due to violation of taboos is common and widespread. Such deaths are frequent in aboriginal Australia, Polynesia, South America, and Africa. In Australia, an aboriginal medicine man points the *magic bone* at his victim. The ceremony is performed in secret, yet the victim usually hears of it. When he does, he will often die as a result of fear. If belief in sorcery, witchcraft, or supernatural sanctions is firmly held, fear alone can kill.

HINDUISM

Hindus follow the 'eternal religion,' an all-embracing way of life and culture which leads them through the cycles of life, death and rebirth.

The word 'Hindu' is derived from the Persian word for 'Indian' and 'Hinduism' is the religion of the peoples of India. Precise definition, however, is not so simple. Hinduism is a vast subject and an elusive concept. It has no founder and no creed. But it does possess scriptures, and the most ancient of these, the *Rig Veda*, provides a key to understanding Hinduism as a whole.

Some time between the years 1500 and 1200 BC—roughly speaking when Moses was leading the Israelites out of Egypt—wild charioteering Aryan tribes invaded India from the north-west and settled in what is today the Punjab. They had an important class of priests who composed hymns to their gods for use at sacrifices. Over the years these hymns were committed to memory and remarkably preserved until in later centuries 1,028 of them were enshrined in writing in the *Rig Veda*, the world's oldest living religious literature and Hinduism's most sacred book.

The religion develops

However, as Aryan religion spread, it absorbed elements from the cultures already present, for example from the Indus Valley in the north and the Dravidian in the south. So Hinduism as we know it today is like a great, deep river into which, over a period of more than 3,000 years, many streams have flowed. The streams are the beliefs and practices of the numerous races, ethnic groups and cultures of the Indian sub-continent. This means that there are almost as many versions of Hinduism as there are villages or groups of Hindus.

The underlying and dominant current providing unity is the religion which grew out of the *Rig Veda* and later Vedic scriptures. This means that Indian religion has certain discernible features. One of these is the doctrine of reincarnation: the belief that at death the soul always passes into another body until released from the continuous wheel of rebirth.

The many ways of salvation

Hindus number about 400 million. They are mostly to be found in India, but also in other parts of Asia, Africa, the West Indies and more recently to some degree in Europe and the West. Hinduism offers, broadly speaking, three ways of salvation from the wheel of rebirth. These are: philosophy or knowledge, works of religious observance, and devotion.

The *Ramayana* developed around an old heroic tale. The god Vishnu appears as Rama, the brave prince. He gallantly rescues his devoted wife Sita from Ravana, the demon king of Lanka, with the help of Hanuman the monkey-god. Then he returns to rule his kingdom well. In India and South-east Asia this story of the triumph of good over evil is enacted annually scene by scene.

The *Mahabharata* developed around an old martial story. The god Vishnu appears as Krishna, the much-loved friend and counsellor of the five Pandava brothers. The brothers are the heroes in the great battle between the Pandavas and Kauravas. Here, Krishna delivers his sermon—the *Bhagavad Gita*—to Arjuna before the battle.

The rituals of the Vedic Scriptures are still carried out today. High caste Brahmin priests perform a fire ritual to ensure a good harvest.

So existing side by side in Hinduism we find the heights of philosophical reasoning concerning Ultimate Reality, the most patient discipline of concentrated meditation or religious observance, and the dedicated devotion of image-worship associated with countless popular gods. Since the early nineteenth century various reform movements have also arisen as Indians have come into contact with Western culture.

Yet, essentially, to be a Hindu today is to believe in the Hindu way of life and to follow it to the best of one's ability.

HINDUISM

Beliefs

Hindus are monotheists at heart; they believe in one High God—Brahman, 'the Absolute'—who rules over the world with the aid of many lesser gods. To the educated Hindu the lesser gods have a status similar to that of saints and angels in certain branches of Christianity. To the ordinary believer or 'village Hindu', however, they are considerably more important.

The religion of these people—popular Hinduism—may be divided into three branches or sects, each with its own view of the nature and name of the High God: Vishnu, Shiva or Shakti. Families, by long tradition, support one branch or another. All branches are to be found in every part of India, though Shaivism is particularly strong in Kashmir in the north and Tamil in the south, and Shaktism in Bengal and Assam. The three sects continue together more or less in harmony, with devotees of one god occasionally worshipping at the shrine of another. Educated Hindus believe that the three gods are merely differing ways of looking at the same High God or Ultimate Reality.

The three sects

Vishnu is generally worshipped in the form of one of his ten incarnations. Wholly of goodwill, he sits enthroned in heaven beside his wife, the goddess Lakshmi. But because of his concern for the world he descends from time to time in the form of an incarnation.

Shiva differs in character from Vishnu. He has a dark and grim side to his nature, which seems to be derived from Rudra, the Vedic god of mountain and storm. Shiva is often described as lurking in horrible places such as battlefields and cemeteries. In sculpture he is often shown wearing a garland of skulls and surrounded by evil spirits as he dances the grim dance by which he destroys the world. At other times he is seen as the great ascetic, rapt in continuous meditation in the Himalayas. Devotees worship Shiva in the form of an image and also in his emblem, the *linga*, a short, rounded, phallic pillar which represents the creative power of God. Shaivism has its unpleasant sides too. There is animal sacrifice, and some ascetics deliberately inflict pain on themselves. Most devotees, nonetheless, look on their god as loving and gracious.

The tradition of asceticism is strong in India. The followers of the tradition are called *yogi*. In their search for mystical experience they will impose all sorts of hardships on their bodies.

There are ten incarnations (*avataras*) of the god Vishnu. Matsya the fish; Kurma the tortoise; Varaha the boar; Narasimha the man-lion; Vamana the dwarf; Parasurama, 'Rama with the axe'; Rama the prince; Krishna, the most important avatara; Buddha, the last historical avatara; and Kalki, the avatara yet to come.

To her devotees, Shakti, the great Mother Goddess, is the supreme deity. From their point of view the god in his male aspect is not active in the world and does not need worship. His wife Shakti is worshipped instead, in the fierce form of Durga or Kali and in the mild form of Parvati or Uma. In her fierce form Shakti is often depicted as a repulsive hag, bearing an assortment of weapons and trampling on a demon. Even today her worship is often accompanied by animal sacrifice. In the past, human sacrifice to Durga was not unknown. In her mild form Shakti appears as a beautiful young woman. For although she may unleash her fury on sinners she is loving and benevolent to her devotees.

Other major gods are also worshipped, for example Brahma the Creator, Ganesh the elephant-god, Hanuman the monkey-god and Surya the sun-god.

Hindu women, though respected, are reckoned inferior to men. The most notorious consequence of this belief was the practice of *suttee*, which is now forbidden. A widow would offer herself to be burnt on her husband's funeral pyre to ensure salvation for both of them.

At a village shrine, men offer food to the elephant god, Ganesh.

SCRIPTURES

The Vedas The *Rig Veda* consists of hymns completed by about 900 BC.
The *Sama Veda* consists of verses mainly taken from the *Rig Veda* and re-arranged for chanting at sacrifices.
The *Yajur Veda* is written in prose and gives instructions for those officiating at sacrifices.
The *Atharva Veda* contains magical formulae, written in verse, to help cure disease and bring success in war.
The *Brahmanas* are supplements to the Vedas, containing elaborate explanations of the sacrificial rituals.
The *Upanishads*, dating from about 600 BC, are based on the Vedas but reflect a movement away from rituals to philosophy, particularly the doctrine of reincarnation.

The Law Codes These attempt to regulate Hindu society.

The Great Epics The *Mahabharata* and the *Ramayana* portray in epic stories all the complexity of Hindu belief and practice. The *Mahabharata* contains the best-known and best-loved scripture of modern Hinduism, the *Bhagavad Gita*.

The Puranas These develop the mythology of classical Hinduism in a series of lengthy versified texts from the medieval period.

KEY WORDS

Brahman The all-pervading, self-existent power, the cosmic unity.

Atman The essence or principle of life: reality in its individual forms, as distinct from *brahman*.

Maya Literally 'illusion'; this world is neither real nor unreal.

Advaita Only one reality exists. All things are one. A strict form of this belief called 'monism', was taught by the Vedanta philosopher, Shankara.

Dharma Moral and religious duty.

Karma Literally 'action'; the inexorable moral law of cause and effect governing the future: bad actions lead to rebirth in the lower orders, perhaps as an animal; good actions lead to rebirth in the higher orders, perhaps as a priest.

Samsara The bondage of life, death and rebirth, governed by the law of *karma*.

Moksha Literally 'release'; liberation from the continuous round of rebirths.

Bhakti Devotion or worship offered to a single deity. Liberation by faith as distinct from liberation by works or knowledge.

In popular Hinduism, festivals are of great importance. This man is on his way to the temple during a festival in Southern India.

A way of living

Hinduism is a way of life. It is a path of duty to be followed within a divinely ordered society. The basic unit of society is the family. And so an individual's life is marked at every stage by domestic ritual. Birth, initiation, marriage and death—each has its ritual, as well as rites of daily worship and annual festivals. The individual is reminded that he is part of a family. He is also made aware that the family is part of a caste and the caste part of a social class.

There are four great classes: the priests (*brahmins*), the nobles (*kshatriyas*), the merchants and peasants (*vaishyas*), and the manual labourers (*shudras*). There are also outcastes and unclassified peoples. All are divided into several castes or sub-classes, each with its appropriate duty. Traditionally, the four classes were looked on as totally separate species. A member of one class would not marry a member of another class—nor even eat a meal with him. Nowadays, however, at least theoretically, such distinctions have been abolished.

A man of the upper three classes, goes through four stages in his life. There is the stage of the celibate student, the householder, the hermit, and the homeless religious beggar. The first stage is entered at the time of initiation. From then on the man will wear the sacred thread which passes over his left shoulder and under his right arm. Marriage is important, and the wedding ceremony one of the most solemn and complicated rites in Hinduism, because it ensures not only the continuity of the family but also the welfare of its dead members in the other world. Only a son can perform the funeral rites which provide the soul of his dead father with a new spiritual body with which to pass on to the next life.

No Hindu village is without its temple or shrine. In larger temples where there are many attendants, the god is awakened at dawn and taken from the bedroom where he has been sleeping with his wife. In the shrine-room he is washed and dried, dressed, offered sacrifices and fed. He is believed to eat the immaterial part of his food and the remainder is distributed either to the worshippers or to the poor.

The wedding ceremony has great personal and religious significance for a Hindu.

Hinduism in the home

All the most important Hindu rites are performed in the home, not least worship (*puja*). Hindus worship as individuals and families, not as congregations—except in modern reform sects. Most houses have either a room or a corner in which there is a family shrine. The shrine contains an image or emblem of the deity. It may be the spiral marked stone representing Vishnu or the stone pillar representing Shiva. There are brightly-coloured pictures illustrating Hindu mythology or depicting the exploits of the gods. First the worshipper anoints the god, while reciting texts. Then he sits down in front of it to meditate. Incense or joss sticks are lit and flowers and food are placed in front of the shrine. Worship in the temple follows a similar pattern.

The path of duty is the way to salvation: it obtains the release of the soul from the continuous cycle of life, death and rebirth.

BUDDHISM

In some of its many different forms, Buddhism is the religion without a god.

The Golden Pagoda of Rangoon is the largest and oldest shrine of its kind in the world. It is the spiritual heart of Burma. Its special sanctity arises from the belief that it enshrines relics not only of Gautama the Buddha, the founder of Buddhism, but also of the three previous Buddhas.

Pilgrims arrive on foot and by bus at the hill over which the pagoda is spread in all its splendour, with its courtyards and many chapels. Giant lions guard the pinnacled gateways to the four main entrances. The worshippers remove their shoes and climb long flights of stone steps to a courtyard above. From stalls beside the steps they buy a variety of religious and secular objects: gold leaf to stick on the pagoda, incense sticks, flowers, paper lanterns, images, prayer beads, bells, dolls, drums, combs, buttons and orangeade. At the top each pilgrim strikes a great bell to call heaven and earth to witness his acts of piety.

The layman and the monk

For the lay pilgrim, worship (*puja*) is a way of earning merit, and consists of offering gifts and services to the Three Jewels. The worshipper places a large vase of flowers in front of an image of the Buddha. He joins his hands in front of his face, bows, kneels and prostrates himself. He chants the liturgy and passages of scripture, performs ritual acts of reverence and burns

THE THREE JEWELS

Buddhism's Three Jewels or *triratna* are the Buddha, the Dharma (his doctrine) and the Sangha (the order of monks).

At every Buddhist shrine and meeting the Three Jewels are invoked three times in the simple formula which, it is believed, Gautama gave to his first missionaries:

'To the Buddha for refuge I go,
To the Dharma for refuge I go,
To the Sangha for refuge I go.'

incense. In an offering of inner worship, he contemplates an image of the Buddha.

Outside the pagoda, at the foot of one of the giant guardian lions, is a young monk, or *bhikku*, chanting the liturgy as he counts the beads of a rosary. For him, as for the pilgrim, worship is individual, not communal. Moreover, acts of worship are in origin performed by monks, not by lay people. For the monk is Buddhism's norm, perhaps the only true Buddhist. It is said that if a layman gains the Buddhist bliss (*nirvana*) it is because he has been a monk in a previous existence.

The monk is marked out by his yellow or saffron robes, consisting of three garments, his shaven head, and beard. His only possessions are his robes, an alms bowl, a razor, a needle and a water-strainer. He begs for his food. In the Buddhist lands of south-east Asia, every morning monks are to be seen on their begging-round, holding their lacquer-ware alms bowls in outstretched hands.

Monks enter the order (*sangha*) by means of special ordination ceremonies. They are not, however, bound to the monastic life for ever: they may leave whenever they wish. In certain countries, all boys spend some time, perhaps as little as a week, in a monastery as part of their religious education. Others enter a monastery during the rainy season in order to meditate.

The two Buddhisms

There are two distinct types of Buddhism, Theravada and Mahayana, springing from a common root. Theravada is often called the 'Little Vehicle' and Mahayana the 'Great Vehicle', since the Buddhist doctrine is conceived as a vehicle, a raft or ship, which carries us across the ocean of the world of suffering to a 'Beyond'—to salvation, to bliss.

Theravada is the earliest form of Buddhism. Its teaching is based on a collection of doctrines, which was approved at an important conference held soon after Gautama's death and offers salvation to the monk alone. Mahayana belongs to the second phase of Buddhist thought. Its crystallization coincides with the beginning of the Christian era and its teaching opens up the way of salvation to all.

The vast majority of Buddhists adhere to Mahayana and belong overwhelmingly to the northern countries of Nepal, Tibet, Vietnam, China, Korea and Japan. Theravada is dominant in the south-east Asian countries of Sri Lanka, Burma, Thailand, Laos and Kampuchea. In India, land of its birth, Buddhism is a minority religion currently undergoing revival. In China, Tibet, Vietnam, Laos and Kampuchea, Buddhism is under threat and its survival uncertain. And in the West Buddhism is enjoying increasing acceptance. Estimates of the extent of Buddhism vary from 200 million to one third of the world's population.

This enormous image of the Buddha is in Sri Lanka, the chief centre of Theravada Buddhism today.

The famous Golden Pagoda, or Shwe Dagon, in Rangoon is a magnificent building, rising over 300 ft/100 m, gilded from base to summit. It is said to contain 25 tons of gold in its images and an 'umbrella' top inlaid with more than 4,000 diamonds. Pagodas (*dagobas* in Sri Lanka, *wats* in Thailand) are essentially shrines which enfold relics. The Golden Pagoda is reputed to contain hairs of the Buddha, a sandal, and robes of previous Buddhas, kept in a barred underground basement.

In the countries of South-east Asia where Buddhism has become the national religion—Sri Lanka, Burma and Thailand—it has often had considerable influence on political life. In Thailand, state occasions are marked by Buddhist rituals.

Gautama the Buddha

According to tradition the founder of Buddhism was Siddhartha Gautama who, most probably, lived from 563 to 483 BC. What is known of his life and teachings is based on the scriptures of Theravada Buddhism. These were written in the ancient Pali language about 400 years after Gautama's death, and until that time had been carried in the memories of successive generations of disciples. For early Buddhism it was the word of its founder, rather than his life, which was of greatest importance. Consequently, there was no full-scale biography until the second century AD. However, we may be reasonably certain about the essential facts of his life.

Son of a wealthy leader belonging to the Sakya clan, Gautama was born and brought up in a little town in the foothills of the Himalayas in what is now Nepal. Throughout his early life his father sought to protect him from the sorrows of the world. He was reared in delightful palaces, schooled in the princely arts and married to a beautiful princess who bore him a son. However, while his son was still an infant, Gautama began to be disturbed by the problem of suffering. Despite his father's efforts, he eventually escaped his sheltered environment. Outside he met, one after the other, an old man in the last stages of senility, a sick man afflicted by disease, a corpse being carried to the cremation ground and, finally, a shaven-headed, wandering religious beggar, clad in a simple yellow robe, but radiating peace and joy.

Buddhist monks collect alms daily to support themselves.

BUDDHISM

Renunciation and enlightenment

Then came *the great renunciation*. Gautama resolved to leave his wife and infant son and to live the life of an ascetic. For six years, with five companions, he strove to find release from the weariness of existence. By the end he was reduced to skin and bones; yet he had not attained his goal. He therefore left his companions and went to meditate under a Bo-tree by the River Gaya. It was there that he received *the great enlightenment*. He discerned that suffering and its cause, desire, were at the root of man's troubles. Moreover, desire could be stopped by following the Middle Way between the extremes of sensuousness and asceticism.

Gautama then went to the deer park at Benares. There he preached his first sermon to his five former companions, so as to 'set in order the Wheel of Dharma'. The five became his first disciples (*arhats*) and were joined a few days later by a band of 60 others. Thus was founded the nucleus of the Buddhist order of monks. For eight months of the year they would travel from place to place preaching, and then for the four months of the rainy season they would live in bamboo huts in great parks donated by wealthy lay followers—a basis for the great monasteries of later years.

Throughout the Buddhist world, images of the Buddha are similar. The largest image is the Daibutsu in Japan, which was cast in bronze over 700 years ago.

The great size of many Buddha images comes from the belief that the Buddha's 'glorious body' was 18 ft/6 m high. This body was golden in colour. Between the eyebrows was a woolly curl (*urna*) which is usually represented by a single dot or by a jewel, later interpreted as the 'eye of wisdom'.

Early Buddhists (Theravada) aimed at the ideal of the *arhat*—the being who had become perfected. But that ideal was gradually replaced in Mahayana Buddhism by the ideal of the *bodhisattva*. This is a being who on reaching complete enlightenment, gives up entry into *nirvana*—the state of bliss—out of compassion for his suffering fellow creatures.

In protest against government persecution of his religion, a Buddhist monk burnt himself to death in Saigon in June 1963.

Gautama died at the age of 80. His body was cremated by his disciples and the ashes divided between eight clan groups. Each built an elaborate sacred cairn or *stupa* to house the relic. For lay Buddhists these *stupas* became the focus of devotion and were later developed into the pagodas.

The way to release

Buddhism's Middle Way appears to be a religion of self-effort without reference to the gods. Yet this statement needs to be qualified, because the idea of the self in Buddhism is distinctive. The self or soul is made up of five elements or *skandhas*—body, feelings, perception, impulses

THE FOUR NOBLE TRUTHS

1 The noble truth of suffering. All mortal existence is characterized by suffering.

2 The noble truth of the origin of suffering. Suffering arises from craving or desire.

3 The noble truth of the cessation of desire. To stop desire means to stop suffering.

4 The noble truth of the way to the cessation of desire. The stopping of desire comes by following the Noble Eightfold Path pioneered by the Buddha.

SCRIPTURES

The teachings of Buddhism are found in collections of scriptures called the 'three baskets' or Tripitaka and also in the scriptures of the different schools of Buddhism.

The Tripitaka *The Vinaya Pitaka* deals with monastic discipline. *The Sutra* (or *Dharma*) *Pitaka* deals with doctrine, for example the Buddha story, theories of the self and rebirth, the Three Jewels and the Precepts.

The Abhidharma Pitaka deals with advanced doctrine and philosophy.

The Dhammapada or 'path of Nature'. This is the oldest Buddhist text. It is quite short but of great importance and contains the Four Noble Truths, the Noble Eightfold Path and many teachings on practical morality and self-discipline.

THE NOBLE EIGHTFOLD PATH

The earliest and most basic description of the Path is that it is threefold. The three parts, morality, meditation and wisdom, are to be pursued simultaneously.

1 Right View
2 Right Resolve

3 Right Speech
4 Right Action
5 Right Livelihood

6 Right Effort
7 Right Concentration
8 Right Contemplation or Ecstasy

Wisdom Grasping the Four Noble Truths and resolving to observe them.

Morality Expressed in the Five Precepts.

Meditation Liberation, mind control and the cessation of sense experience.

THE PRECEPTS

Regularly, in their devotions, monks and lay people undertake to refrain from five things:

● Causing injury to living things.
● Taking that which is not given.
● Sexual immorality.
● Falsehood.
● The use of alcohol and drugs since they tend to cloud the mind.

Some lay people follow a more advanced degree and, especially on holy days, undertake with the monks to abstain from:

● Taking food after midday.
● Dancing, singing and amusements.
● The use of garlands, cosmetics and personal adornments.

Monks also undertake to refrain from:

● Accepting gold and silver.
● The use of a luxurious bed.

The Buddhism of Tibet and Nepal is distinctive because of the important role played by the monastic leaders, the *lamas*. These Tibetan Buddhists are celebrating their New Year.

and consciousness—and it is constantly changing. It is not a 'permanent self' which connects a man's new life to the life of his former existence. Rather it is the 'deeds' of *karma* (the inexorable law of cause and effect) which link one existence to another. The goal of human existence is *nirvana*, the state of bliss arrived at when desire ceases and *karma* is no more. *Nirvana* is not annihilation, not nothingness, and yet it is formless and uncreated.

It was inevitable that later Buddhism should develop a doctrine of salvation attainable by all men, not just by the monks. It is a doctrine of salvation by faith and not by works and is exemplified in the Buddhism of China and Japan.

CHINA

Today, after 30 years of suppression, religion is once more coming to life in China.

Before going into the Taoist temple, this Taiwanese girl lights an incense stick.

A meeting of Confucius, Lao Tzu and the Buddha. This, although not historically possible, illustrates the intertwining of China's three teachings.

China is the land of the three 'ways': Confucianism, Taoism and Buddhism. In their origins, the three are distinct. Confucianism gave new impetus to the ancient practice of ancestor worship, Taoism provided a mystical interpretation of the world and Mahayana Buddhism brought the possibility of salvation to all by grace through faith and devotion. But in their development, all three have intertwined or even merged with each other and with the folk religion which centred on home and farm.

In recent centuries, world religions such as Christianity and Islam have also exercised some influence. And, more recently still, Marxism has displayed all the influence and appeal of a fourth religion. Yet what the future holds is unknown. Since the republican revolution of 1911 the State rites have disappeared and ancestor veneration has dwindled. Since the communist revolution of 1949 Confucianism has been condemned as impeding progress and social change, Taoism has been controlled and Buddhism tolerated. Yet

Confucius' tomb was restored in 1962, the temples of Peking have been beautified and re-opened to the public and at least 50 million people profess to be conscientious devotees of the Buddha.

Confucianism

The founder of Confucianism, K'ung-fu-tzu, or Confucius as Christian missionaries called him, was born in 551 BC in the city-state of Lu in northern China, and died in 479 BC. Although later legend made him of aristocratic descent, he himself is reputed to have said: 'When young I was without rank and in humble circumstances.' He was to become one of the world's most famous teachers.

His times were fraught with chaos and uncertainty and the administration of China was taken over by experts in writing and ritual called *Ju*. It is thought that Confucius was one of these; but he failed to secure a place in administration and so took up teaching. He gathered round him a group of students to discuss the moral, social and

The dragon is China's ancient animal symbol.

CONFUCIAN SCRIPTURES

Six Chinese Classics
- The Book of History (*Shu Ching*)
- The Book of Poetry (*Shi Ching*)
- The Book of Changes (*I Ching*)
- The Book of Rites (*Li Chi*)
- The Book of Music (*Yueh Ching*)
- Spring and Autumn Annals (*Ch'un Ch'u*)

Four books
- The Analects (*Lun Yu*)
- The Great Learning (*Ta Hsueh*)
- The Doctrine of the Mean (*Chung Yung*)
- The Book of Mencius (*Meng Tzu Shu*)

political problems of the day. He taught more by debate than by systematic lecturing and his teaching in its most original form is to be found in *The Analects*, a collection of discussions and sayings.

Confucius taught the importance of *li*, which means propriety or orderliness. And the Confucian ideal of the 'gentleman' whose life is governed by propriety gradually emerged. The gentleman is serious in personal conduct, respectful to superiors, just and kindly disposed to the people. He is also concerned with 'filial piety', his duty as a son to care for his parents, and he venerates the ancestors. This emphasis on filial piety led to the association of Confucius' name with the ancestral cults, although of course they had existed before his time.

As so often happens, Confucius' students experienced greater success than their master. It was his successors Meng Tzu (Mencius, about 390–305 BC) and Hsun Tzu (about 312–238 BC) who spread his fame and enlarged his ideas.

CONCEPTS IN CONFUCIANISM

Li Literally 'rites', but for Confucius it came to mean 'good manners', propriety, the code of gentlemanly conduct.

Jen Goodness or virtue in the sense of unselfishness, deference towards others, courtesy and loyalty to family and prince.

Hsaio Filial piety, from which developed the *five relationships*:
(1) between father and son;
(2) between elder and younger brothers;
(3) between husband and wife;
(4) between elder and younger;
(5) between ruler and subject.

Chan-tzu The superior person, the virtuous, the gentleman.

T'ien Heaven, that which inspired Confucius. Most likely it included a supreme providential Being.

Tao The way, the pursuit of virtue and harmony in social living.

Shu The principle of 'reciprocity'. It is summed up in Confucius' negative expression of the Golden Rule: 'What you do not want done to yourself, do not do to others.'

Many Confucians believe Confucianism to be a way of life, a code of moral and social behaviour, rather than a religion. Thus they need not believe in any god. Alternatively they may follow their master, Confucius, and at the same time profess another religion.

The Way

The word 'Tao' means literally a path or a way. It may denote a way of acting or a principle of teaching. Confucianism emphasizes the former and Taoism the latter. Tao is the inexpressible Source of all being, the First Cause, the Ultimate Reality. It is the Principle which moderates and controls the universe, the Way in which men live in harmony with the universe.

The original teachings of Taoism are to be found in China's most influential book, the *Tao Te Ching*. The book is attributed to Lao Tzu (born 604 BC), but is now believed to be an anthology of brief passages dating from about the fourth century BC. Lao Tzu's very existence is disputed today: his name means 'Old Master', a title applied to a number of teachers in the period following Confucius.

To follow the Tao is to follow the way of nature, the 'watercourse way'. Water flows softly and effortlessly to humble places; yet even so it can be the most overpowering of substances. So, too, with the follower of *philosophical Taoism*. He is likely to be mystical and quietist: by stilling himself, his senses and his appetites, he can gain an inner perception of the Tao, a oneness with the Eternal, a harmony with the Principle underlying and penetrating the whole world. He attains a kind of enlightenment not unlike the Buddhist engaged in yoga.

'Te' means virtue or power, and the follower of *popular Taoism* seeks to harness this power through magic and ritual. He is likely to be preoccupied with death and the quest for immortality.

The New Buddhism

Mahayana Buddhism penetrated China from outside around the first century BC. At first, it met with resistance. Its doctrine of rebirth and emphasis on the monastic life appeared to conflict with Chinese respect for the ancestors and the importance of the family. But later it was to make

KEY CONCEPTS IN TAOISM

Tao The way. This is threefold in meaning: it is the Ultimate Reality; the Principle controlling the universe; and the way of living in harmony with the universe.

Te Virtue, power, the psychic magnetism of the human personality.

Wu wei Actionless activity, passivity. The basis of the Taoist ethic is for man to imitate the effortlessness of nature.

Laissez-faire government Actionless activity applied to the political sphere. This implies a form of anarchy: 'ruling by not ruling'.

Yin and yang The ancient principle of activity and passivity. *Yang* denotes the active masculine energy and *yin* the passive feminine one; heaven is active and earth passive. Taoism is *yin*-like. Good is often identified with the *yang* and bad with the *yin*.

TAOIST WRITINGS

Chuang Tzu The formal treatise of philosophical Taoism.

Tao Te Ching (*The Way and its Power*). The classic of mysticism, of first importance in religious Taoism.

Ancestral veneration, part of China's ancient religious heritage, takes on a number of forms today. Funerals, for example, are elaborate, with huge funeral processions.

A Taoist temple in Taiwan.
In popular Taoism the traditional gods of China find their way into Taoist belief. Three gods, one of which is Lao Tzu, and eight spirits of earth and heaven are given greatest importance.

Temples are attended by priests and worshippers visit them to seek cures for illness and power over death. To do this they use incantations, spells, charms, necromancy, spiritualism and sorcery.

great progress because of its liberal doctrines.

In the most important of Mahayana scriptures, the *Lotus Sutra*, Sakyamuni, the glorified Buddha, declares a new revelation: salvation is by faith. All men are called to bliss. All men will one day become Buddhas.

This new teaching included countless Buddhas. Maitreya, the Buddha-to-come, or laughing Buddha, is a popular figure, for he will bring happiness and good fortune. So too is Amitabha who presides over the Pure Land or Western Paradise beyond the west China mountains. Devotees pray to Maitreya for wealth and to Amitabha for guidance in the ship of salvation over the sea of sorrows to Paradise. The Bodhisattvas are also important. They are the enlightened beings who have denied themselves *nirvana* out of compassion for struggling humanity.

One reason why Buddhism was accepted was its common ground with Taoism—quiet and meditation. The special Chinese brand of Buddhist meditation called Ch'an is better known to the modern world by its Japanese name, Zen.

The anonymous 'Paradise of Amitabha', a hanging scroll in ink and colours on silk, now in the British Museum, depicts the Pure Land of Chinese Mahayana Buddhism, the paradise offered to faithful devotees.

JAPAN

Once the tool of the powerful emperor, religion in Japan now has a new vitality.

On the surface it would appear that the people of modern, industrialized Japan take little interest in religion. But to judge by the great number of religious groups and the multitudes of worshippers seen entering temples and shrines, particularly on such occasions as New Year, this first impression is false. The religiosity of the Japanese is confirmed by the 1970 census which gives a total population of just over 100 million and a religious affiliation of 177 million! Such multiplicity and complexity is undoubtedly related to the tendency of Japanese culture to borrow and assimilate.

Japan, like China, presents us with a mingling of religious traditions. The three most important are Shinto, Buddhism and Confucianism. Shinto has been Japan's own religion for over 2,000 years. Buddhism and Confucianism have both profoundly influenced the spiritual and social life of the Japanese people since the sixth century AD. Christianity has been an important cultural and intellectual influence since its introduction first in the sixteenth century and again in the nineteenth. In addition to these there are the New Religions, which have developed during transitional and unstable periods, and the Folk Religion which can be seen in the syncretistic beliefs of the common people.

Shinto

Shinto is not a Japanese word. It was coined from the Chinese *shen* (gods) and *tao* (way) when Buddhism first entered Japan. The intention was to distinguish the older religion, 'the Way of the Kami' from the new Buddhism. Kami is a difficult word to translate. It is applied to animals, birds and plants; seas and mountains; all natural phenomena; and even to the ancestors. It expresses a feeling of awe and wonder, a sense of the 'numinous'. According to popular belief there are 8 million Kami.

Ancient Shinto combined this veneration of nature with rites of an early agricultural fertility cult. Traces of both can be seen today in worship of one of the foremost Kami, the Sun Goddess Amaterasu, at the famous shrine of Ise; at pilgrimage to the summit of the holy Mount Fuji; in planting and harvesting ceremonies; and in the veneration of sacred trees.

In the heart of industrial Tokyo, thousands pass through this huge Shinto shrine every day.

As the worshipper approaches a Shinto shrine, which is usually situated in a grove, he will walk along a pathway lined with lanterns and pass through one or more gateways (*torii*) made of two horizontal beams supported by two pillars. The inner shrine, or *honden*, contains a Kami symbol, usually a mirror representing Amaterasu. Only the priest may go in—the worshipper remains in an outer room. He purifies himself, claps his hands and bows his head in reverence as he makes his petition.

SHINTO WRITINGS

Shinto has no collection of Scripture. It has instead a mythology recorded in two texts from the early eighth century AD (*Kojiki* and *Nihongi*) and a manual of ritual prayers (*Engishiki*) dating from AD 927.

According to Shinto mythology, the age of the Kami began when the cosmos emerged out of chaos. The most important Kami was the Sun Kami, Amaterasu-O-mikami. The age of human history began when Ninigi, grandchild of the Sun Kami descended to the lower regions and his great-grandson, Jimmu Tenno, became the first emperor of a unified Japan.

The Kami are still important in Japan today. This shrine is in the home of a wealthy farmer. At the appropriate season he will pray to the Kami of his fruit trees and at rice-planting there will be important ceremonies to ensure a good crop.

Buddhism in Japan

Mahayana Buddhism came to Japan by way of Korea. Between AD 550 and 600, various Korean princes sent gifts of images, scriptures and missionaries to the Japanese imperial court. The princes assured the emperors that Buddhism was a charm to ensure national welfare. For some time its fortunes varied, until a pro-Buddhist clan won control of the imperial house. First, under the devout and statesmanlike regent, Shotoku, and later for a period of more than 1,000 years, Japan honoured Mahayana Buddhism as the state religion. Buddhist priests took over Shinto shrines and re-interpreted Shinto beliefs according to Buddhist doctrine. However, because of Buddhism's characteristic tolerance, Shinto rites underwent few changes and Shinto shrines were carefully preserved. This is often called *Dual Shinto*.

SECTS OF JAPANESE BUDDHISM

Tendai Introduced by Dengyo (AD 767–822). It stresses one ultimate reality and teaches that salvation comes through meditation and faith.

Shingon This sect drew on many sources. It was introduced by Kobo (AD 774–835), and affirms that at the heart of the universe lies mystery, which is expressed through symbol and ritual.

Jodo Begun by Honen (AD 1133–1212). It stresses faith in Amida (Amitabha) Buddha and teaches that salvation for all can be given from outside; repetition of Amida's name leads to birth into the Pure Land.

Jodo Shinshu Founded by Shinran (AD 1173–1262), one of Honen's favourite disciples. With its emphasis on faith as complete passivity it appeals to lay people.

Zen Flourished with Eisai (AD 1141–1215). It teaches that enlightenment comes from within, through meditation.

Nichiren Founded by Nichiren (AD 1222–1282). It emphasizes devotion to the Buddha, doctrine and scripture, and is marked by nationalist emphasis, syncretistic tendencies, and the emergence of lay Buddhism.

Zen gardens, with their pure white raked sand are an aid to meditation.

Religion and nationalism

For many centuries, Buddhism dominated Japan. But its supremacy was to end. From the fifteenth century onwards, influences for change came from both inside and outside Japan.

But it was the opening up of Japan to western influence in the eighteenth and nineteenth centuries which proved decisive. Japan's heritage was recovered and restored to its former glory. Pure Shinto was revived. Its spokesmen were interested above all in instilling love of country, reverence for the emperor, filial piety and loyalty to the government. They wanted to reinforce the nationalist concept of a strong centralized State. And so in 1890 an imperial edict declared that *State Shinto*, despite its use of Shinto mythology and religious-ceremony, was non-religious. All Japanese citizens must follow it. Christians and others objected to this infringement of religious freedom, but they were assured that the compulsory rites of State Shinto had no significance except as patriotic exercises.

The whole enterprise came to a sorry end when, after defeat in World War II, the emperor was forced to denounce '. . . the fictitious ideas that the emperor is manifest god and that the Japanese people are a race superior to other races and therefore destined to rule the world.'

Religious revival

The state monopoly of religion had left people cold. Now there was a popular demand for some warmth and vitality in religion and this led to the development of *Sect Shinto*. In 1882, religious organizations had been divided into three categories: Buddhist, Christian and Shinto. Those that could not be classified as Buddhist or Christian were classified as Shinto sects. Thus began the distinction between *Shrine* and *Sect*

Zen Buddhists have developed skills such as calligraphy in their pursuit of enlightenment.

All over Japan, Shinto shrines are looked after by priests, who often have a full time secular job as well.

Japanese monks saluting their emperor at the joyful New Year celebrations. Though the emperor is now far less powerful than he once was, nationalism is still an important factor in Japanese religion. In particular, the largest of the New Religions, Soka Gakkai, aims to become the national religion of the country.

SECT SHINTO

The thirteen branches of Sect Shinto divide into five groups.

Pure Shinto This emphasizes loyalty to the throne and veneration of the ancestors.

Confucian Sects A combination of Confucianism and Shinto.

Mountain Sects Groups which believe their gods live in sacred mountains.

Purification Sects They insist on physical and ritual purity.

Faith healing Sects These include the groups founded by Bunjiro (who taught belief in one God and the universal love and brotherhood of all men) and Maekawa Miki (who taught the spiritual nature of sickness and evil, and encouraged purification rituals as a cure). Together they claim 7 million members.

Shinto. Sect Shinto is characterized by diverse elements such as spirit possession, divination, healing and the practice of magic. Today it has thirteen branches or 'churches', most of which have little in common.

However, nowadays, Shinto sects are commonly known as New Religions, although not all the new religions have a Shinto background. Two of the best known, Tenri-kyo and Konko-kyo, arose in the middle of the last century among the peasants and urban workers. Today they appeal to the middle classes as well. There are said to be well over 100 new religions, varying in size but counting their membership in millions. And new ones are constantly arising, encouraged by the granting of religious freedom after World War II.

Japanese Buddhism, meanwhile, is still influential. Over the centuries it has adapted and assimilated many of the Chinese schools of Buddhism as well as developing its own. The best-known in the West, but by no means the largest, is Zen. Zen was adapted from the Chinese Ch'an, whose method of meditation resembled the self-awareness of Theravada Buddhism. Its aesthetic quality has permeated Japanese life. It has become well known for its adaptation of the secular and even the military arts to the pursuit of enlightenment. Examples are its use of archery, flower arrangement, and even motorcycle maintenance! By undergoing the discipline of each art a person is brought to achieve a kind of 'ordered spontaneity'. Zen discipline, together with the Confucian ethic of orderliness, helped to form the ethos of the Japanese warrior class. But, for many, Zen is linked with the calm and orderly ritual of the tea ceremony, or the peace and serenity of the seemingly formless sand-garden.

JAINISM

To the Jain, every living thing is sacred. Cruel actions darken the soul, and the most cruel of all is to take life.

For a religion of only 3 million people, almost all of whom live in India, Jainism has wielded an influence out of all proportion to its size and distribution. This influence has been felt most keenly in the modern world through Mahatma Gandhi who, although not a Jain, followed its most distinctive doctrine—non-violence to living things, *ahimsa*.

The eternal universe

Jains believe that the universe is eternal, without beginning or end. It is uncreated and so there is no Creator. The universe passes through an infinite number of cosmic cycles, each divided into phases of ascent and descent, during which civilization rises and falls. At the peak period, men reach an enormous size and a tremendous age. In each cycle, 24 Tirthankaras, or 'fordmakers', appear, to gain liberation for themselves and to guide others across 'the river of transmigration'. The final three 'fordmakers' of the present phase (of rapid decline) are well known in the history of ancient India; the last, Vardhamana Mahavira, died probably in 468 BC. It is from the Sanskrit equivalent to 'fordmakers', *Jinas*, meaning 'conquerors', that Jains derive their name.

Several fine pieces of temple architecture tell of the ancient glory of the Jains. They include the magnificent complex at Mount.Abu, famous for the delicate workmanship in marble.

Jain temples do not normally enshrine the images of gods but only of the Tirthankaras, represented either as seated or standing rapt in meditation. The bathing of the images and waving of lamps in front of them to the tune of devotional hymns is not worship but only contemplation. When images of gods are included they are regarded as inferior to the great teachers.

A Jain nun making a pilgrimage on foot. The cloth across the mouth is to keep her from destroying insects. This is extreme, but it is normal for monks and nuns to take a whisk with which to brush insects from the path. According to the Jain doctrine of rebirth animals must be reborn as humans, women as men and laity as monks and so on in order to attain salvation.

Mahavira, the last fordmaker

Mahavira was a contemporary of the Buddha.
Like the Buddha, he rejected the religious way of
the priests (*brahmins*) for the atheistic way of the
possessionless teachers (*shramanas*).

Of noble birth, according to one tradition he
was a life-long bachelor; according to another he
was married to a princess who bore him a son.
Either way, at the age of 28 he plucked out his
hair, put on a single garment and set out to live
the life of an ascetic. In the thirteenth month he
discarded the encumbering garment in favour of
nudity, and in the thirteenth year he attained the
knowledge of all things—omniscience. Then, for
the next 30 years, he taught a great number of
followers, monks, nuns and laity alike, the path to
'passionless detachment'. At the age of 72 he
starved himself to death. He is regarded as a
great teacher and the great example to be
followed.

Salvation through non-violence

Jains believe that the individual consists of a soul
closely bound up in matter. Salvation is to be
found by freeing the soul from matter, so that it
may enjoy omniscient self-sufficient bliss for all
eternity—the Jain *nirvana*.

The soul is naturally bright and omniscient,
but it is liable to get clouded over by *karmic*
matter, the result of all action. Selfish, careless or
cruel actions darken the soul, but selfless,
thoughtful and kind actions can help to lighten it.
The most cruel of actions is to take life. And as all
living things have souls, including plants and
everything derived from the earth, Jains are
strongly vegetarian and restricted in their
possible work. The most preferred jobs are trading
and money-lending and so many Jains have
become wealthy merchants and bankers.

There are two main sects of
Jains, each with its own
collection of sacred texts. They
differ not about fundamental
doctrine but about ascetic
discipline. Both sects believe
that ideally the monk should be
completely naked. However, the
Svetambaras ('white-clad')
believe that owing to the present
state of decline of the universe
nudity is no longer possible.
The Digambaras ('sky-clad')
maintain in theory that total
nudity is right and proper when
practicable. Jains are
concentrated in certain regions
of India: the Svetambaras in
Gujerat and Rajasthan, and the
Digambaras in and around
Mysore.

FIVE VOWS OF THE MONK

The life of the Jain monk is strict in
the extreme. He vows to renounce
five things:

- Killing
- Stealing
- Lying
- Sexual activity
- The possession of property

SIKHISM

In the West, as in their native India, Sikh communities are a vigorous, active influence on society.

Sikhs can be found in almost every part of the world. Their temples adorn the cities of Britain, East Africa, Malaysia, the west coast of Canada, and the United States. The vast majority of Sikhs, however—about 10 million of them—live in India. And of these, about 90 per cent are to be found in the Punjab: 'a tiny island in the sea of Hinduism'. Yet their influence in the life of India greatly exceeds their numerical strength. They are renowned for their progressive farming, their role in the armed forces, sport and the transport industry, and to a lesser extent in manufacturing industry, commerce and the professions.

Stylized religious pictures of Guru Nanak are very popular and few Sikh homes are without one.

Guru Nanak
Sikhs trace their origin to Guru Nanak who was born in AD 1469. Nanak spent his childhood in the village of Talvandi, 40 miles south-west of Lahore. Before leaving the village he was married and had two sons. But at some point close to the year 1500 he forsook his married life for that of a wandering ascetic. Like a Hindu holy man he wore the saffron robe but like a Muslim he also wore a turban and carried a rosary.

It would be too simplistic to say that Guru Nanak formed a synthesis of these two major religions. But it is true to say that he owed a great deal to a synthesis already in existence, the Sant Tradition of Northern India. This tradition combined elements from the personal devotion of popular Hinduism (*bhakti*), the contemplative experience of mystical Islam (*Sufism*) and the controlled ritual practices of Tibetan Buddhism (*Tantrism*). Nanak expressed the synthesis in a new way, with great beauty and clarity.

Nanak's teaching
It was particularly the ideas about salvation which he brought to maturity. The theory held by the Sant tradition was at best incomplete and often naive. Salvation depended on the single repetition of a particular divine name. Underlying Guru Nanak's new doctrine of salvation were two sets of basic assumptions—concerning the nature of God and the nature of man.

God is single and personal, the transcendent Creator with whom the individual must develop the most intimate of relationships. Guru Nanak expressed this understanding of God in a number

All Sikh temples provide free food for travellers and pilgrims. Volunteers serve in the community kitchen attached to the temple.

of important terms: God is without form (*nirankar*), eternal (*akal*) and ineffable (*alakh*). Great emphasis is given to the third idea: essentially, God is unknowable. How then can he be known? He can be known because he is a God of grace, concerned that men should possess the means of salvation. He therefore reveals himself, in a way that is visible to all who will open their eyes and see. He is 'everywhere present', pervading all creation, particularly the human heart.

But men are wilfully blind. They shut their eyes to this divine revelation which lies within and without. They know that they need salvation but seek it through futile religious exercises, such as worship at Hindu temples or prayers in Muslim mosques. But externals of this kind only bind them even more firmly to the wheel of birth, death and rebirth.

KEY TERMS

Amrit The 'nectar of immortality', sugar crystal and water solution used at initiation (*pahul*).

Karah parshad A food made of flour, sugar and ghee in equal proportions, shared at the end of Sikh gatherings to symbolize

casteless equality and brotherhood.

Langar Free kitchen.

Mela Fair, festival.

Seva Service.

THE TEN GURUS

What we in the West call Sikhism, Sikhs call *Gurmat*, 'the Guru's doctrine'. God, the original Guru, imparted his message to his chosen disciple, Nanak, and thereafter to a series of ten gurus:

1 Nanak (1469–1539), a strict monotheist, mystic and opponent of asceticism.

2 Angad (1504–1552), a consolidator, compiler of hymns and builder of temples.

3 Amar Das (1479–1574), the divider of the land, initiator of communal meals. He emphasized the equality of mankind.

4 Ram Das (1534–1581), a social reformer and founder of Amritsar, the place of worship and pilgrimage.

5 Arjan (1563–1606), the first guru born a Sikh, builder of the Golden

Temple at Amritsar, compiler of hymns and teachings of the Gurus to form the Adi Granth.

6 Hargobind (1595–1644), the founder of the army which was advised by his father.

7 Har Rai (1630–1661).

8 Har Krishan (1656–1664).

9 Tegh Bahadur (1621–1675), brave and generous.

10 Gobind Singh (1666–1708), the founder of the Khalsa, installer of the Granth as Guru, reviser of the Granth.

Devout Sikhs express their worship in three ways: daily recitation of set passages of Scripture, daily family worship, and regular attendance at the temple (*gurdwara*).

The temple contains no images of any kind. Instead, the *Adi Granth*, a collection of hymns containing the Gurus' teaching, is revered as the *Guru Granth Sahib*. It is kept in the position of honour on a cushion under a canopy.

SIKHISM

The way to the divine harmony

Guru Nanak's teachings about salvation are expressed in a number of key words which recur throughout his works. They are the name (*nam*), the word (*sabad*), the teacher (*guru*) and harmony (*hukam*). *Nam*, the divine Name, and *sabad*, the divine Word, together express the whole nature and being of God. But man, because of his nature, fails to recognize this divine presence, so he needs a *guru*, or divine Preceptor. The divine Preceptor is the 'voice' of God mystically uttered within the human heart. Once awakened, the enlightened man looks around and within himself, to see the *hukam*, the divine Order, or harmony. Salvation is then a matter of bringing himself within this pattern or harmony through regular, disciplined meditation on the divine Name. Ultimately this results in the devotee uniting himself with the divine harmony and the wheel of transmigration stops.

The community develops

Before his death Guru Nanak appointed a disciple to succeed him. And from that time, for more than a century and a half, leadership in the Sikh community was exercised by a succession of gurus. The tenth of these, Guru Gobind Singh (1666–1708), brought the line to an end and transferred authority to the community (*Khalsa Panth*) and the scripture (*Guru Granth*). Today, it is the scripture which is most important.

The Sikh community evolved between the time of Nanak and that of Gobind Singh. Its identity was forged in the context of the cultural, political and military development of the Punjabi people. The community struggled for survival in the face of Muslim Mughal emperors, it was incorporated into the community of the martial Jat caste, and then exposed to the Sakti (power) culture of the Shivalik hills area. The beards, turbans and

The outward symbols of the Khalsa brotherhood are the Five Ks. These are the *kesh* (uncut hair), the *kangha* (a comb to hold the hair in place), the *kirpan* (dagger), the *kara* (steel bangle) and the *kachh* (under-trousers).

The prohibitions are also important. They include abstinence from tobacco, hemp, opium, alcohol, beef and pork.

martial valour commonly associated with Sikhism today are marks of this evolution. The climax came with the setting up of the Khalsa brotherhood, probably by Guru Gobind Singh in 1699. Members of the brotherhood had to accept baptism and a new code of discipline which included the Five Ks and a set of prohibitions.

One small dissenting group within Sikhism—the *sahaj-dhari*—does not honour the code in its fulness but claims to follow the teachings of the gurus in their pristine purity. If, in modern society, Sikhs abandon the externals of their faith, they run the risk of being called 'fallen' by the orthodox.

In other ways, too, Sikhism stood out from the common culture. It encouraged the elimination of caste distinctions and affirmed the equality of women. Concerning women, Guru Nanak is said to have observed: 'How can she be called inferior who begets kings?'

CEREMONIES

Naming When the mother has recovered after childbirth, the family visits the gurdwara to give thanks and name the child.

Marriage This is not just a social contract but a spiritual union. It is both a social and religious occasion.

Cremation Normally held the day after death; a family occasion, marked by readings from the scripture.

Initiation At puberty young Sikhs enter the Khalsa, or community; boys add *Singh* and girls *Kaur* to their surnames.

FESTIVALS

Baisakhi The New Year and spring harvest, adapted from Hinduism, marked by an animal fair at Amritsar.

Divali The Hindu New Year, adapted by Sikhs for assembly in the gurdwaras.

Hola Mohalla Guru Gobind Singh adapted the Hindu Holi to give it a martial flavour; today it is marked by fairs and carnival processions.

The Golden Temple at Amritsar is the central shrine of Sikhism and its most important place of pilgrimage.

PARSISM

Parsism today seems a mixture of unrelated elements.
Yet down the years, the influence of its founder,
Zoroaster, has been enormous.

On the extreme edge of the western Iranian desert, in and around Bombay in India, in East Africa, and in many of the major cities of the world are pockets of a small community totalling no more than 120,000 members worldwide. They are the Parsis, or 'Persians', followers of the great Persian prophet, Zoroaster. From the eighth century onwards, in the face of Muslim persecution, the majority of them have fled from Iran to tolerant India and beyond.

Zoroaster

Zoroaster ('Zarathustra' in Persian) is commonly believed to have lived during the sixth century BC, a period remarkable for its prophetic endeavour and spiritual enlightenment. Modern scholars, however, tend towards a much earlier date, somewhere in the period 1500–1000 BC.

Zoroaster called for righteousness and allegiance to Ahura Mazda, the 'Wise Lord'. But he also believed in various good and evil spirits, particularly Angra Mainyu, the 'Evil Spirit', to whom he appeared to give equal status with the Wise Lord. Both are eternal. This is why Parsism is often considered dualistic—believing in two opposing, and equally balanced, forces of good and evil in the world. Yet, because he did not believe that matter was essentially bad, Zoroaster taught that in the end Good would triumph over Evil. This is why Parsism claims to be monotheistic—believing in one Almighty God.

Moreover, man has a part to play in the triumph of Good over Evil: because Ahura Mazda created the world in order to help him overcome Angra Mainyu, man is constantly summoned to combat evil. So Parsis are seekers of the 'Good Life'—'good thoughts, good words and good deeds'.

The fire ritual is the first of Parsism's two central rites. Fire is the symbol and the son of Ahura Mazda and must be kept from all defilement—from the sun and unbelieving eyes; and so it is kept in a Fire Temple where it is lovingly attended.

There are three kinds of temple: the *Atash Dadgah*, often an ordinary home used for worship; the *Atash Adaran*, built where ten or more Parsi families live together; and the *Atash*

Parsi boys enter fully into their faith at the New Birth ceremony, when they are given a sacred shirt and a sacred thread.

The ancient Parsi Village of the Dead was recently excavated in Iran. Above it towers the huge Tower of Silence.
Parsis do not cremate their dead, that would be to defile the elements (earth, water, air and fire). Instead, they leave dead bodies in a Tower of Silence, exposed to sun and vultures.

Living the Good Life

Good deeds will be rewarded and bad deeds punished. The injustices and inequalities of this world will be set right in the next. For Parsis believe firmly in life after death, the coming of a Saviour, a day of judgment, a bodily resurrection and the salvation of all mankind to praise God for ever.

Because Parsis pursue the 'Good Life', Parsism is a highly moral religion and Parsis are renowned for their intelligence, integrity, industriousness, and philanthropy, and their contributions to commerce, industry, education and social work. Because Zoroaster's teaching most probably influenced Judaism (and therefore Christianity and Islam indirectly), especially during the period of Jewish exile in Babylon, and particularly concerning belief in life after death, Parsism has abiding significance and relevance for the contemporary world.

Ritual and tradition

But Parsism also owes much to the popular religion of ancient Iran. And so today, while reformists stress the importance of monotheism and morality, orthodox Parsis lay strong emphasis on ritual and tradition, for example, purification, worship and sacrifice. They pray at the five divisions of the day and ritualize all the great moments of life: birth, puberty, marriage, child-bearing and death. As part of their daily dress they wear a sacred thread, reminding them of their scriptures, and a shirt, symbolizing their religion, both received at initiation. Their priests, in addition, wear white robes and turbans. They are a distinctive people. They do not seek to win others to their faith because they believe each person should follow the religion into which he was born.

Behram or 'king of fires'—only ten exist today.
The priest holds symbols of the sacred barsom twigs, his nose masked to prevent defilement from his breath.
The haoma sacrifice is the second of Parsism's two central rites. The plant haoma is the god come to earth. As he is pounded he is ritually sacrificed. From the juice comes the drink of immortality.

SCRIPTURES

The Parsi scriptures, known as the *Avesta*, are very varied, and arose over a vast period of time.

Yasna Mainly liturgical texts recited by the priest during rituals. They contain the *Gathas*, 17 songs attributed to Zoroaster and reckoned to be the oldest part.

Vendidad Mainly liturgical texts dealing with purification rites and the punishment of offenders.

Yashts Hymns of praise and prayers of the laity.

FESTIVALS

Ghambars Six seasonal festivals, including New Year, celebrated with services and feasts.

Farvardega Days in memory of the dead, marked by taking sandalwood to the temples and flowers to the temples of silence.

Jashans Anniversaries, for example in praise of Zoroaster.

JUDAISM

*Judaism is the religion of a nation –
God's chosen people. Yet for more than
half their history, the Jews have had no
homeland.*

Judaism is the religion of the Jewish people.
There are 12 million Jews in the world, 6 million
in the USA, 2 million in Israel, and 4 million
dispersed throughout the world, many of them in
Russia and Eastern Europe. In the holocaust of
1939–45, 6 million Jews were annihilated in the
concentration camps of Nazi Germany, as Hitler's
Gestapo sought to 'purify' the race.

In the aftermath of war, in 1948, the tiny state
of Israel was born. It was created to secure a
permanent homeland for Jews. Israel's short
history has been one of remarkable economic
achievement, and of painful struggle—for
recognition, identity and survival.

The 'Jewish story', their early history, is told in
the Hebrew Bible, in particular in the
'Pentateuch', known as the Five Books of Moses,
or the Torah (Law).

The patriarchs, Abraham, Isaac and Jacob, are
revered as the founders of the Jewish people. In
their daily prayers, Jews claim to be 'children of
Abraham', the friend of God, and their nation is
called Israel—the name God gave to Jacob.

Abraham crossed from Mesopotamia in about
1800 BC to settle in Canaan, 'the promised
land'—later known as Palestine, which had much
the same extent as the present state of Israel. In
time of famine the 12 sons of Jacob took refuge in
Egypt, where they later became slaves.

Then, probably about 1250 BC, their
descendants, the Hebrews, were led out of Egypt
by Moses. This was the 'exodus'. On the way, on
the top of Mt Sinai, the God of the patriarchs, now
known as 'Yahweh', made a covenant with Israel.
It was enshrined in the words of the Ten
Commandments, engraved by Moses on stone

tablets, and sealed with the blood of a sacrifice. The God of Israel revealed himself as the God of history: not simply a tribal deity or nature spirit, but the Creator in control of his world. From that time on, Israel's national identity and its religion have been indissolubly linked.

Moses himself did not enter the promised land. It was his successor, Joshua, and the Judges (later leaders raised up by God) who moved into the land and settled the people. They were in turn succeeded by a line of kings. The first three, Saul, David and Solomon, ruled Israel. Their successors ruled the divided kingdoms of Israel and Judah.

But Palestine, at the crossroads of East and West, was to be occupied in turn by Persia, Greece and Rome. Time after time her people were sent into exile, first to Babylon in the sixth century BC and, from the second century AD onwards, to the four corners of the earth. Yet, conscious of being God's chosen people, they retained their racial, cultural and religious identity wherever they went and whatever they suffered.

DIVISIONS OF JEWRY

Orthodox This is the strictly traditional Judaism which accepts the Law and rabbinic authority.

Progressive This is represented by two movements.
Liberal Judaism arose in continental Europe out of the eighteenth-century Enlightenment. It stressed biblical criticism, and emphasized the ethical and generally applicable aspects of Judaism over against the ritualistic and limited.
Reform Judaism continues this tendency. It welcomes the methods of historico-critical research and plays down the observance of ritual. It also plays down the 'particularist' or 'nationalist' elements of Judaism—the hope of a return to Zion, the restoration of the sacrificial system and the coming of a personal Messiah.

Conservative This branch originated in the nineteenth century, especially in America, and steers its way between Orthodox and Progressive. It pleads for modification of ritual but accepts rabbinic tradition.

Mystical This is represented by two movements.
The Kabbalah emerged in thirteenth-century Spain and emphasizes union with God through meditation and contemplation.
The Hasidim emerged in eighteenth-century Eastern Europe and emphasizes communion with God through enthusiastic prayer.

Zionist Cutting across all other divisions, Zionism is a nationalist movement, with spiritual overtones. It arose out of the persecutions of nineteenth-century Eastern Europe, stressed Jewish nationhood as well as peoplehood and culminated in the return to the land of Israel.

Jerusalem's Wailing Wall, the remains of the temple destroyed by the Romans in AD 70, is a place of pilgrimage for Jews. A central feature of Israelite religion had been the offering of sacrifices by the priests in the temple at Jerusalem (Zion). First, during the exile in Babylon, and then, once the temple and its sacrifices had gone, Judaism became a much more decentralized religion, centred on worship at local meeting-places, 'synagogues'.

Throughout their history, the Jews have been cruelly persecuted. In concentration camps such as Belsen in the Second World War, 6 million Jews were killed.

Moses is a prophet revered by Jews and Muslims alike. In 1978, President Sadat of Egypt and Premier Begin of Israel met on the traditional site of Mt Sinai, where Moses is believed to have received the Law. There they prayed together for the peace of the world.

God and his law

The Bible does not argue for the existence of God: God is. He is one and eternal, creator and ruler of the universe. He is both all-powerful and all-loving. He created the world, including man, for the manifestation of his glory.

God makes himself and his purposes known to man through revelation. Man responds and communicates with God through prayer and meditation. By means of this two-way process God gave man his Law, the Torah. To keep this Law is to hasten the establishment of God's kingdom (rule) on earth. A personal Messiah ('anointed one'), descended from David, Israel's greatest king, will herald the coming of the kingdom. So, in the scheme of salvation, the Jewish people play a special role, since it was to them that God revealed the Law.

The Law and obedience to it is therefore central to Judaism. It consists of 613 commandments (*mitsvot*)—248 positive and 365 negative. They are the expression of God's will and are therefore binding on the believing Jew. Jews have a duty to both God and man to lead a life in accordance with God's will. In so doing they bear witness to God and his purpose in the world. This is the essence of the idea of Israel's 'election'—their position as God's chosen people.

God and his world

According to the Jewish view of human society all men are created in God's own image. All men are created equal. All have dignity. And so the Law commands respect for all. It also commands special care of the under-privileged—the sick, the widow, the orphan, the stranger, the distressed, the captive and the poor. This is emphasized through constant reference to Israel's own

In the annual Jerusalem March, a procession of thousands is headed by a group carrying the scrolls of the Law.

When he is 13 years of age a Jewish boy becomes *bar-mitzvah*, a 'son of the commandment'. During the synagogue service he is called to the reading-desk to read from the Law. From that time on he is held to be an adult, with all the privileges and responsibilities —religious and social—which this brings. Girls, too, have their own initiation ceremony.

history: for example, as God's people were themselves 'strangers' in Egypt so they must be hospitable to strangers.

According to the Jewish view of human nature, all men are created free, with the ability to choose between good and evil, and without the 'inheritance' of a burden of sin. And the world in which man is placed is a good world, created by God for man's benefit. Man must therefore enjoy its bounty and use its gifts both for the betterment of mankind and the service of God. Unlike Indian religion, therefore, Judaism is a world-affirming and not a world-denying faith. Salvation is to be achieved in and through this world. Thus, although Jews believe in the resurrection of the dead and the immortality of the soul, they pay far more attention to living life well here and now than preparing for the life to come.

KEY BELIEFS

The medieval Jewish philosopher, Moses Maimonides (1135–1204), drew up thirteen articles of faith, which are generally considered to sum up the essentials of Jewish belief.

1 The existence of the Creator.

2 His unity.

3 His incorporeality (God is spirit).

4 His eternity.

5 The obligation to serve and worship him alone.

6 The existence of prophecy.

7 The superiority of Moses to all the prophets.

8 The revelation of the Law to Moses at Sinai.

9 The unchanging nature of the Law.

10 The omniscience of God (God is all-knowing).

11 Retribution in this world and the next.

12 The coming of the Messiah.

13 The resurrection of the dead.

SACRED JEWISH WRITINGS

Bible ('books') A collection of books written over a period of 1,000 years and given the status of scripture about AD 100.

Torah ('law') The first five books of the Bible, attributed to Moses.

Mishnah ('repetition') Ethical and ritual teaching based on the Bible, dating from the second century AD onwards.

Talmud ('study') In two versions, one Palestinian and one Babylonian, based on the Mishnah, with further reflections.

Wherever ten or more Jewish men live near together a synagogue can be formed. The worship, teaching and social functions of the synagogue hold the community together.

Congregations are served by teachers or lawyers (*rabbis*) who are chief officers of the synagogue, readers (*chazzan*) who read lessons and recite prayers and priests (*cohen*, descendants of the temple priests).

Here a rabbi stands in front of the Ark, which contains scrolls of the law.

The home

The centre of Jewish religious life is the home—even more than the synagogue. Jews lay great emphasis on the family and family relationships, and so many Jewish festivals are family festivals. Most notable is the weekly Sabbath.

Sabbath means 'rest', and 'the Sabbath' is a weekly day of rest from work and a festival of religious and family significance. The Jewish day begins and ends at sunset, so the Sabbath, which falls on Saturdays, begins on Friday evening.

Before sunset, the woman of the house kindles the 'Sabbath lights'. As she does so, she prays for God's blessing on her work and her family. The male members of the household may be with her, or they may be attending the synagogue. The Sabbath table is spread with a clean cloth and laid with two loaves and a cup of wine. Before the evening meal, the husband chants the praise of a virtuous wife and recites verses from the Bible about creation and the Sabbath rest. He then takes the cup of wine and blesses it in the name of God. He also blesses the bread, taking his portion of wine and bread before handing them round.

The synagogue

Synagogue means 'assembly'. It is the centre of public worship and social life for the Jewish community. Jews gather in the synagogue for Sabbath services held on Friday evening and Saturday morning.

Jewish families gather together for the *seder*, the home service of Passover. On the candlelit table are unleavened cakes, a shankbone of mutton, bitter herbs, paste made from apples, almonds, cinnamon and other spices, raisins, and salt water, all to commemorate Israel's slavery in Egypt. The story of the slavery from which God delivered them is recounted, psalms sung, and food and wine are shared.

FESTIVALS

Passover (*Pesach*) An eight-day spring festival, commemorating the deliverance of Israel from slavery in Egypt.

Pentecost (*Shavuot*) (Feast of Weeks) Held seven weeks after Passover, to celebrate the end of the corn harvest; it is also associated with the giving of the Law at Sinai.

Tabernacles (*Succot*) A joyful autumn festival celebrating the fruit harvest. Prayers are made for good rain, and for the dead. The celebration includes camping out in tents ('tabernacles') made of branches, to commemorate Israel's pilgrimage through the desert.

Dedication (*Hannukah*) (Lights) Winter festival, commemorating the rededication of the Second Temple by Judas Maccabaeus in 165 BC after the occupying Greeks had defiled it.

Purim Commemorates the deliverance of the Jews of the Persian Empire as recorded in the book of Esther. Held in the early spring, it is marked by carnivals.

New Year (*Rosh Hashanah*) The beginning of the religious calendar, in the early autumn. It is the time to put one's life in order.

Day of Atonement (*Yom Kippur*) The tenth day of the New Year, the highest of all holy days; it is marked by 24 hours of abstinence from food and water as a sign of penitence before God for the sins of the individual and of the community.

The building may be square or oblong. At the end facing Jerusalem is the Ark, containing scrolls of the Law. Pews are arranged on three sides, placed so that the worshippers face the Ark. In front of the Ark is a reading-desk (*bema*) from which prayers are said and the Law read. Normally during the service men wear hats or skull caps, and white prayer shawls round their shoulders; women wear hats but no shawls. In orthodox synagogues, women sit separately from men.

During the service, all members of the congregation rise to repeat the *shema* (which all Jews recite twice daily): 'Hear, O Israel: The Lord our God, the Lord is One; and you shall love the Lord your God with all your heart, and with all your soul, and with all your might.' At the climax of the service the Ark is opened and the scroll of the Law is taken out and carried round the synagogue. The people bow as it passes each pew.

First, the priests and members of the priestly line (Levites), and then, any lay man, may stand up and read the Law.

Religious observances

In addition, the religious life of a devout Jew is marked by prayer three times daily and the keeping of strict laws on diet, involving the declaration of all food as clean (kosher). As a sign of the covenant made between God and Abraham, all Jewish boys are circumcised eight days after birth. Traditionally, the ceremony took place in the home or in the synagogue, but nowadays, it usually takes place in hospital, in the presence of a rabbi.

CHRISTIANITY

Christianity offers the world today a message concerned with changing both the individual and society.

Christians take their name from Jesus Christ. Jesus was born in Bethlehem, in Judea, sometime between 6 and 4 BC, to a devout Jewish couple named Mary and Joseph, descendants of King David. He grew up in Nazareth, in Galilee, and at the age of 30 was baptized in the River Jordan by a prophet called John the Baptist. John had been preaching and baptizing people as a mark of repentance for sins. He heralded the coming of one greater than himself.

After his baptism, Jesus gathered round him a band of twelve disciples (the 'apostles'), and went about the countryside preaching, teaching and healing the sick. He announced the coming of God's rule and declared the need for people to repent of their sins and believe the good news of God's kingdom. When, after many months together, Jesus asked his disciples who he was, their leader, Peter, declared 'You are the Christ'—the 'anointed one', the Messiah of Jewish expectation.

At the age of 33 Jesus was arrested, tortured and put to death by the Roman authorities, with the collaboration of Jewish secular and religious leaders, probably about AD 29–30. He died by crucifixion, a common but very painful method of execution. But he rose from the dead three days later, appeared to some women followers and his disciples on a number of occasions during the next 40 days, and then returned to his Father in heaven.

Christians therefore believe in a living Christ, not a dead hero. The crucifix and the cross have become symbols of the suffering Saviour and the risen Lord. Friday and Sunday, the days on which respectively he died and rose, have become 'holy' days.

Who was Jesus?

Christians believe that Jesus Christ is both 'Son of God' and 'Son of Man'—fully human and fully divine and without sin. In him, the One God, Creator of heaven and earth, came down to men, in order to raise men to be with God. This is the *incarnation*, achieved through his birth of a virgin mother, conceived by the Holy Spirit. Jesus took on himself the limitations of human nature.

Christians go through the waters of baptism (either by 'sprinkling' or by 'immersion') to symbolize dying and rising with Christ and being born to new life. The early Christians probably confessed their faith at baptism in the words of the exclamation 'Jesus is Lord!' Since the fourth century, Christians in the West have used a creed approximating to the 'Apostles' Creed' for the same purpose.

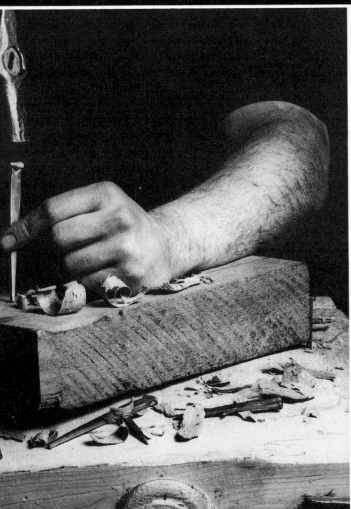

He also took responsibility for the sins of the human race, reconciling God with men and men with God. This is the *atonement*, achieved through his death. But he died only to rise again to new life. This is the *resurrection*.

Those who believe in Jesus are not only saved from their sins but will be raised to new life when Jesus comes again. Meanwhile, through the Spirit of God living in them, they are guided and strengthened in their pilgrimage on earth.

KEY BELIEFS

The Christian creeds express the essence of Christian belief. They fall into three sections, concerned with God, Jesus Christ and the Holy Spirit. The familiar 'Apostles' Creed' is used only in the Western church; the Nicene Creed, which follows, is used in the church worldwide, although the Eastern church omits the 'filioque' clause (in brackets).

We believe in one God,
   the Father, the almighty,
maker of heaven and earth,
   of all that is,
   seen and unseen.

We believe in one Lord, Jesus Christ,
   the only Son of God,
   eternally begotten of the Father,
God from God, Light from Light,
true God from true God,
   begotten, not made,
   of one Being with the Father.
Through him all things were made.
For us men and for our salvation
   he came down from heaven;
by the power of the Holy Spirit
   he became incarnate of the Virgin Mary, and was made man.
For our sake he was crucified under Pontius Pilate;
   he suffered death and was buried.
On the third day he rose again
   in accordance with the Scriptures;
he ascended into heaven
   and is seated at the right hand of the Father.
He will come again in glory
   to judge the living and the dead,
   and his kingdom will have no end.

We believe in the Holy Spirit,
the Lord, the giver of life,
   who proceeds from the Father (and the Son).
With the Father and the Son he is worshipped and glorified.
He has spoken through the Prophets.

We believe in one holy catholic and apostolic Church.
We acknowledge one baptism for the forgiveness of sins.
We look for the resurrection of the dead,
   and the life of the world to come.

Christianity is a world faith. As it has spread, new believers have come from all sorts of backgrounds. This Malaysian girl had been tatooed with kerosene when she was three.

The influence of Christianity on the arts has been considerable throughout the world. This is a page from the *Book of Kells*, a finely ornamented manuscript of the Gospels, copied in Ireland in the eighth century. It reminds us both of the importance of the scriptures for Christians and the significant contribution of Irish Christianity to Europe during the Dark Ages.

The birth of the church

After Jesus had ascended to his Father in heaven, his followers gathered in Jerusalem to await the coming of the Spirit of God whom Jesus had promised. Ten days later, the Holy Spirit came, and Peter, leader of the twelve apostles, filled with new boldness and power, addressed the crowds. He told them that Jesus, whom they had crucified, and whom God had raised from the dead, was the promised Messiah, and called on them to turn from their sins and be baptized in his name. Three thousand responded to this first preaching of the Christian message and were baptized.

From Jerusalem the church spread outwards until, by the close of the century, it was strong in Asia Minor, Macedonia, Greece and Rome. The expansion was due largely to the efforts of Paul, the first great Christian missionary. Paul made known the good news about Jesus—the 'gospel'. He used to full advantage the widespread law and justice which resulted from the 'Roman peace', the ease of communication made possible by the Greek language, and the privileged position accorded to the Jewish religion.

And the churches which he founded in turn preached the gospel, so that by the end of the second century the church had spread throughout the Mediterranean world, into Egypt, North Africa and even France. Christianity was providing a real reason for living: life in this world and hope in a world to come.

The church worldwide

Yet, success was not without cost. Persecutions were common. And they, more often than not, led to quarrels and disputes which divided and weakened the church, sometimes irretrievably.

But then, with the issue of the Edict of Milan by the Emperor Constantine in AD 313, persecutions ceased. Christianity was now officially tolerated and before long became the state religion. On the one hand, the church's alliance with the state had a high price: until that time Christians had been a persecuted minority; from now on it would be convenient to be a Christian for political, economic and social reasons. On the other hand, the alliance, first in the form of the Holy Roman Empire and later through national churches, resulted in the flowering of Western Christian culture—Christendom.

With the growth of the Holy Roman Empire developed the power of Christendom's chief religious leaders—the Pope of Rome and the Patriarch of Constantinople—and a struggle for supremacy. In 1054 the Pope excommunicated the Patriarch and the Patriarch did the same to the Pope. This formalized the separation of the Greek and Latin churches. They became the Eastern Orthodox and Roman Catholic churches respectively, and the break is known as the great East-West Schism.

THE WAY

When his disciples asked him to teach them to pray, Jesus gave them this 'model' prayer:

Our Father in heaven,
   hallowed be your name,
your kingdom come,
   your will be done,
   on earth as in heaven.
Give us today our daily bread.
Forgive us our sins
   as we forgive those who sin against us.
Lead us not into temptation
   but deliver us from evil.
For the kingdom, the power,
   and the glory are yours
   now and for ever.

Jesus summed up the Law in two short commandments. His summary is often called the Great Commandment:

'The first commandment is this: "Hear, O Israel, the Lord our God is the only Lord. You shall love the Lord your God with all your heart, with all your soul, with all your mind, and with all your strength." The second is this: "Love your neighbour as yourself." There is no other commandment greater than these.'

CHRISTIANITY

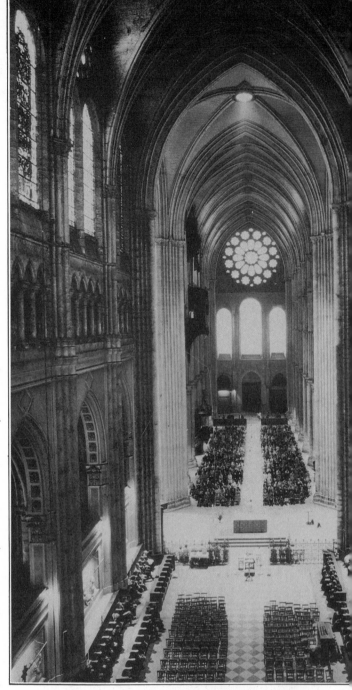

Chartres cathedral in France is one of the finest examples of Gothic architecture in the world. As in all Roman Catholic churches, the main service is the celebration of the mass; the altar stands out as the main focus of the building.

Division and growth

Along with the rest of Europe, the church emerged from the darkness of the Middle Ages into the light of the Renaissance. But it found itself suddenly confronted with the stirrings of physical and spiritual freedom, and individual and national independence. In 1515–1516 in Germany, a young monk and scholar named Martin Luther became convinced, while preparing lectures on Paul's Letter to the Romans, that salvation could come only by faith, not by good works as the church was teaching. When challenged, he refused to submit to the Pope's authority. The Reformation had begun, the movement from which churches of the Protestant tradition spring.

Today, although in decline in Europe and North America, Christianity is rapidly gaining converts in Africa, South America and parts of Asia. It claims a world membership of 900 million.

The community of believers

Christians worship together. Any group of Christians, meeting together regularly, whether in a home, a school hall or in the open air, is called a church. Special buildings for Christians to meet in have also come to be called churches.

Down the centuries, the building of churches has made an important contribution to the artistic and architectural heritage of the world. Churches are usually among the most beautiful and outstanding buildings in the villages, towns and cities of Europe, America and Australasia. Their towers and spires rise above the neighbouring houses, pointing people to God, and the great ornamented cathedrals of the Western world are rivalled only by the great sculptured temples of southern India. One usually enters a church or cathedral by the west door. At the far end, directly facing the west door, is a table on which is placed a cross and two or six candles, or simply two vases of flowers. To left and right are pulpit and lectern.

Whether in a church building or elsewhere, Christians meet together to worship God, to learn together and to celebrate their beliefs. Shortly before he died, Jesus commanded his disciples to commemorate his death until his return to earth at the end of the present age. Ever since that night, Christians have done this in the celebration known as the Mass, the Eucharist, Holy Communion or the Lord's Supper.

For churches of the Catholic and Orthodox traditions, this is the main service, often held daily. It is the main way in which the faithful receive help from God and feel his presence. Prayers are said, passages from the Bible are read and explained, hymns are sung, and bread and wine are consecrated to represent the body and blood of Christ. The priest then distributes the bread and the wine (or the bread only) to the faithful who gather round the table.

In churches of the Protestant tradition, the emphasis is different. Holy Communion may be celebrated less frequently: in some fortnightly or monthly or only twice a year. The main way in

The Christian church is flourishing in Korea. As in all Protestant churches, preaching is a central part of the church's activity.

The Christian message is one of practical as well as spiritual help. In Southern India, the Christian relief agency *TEAR Fund* has supplied vital water drilling rigs.

which believers receive spiritual nourishment is through hearing the word of God and obeying it.

In the main service on Sundays the preaching of the 'Word of God' is of chief importance. Prayers are said, passages from the Bible are read, hymns are sung and then a sermon is preached. The preacher concludes with a call to the people to hear the word of the Lord.

Christians also worship individually. They experience God in private prayer and devotion as well as in corporate worship with other believers.

Service

But Christian worship involves serving people as well as God. Medical, educational and relief work has always been a vital part of Christian activity worldwide. Christianity is a world-affirming and not a world-denying religion. God created a good world. It was man who succumbed to temptation and introduced sin. Yet, God so loved the world that he sent a redeemer. And salvation is achieved through God's redeeming the world and not by man's renouncing it. For this reason Christians work for the physical as well as the spiritual well-being of mankind.

SACRAMENTS

A sacrament is an 'outward and visible sign of an inward and spiritual grace'. Catholics and Orthodox recognize 7 sacraments: baptism, confirmation, the Eucharist, penance, extreme unction, holy orders, and marriage. Protestants generally recognize the two of these believed to be specifically commanded by Jesus: baptism and the Eucharist.

SCRIPTURES

The Christian canon of scripture, known as the Bible, was finally agreed on between AD 170 and 220. It contains 39 books of Jewish scriptures (the Old Testament) and 27 books of Christian scriptures, (the New Testament). Some people add to these the Apocrypha, a collection of Jewish writings which formed part of the Greek version of the Jewish scriptures, but which were excluded from the accepted Hebrew canon.

The New Testament consists of four Gospels, the Acts of the Apostles, the Letters of Paul, the General Letters, and the Revelation of John. Christians believe that the Bible is the written Word of God, which bears witness to Jesus, the living Word (Logos).

CALENDAR

The main events in Jesus' life are celebrated in the festivals of the Christian church.

Advent Prepares for the coming of Christ (the Messiah).

Christmas Celebrates the birth of Jesus and is held on 25 December.

Lent A period of spiritual discipline leading up to Easter.

Easter Commemorates the death and resurrection of Jesus.

Ascension Celebrates Jesus' ascension into heaven; held 40 days after Easter.

Pentecost Marks the coming of the Holy Spirit; held on the fiftieth day after Easter.

ISLAM

To the Muslim, Islam is life. It is submission to Allah. And today, with its oil-power, it is on the march to conquer the world.

Islam is the world's third great monotheistic religion. It sprang from the same root as the other two, Judaism and Christianity. 'Islam', an Arabic word, comes from a root meaning 'commitment' or 'surrender': Islam is a religion of submission. Its followers, 'Muslims', are 'those who commit themselves in surrender to the will of God (Allah)'.

Islam is also a religion which emphasizes success and therefore it is a militantly missionary religion. Conscious of a glorious past and with the newly-acquired power of the Muslim oil-rich states, she is set to conquer the world. Muslims believe that she meets all mankind's religious and spiritual needs.

The Prophet

Islam traces its origin to the Prophet Muhammad who was born in the city of Mecca, Arabia, about AD 571. At that time a power vacuum existed between the two great empires of East and West, Persia and Byzantium; Mecca was a centre of the prosperous caravan trade between Southern Arabia and the Mediterranean.

Orphaned at an early age, Muhammad was looked after by a succession of relatives. Eventually a rich uncle sent him on trading excursions to the north where it is reported that he met Christians. At the age of 25, to his surprise, he was proposed to by a wealthy widow of 40 named Khadija. She bore him three daughters but no son.

In middle life, Muhammad began to show mystical traits and developed the habit of

withdrawing to the hills for contemplation. On one such occasion, at the age of 40, he received a revelation calling him to denounce the paganism and polytheism of Mecca and preach the existence of one God, Allah. He was encouraged by his wife, but in the first ten years only a few others followed him. Some of these were prominent citizens, who are known as 'the Companions'.

Islam takes root

Then in AD 622, at the request of the citizens of nearby Medina, he left Mecca for Medina, accompanied by a few followers. This is the celebrated *hijra* or 'emigration', the event from which the Muslim calendar begins. Over the next few years Muhammad organized his followers and the citizens of Medina as a religious and political community and began to attack the trade caravans from Mecca. Meanwhile, he had expelled most of the Jewish tribes, whom he had hoped to win, and gradually incorporated the Bedouin tribes of Western and Central Arabia into the Muslim community. In 630, he massed an attack against Mecca, which finally surrendered. Muhammad immediately set about eliminating the polytheists. He rededicated the ancient sanctuary of the Ka'aba to Allah, making it the central shrine of pilgrimage for Muslims. It remains so to the present day.

The next two years were spent consolidating the tribes of Arabia. Then, suddenly, in 632 Muhammad died without naming a successor. He was succeeded by a series of caliphs ('successors'), the first two of whom were the Companions, Abu Bakr and 'Umar.

The Ka'aba is the central point of the Muslim holy city of Mecca. It is a stone structure containing a black stone, probably a meteorite, dating from pre-Islamic Arabia. Every Muslim, if resources and circumstances permit, should once in a lifetime make the pilgrimage (*hajj*) to Mecca.

ISLAM

The Qur'an and the Hadith

Soon after the death of Muhammad, the revelations which he had received were put together from oral and written sources to form the Qur'an ('recitation'). The authorized version, written in incomparable classical Arabic, was prepared about AD 650 under the third caliph, 'Uthman. Muslims believe that the Qur'an is the infallible Word of God sent down from heaven and that nothing has changed it. Simply to recite it in the original, whether understood or not, brings the Muslim grace (*baraka*).

Next in importance to the Qur'an is the Hadith ('tradition'), which is the record of the life and activities of Muhammad and the early Muslim communities. It contains the Sunna ('example') of the Prophet, the standard which all Muslims should follow. Qur'an and Sunna have combined to form the Shari'a ('law'), an extraordinarily comprehensive guide to life and conduct.

God and his angels

The doctrine of God is central to the Qur'an. Like the Bible, the Qur'an assumes the existence of God and does not argue for it. God is one and unique, with neither partners nor equals. He is good and all-powerful, as can be seen from natural phenomena, which are 'signs' of God's power and bounty. However, although the Qur'an affirms that God rules over all, it also teaches that man has responsiblity.

The Qur'an states that to God belong the most beautiful names and as Islam developed, the names of God came to play an important role. Ninety-nine names emerged and these are recited whilst using a 'rosary'. Among the most important are: 'the Great', 'the Merciful', 'the Disposer' and 'deity'.

The Qur'an strongly affirms the existence of angels, who are God's messengers. But it also believes in the existence of spiritual beings called *jinn*. These were created from fire and not from clay like men, and their purpose is to serve or worship God. Rebellious *jinn* are called demons. The chief demon is Iblis or Satan, whom God allows to tempt men to evil. Alongside the angels God appoints prophets to be his messengers, beginning with Adam, through Abraham to Jesus, and ending with Muhammad, the 'seal' of the prophets.

Life now and the last day

Next in importance to the doctrine of God in the Qur'an is the doctrine of the Last Judgment. On the last day men will be raised to life and will appear before God to be judged and to be assigned to Paradise or Hell, depending on whether their deeds have been mainly good or mainly bad.

Islam is the main religion of much of Africa.

One of the duties of a devout Muslim is to learn Qur'anic texts from an early age.

When the culture of Islam met the culture of Spain in the ninth century, a particular form of architecture resulted. Today this can be seen in the Granada. A garden symbolizing paradise is a formal way of trying to represent the delights awaiting the faithful in heaven.

Iranian students praying.

The Qur'an also contains regulations for the life of the Muslim community. It deals with religious and social behaviour such as prayer, almsgiving, fasting, pilgrimage, adultery, marriage and divorce, inheritance, food and drink, usury and slavery.

THE EXTENT OF ISLAM

Islam founded by Prophet Muhammad, born in Mecca, about AD 571.

Islam spread to the Mediterranean coast, the Atlantic coast of Africa, to the River Indus in the East and Spain in the West, through military expansion during the eighth and ninth century. Islam spread further into India and to China with the rise of the Turkish Empire and the conversion to Islam of Mongolian princes in the thirteenth and fourteenth centuries. Islam entered Eastern Europe after the fall of Constantinople in AD 1453.

Muslims now number about 500,000,000 worldwide.

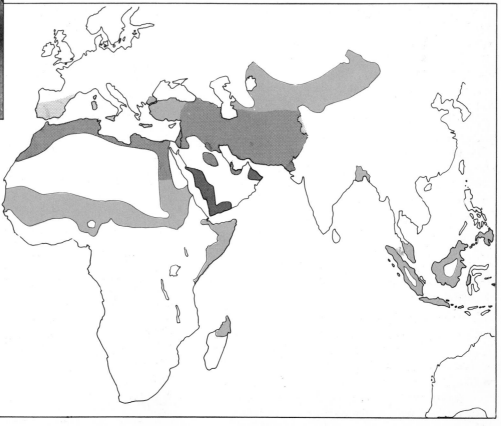

A MUSLIM CREDO

'O believers, believe in God and His Messenger and the Book He has sent down on His Messenger and the Book which He sent down before. Whoso disbelieves in God and His angels and His Books, and His Messengers, and the Last Day, has surely gone astray into far error.'
(*Qur'an IV.135*)

This Bedouin family live in Qatar in the Persian Gulf.

In many Muslim countries women are still treated very differently from men. They still go veiled (*purdah*) and do not attend the mosque.

A law for life

During the first and second centuries of Islam, its theologians and lawyers worked out the Shari'a, the law of Islam. This rests on four foundations: first, the Qur'an; second, the Sunna of the Prophet; third, analogy (*qiyas*) (deriving a new law from an existing law in the first two); and fourth, consensus of opinion (*ijma*) by means of interpretation (*ijtihad*) by experts (*ulama*) on behalf of the whole community.

A fixed code of behaviour developed which all Muslims were to follow. And 'unlike any other system in the world today the Shari'a embraces every detail of human life, from the prohibition of crime to the use of the toothpick, and from the organization of the State to the most sacred intimacies—or unsavoury aberrations—of family life. It is "the science of all things, human and divine", and divides all actions into what is obligatory or enjoined, what is praiseworthy or recommended, what is permitted or legally indifferent, what is disliked or deprecated and what is forbidden.'

For the Muslim there is no distinction between personal and communal, religious and secular, sacred and profane, spiritual and material. This often makes it difficult for the West to understand and appreciate the Islamic and Arab worlds, and vice versa. Muslims believe overwhelmingly in a Creator, whose purpose for the world is all-embracing; men take part in his creative activity as his representatives on earth.

'God is most great, I bear witness that there is no God but God. I bear witness that Muhammad is the Messenger of God. Come to prayer. Prayer is better than sleep.' These words ring out before dawn as the 'crier' (*muezzin*) calls out from the minaret of the mosque. The word 'mosque' means a 'place of prostration' and inside there are no seats, only prayer mats. In fact there is little furnishing—a pulpit and perhaps a reading-desk, on either side of a niche in the wall (*mihrab*) facing Mecca to which all Muslims turn in prayer (*qibla*).

Prayer consists of a fixed number of bowings, interspersed with the confession of faith and the ritual salutations. The bowings have seven movements, culminating in prostration.

JESUS IN THE QUR'AN

Islam believes in Prophets sent by God to preach the unity of God and to warn men of the Judgement. Several of the Prophets rank above others, particularly Adam, Noah, Abraham, Moses, Jesus and Muhammad. According to the Qur'an, Jesus was born of Mary but did not die. Instead, someone died in his place and God raised Jesus to himself. For death would have been failure, and a Prophet cannot be allowed to fail. To believe that Jesus was God would be the great sin of 'ascribing partners to God'.

THE FIVE PILLARS OF ISLAM

1 Confession of Faith (*shahada*) 'There is no God but God, and Muhammad is the Prophet of God.' A mere recital of this confession may be enough to win a new convert.

2 Prayer (*salat*) Muslims pray five times daily—at daybreak, noon, mid-afternoon, after sunset, and early in the night—alone, in company, or in the mosque. Particularly important for adult males is the congregational prayer at noon on Fridays, which usually includes a sermon.

3 Fasting (*Ramadan*) During the month of Ramadan Muslims must not eat or drink, smoke or have sexual relations between dawn and sunset.

4 Almsgiving (*zakat*) Muslims must give two and a half per cent of their income and certain kinds of property to charity.

5 Pilgrimage (*hajj*) A Muslim is required to go to Mecca once in his lifetime.

Discovering God's will

Islam is divided into two groups, Sunni and Shi'ite. The major difference between them is the way in which divine guidance is discovered. Sunni Muslims (who make up about 90 per cent of the total) take their stand on the consensus of the community making known the Sunna of the Prophet. Shi'ite Muslims look instead to inspired teachers or Imams. The Imams were descendants of Ali, the nephew and adopted son of the Prophet, who possessed secret knowledge and special interpretation passed down from Muhammad himself.

Three main groups of Shi'ites survive. The Zaidis of the Yemen, recognize a living series of Imams. The Twelve-Imam Shi'ites, who dominate in Iran, believe that the line ended with the twelfth Imam. The Seven-Imam Shi'ites, or Ismailis of India and East Africa, are the followers of the Aga Khan and believe that the line ended with the seventh Imam.

Both the Seven-Imam and the Twelve-Imam Shi'ites await the appearance of the 'hidden Imam' known as the Mahdi. Meanwhile, because they do not believe in the principle of consensus, their leading theologians, called Mujtahids, are considered spokesmen for the 'hidden Imam' and exercise extensive authority in religious, legal and even political matters. This is seen clearly in the activities of the Mullahs and Ayatollahs of contemporary Iran (many of whom claim to be descended from Ali). The Mujtahids take no account of the opinions of early lawyers but go back directly to general principles contained in Qur'an, Sunna and Hadith. This explains their fundamentalism.

THE WORLD'S RELIGIONS

Ethnic religions
Hinduism
Buddhism
China: Confucianism, Buddhism, Taoism
Japan: Shinto, Buddhism, Sects
Christianity
Islam

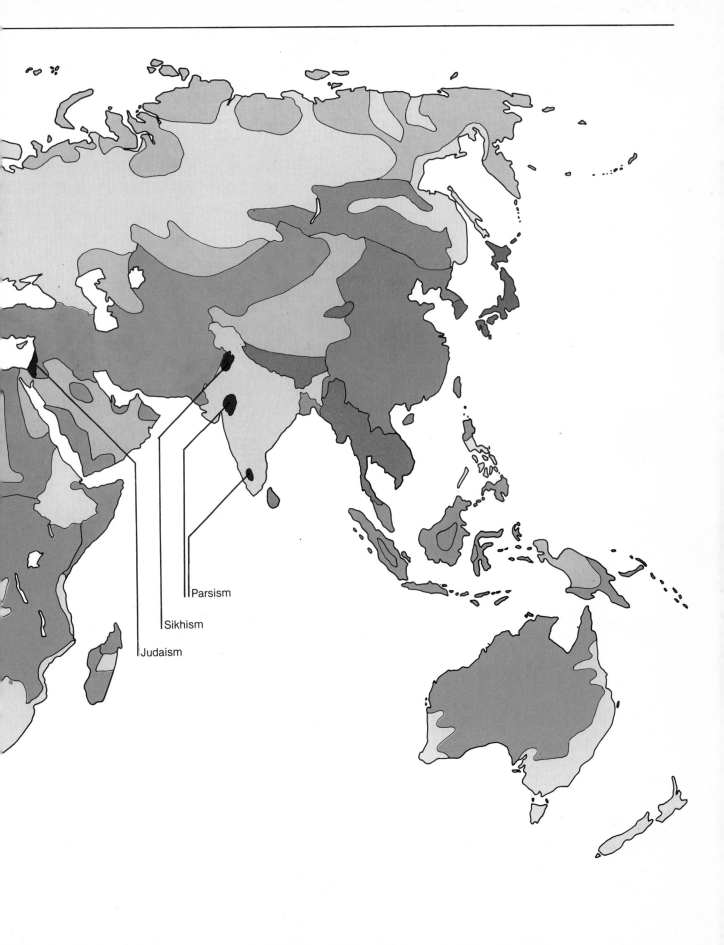

Parsism

Sikhism

Judaism

EPILOGUE

People have called themselves 'Christian' for many different reasons. And I can echo many of them in my own experience. But at heart, to be a Christian is to be a follower of Jesus Christ.

I AM A CHRISTIAN because my parents were Christians before me. I was born and brought up in an Irish village, where it was natural to believe and most unnatural not to. At home, I learnt to pray at my mother's knee. At school, I listened to stories from the Bible and became aware of my Irish Christian heritage. At Sunday school, I mastered the catechism. In church, I discovered what it meant to worship God.

And throughout I learnt to observe and celebrate—with everyone else in the village—the significant moments of the Christian life and the great events of the Christian year. Baptisms, confirmations and holy communions, Christmas, Easter and Pentecost, all stand out as some of the most momentous and memorable occasions of childhood.

I AM A CHRISTIAN because as a teenager I made a conscious decision to follow Jesus. By means of what can be called a conversion experience I entered into a personal relationship with Jesus Christ as Saviour and Lord, receiving the forgiveness of sins and embarking on a new life. I persisted as a Christian through the stormy years of adolescence.

From time to time, doubting the existence of God for intellectual reasons, I suspended belief for brief periods. Later, at college, I took as my motto Anselm's famous maxim: 'I do not seek to understand so that I may believe; but I believe so that I may understand. For I believe this also that "unless I believe, I shall not understand".'

I AM A CHRISTIAN despite the problem of pain. I experienced a time of acute personal suffering in my late twenties and it was then I realized that the Christian God is a God who himself entered into the suffering of the world, so as to redeem it. The cross, the crucifixion of Jesus Christ, is at the centre of Christianity.

I AM A CHRISTIAN because, encountering the world's other religions in Africa, I recognized in Jesus Christ the Word of God (the Logos), the

African Christians singing and praising the Lord

The Rock of Cashel in County Tipperary is crowned by the most imposing of ecclesiastical remains in Ireland.

A POEM OF THE CROSS

The death and resurrection of Jesus is the central fact of Christianity. This hymn from Ireland sums up what his death means to the believer.

There is a green hill far away
  Without a city wall,
Where the dear Lord was crucified,
  Who died to save us all.

He died that we might be forgiven,
  He died to make us good,
That we might go at last to heaven,
  Saved by his precious blood.

We may not know, we cannot tell
  What pains he had to bear,
But we believe it was for us
  He hung and suffered there.

There was no other good enough
  To pay the price of sin,
He only could unlock the gate
  Of heaven, and let us in.

Oh dearly, dearly has he loved,
  And we must love him too,
And trust in his redeeming blood,
  And try his works to do.

Mrs Cecil Frances Alexander

THE SHIELD OF GOD

The Christian follows Jesus Christ. The prayer of Saint Patrick, the patron saint of Ireland, expresses the desire for Christ to be in every part of his life.

Christ for my guardianship today . . .
Christ with me, Christ before me,
Christ behind me, Christ in me,
Christ under me, Christ over me,
Christ to right of me, Christ to left of me,
Christ in lying down, Christ in sitting, Christ in rising up,
Christ in the heart of every person, who may think of me!
Christ in the mouth of every one, who may speak to me!
Christ in every eye, which may look on me!
Christ in every ear, which may hear me!

light who enlightens every person who comes into the world. Religion is not only men's search for God but rather God's finding of men. The Word became flesh and dwelt among us.

I AM A CHRISTIAN despite the fact that we live in a world full of sinful people and marred by unjust social structures. For Jesus came to initiate change: 'to bring good news to the poor, to proclaim liberty to captives and to the blind new sight, to set the downtrodden free, to proclaim the Lord's year of favour'.

I REMAIN A CHRISTIAN because I am convinced that in the person of Jesus Christ is to be found all the fulness of God, in his message is to be discerned hope for our world, and in his church is to be discovered true community.

GLOSSARY

Altar A raised flat-topped structure where offerings are made to the deity; the Communion table in Christian churches.

Anthropology The study of man.

Church A group of Christian believers; the body of all Christians; a building designed for public worship.

Contemplation Concentration of the mind and soul upon God.

Creed A system or statement of belief; particularly a brief formal summary of Christian belief.

Deity A god or goddess; the nature or character of God.

Dualism The belief that reality consists of two basic principles, mind and matter; the theory that the universe has been ruled from its origin by two conflicting powers, one good and one evil, both existing as equally ultimate first causes.

Grace Help or assistance given by God to man, in order to inspire, strengthen or bring spiritual rebirth.

Hymn Songs of praise to God, especially Christian.

Image A representation or likeness of a person or thing.

Lectern A reading-desk, especially in a church.

Magic The art of using spells to influence events by supernatural means.

Meditation Deep reflection on spiritual matters, especially as a religious act.

Monism The belief that reality consists of only one basic substance.

Monotheism The belief that there is only one God.

Mosque A Muslim place of worship.

Mysticism A system of contemplative prayer and spirituality aimed at achieving direct intuitive experience of the supernatural or the divine.

Polytheism The worship of or belief in more than one god.

Prayer A personal communication or petition addressed to a deity.

Priest A person who acts as a mediator between God and man by administering the sacraments, preaching, blessing, guiding, making offerings and so on.

Prophet A person who speaks by divine inspiration; especially one through whom God reveals himself and expresses his will.

Pulpit A raised enclosed platform from which the preacher delivers a sermon.

Rabbi The spiritual leader of a Jewish congregation; an early Jewish scholar.

Reincarnation The belief that at death the soul is born again into another body.

Resurrection The rising again of the dead at the Last Judgment.

Ritual The prescribed way of performing a religious or other rite.

Sacrament An outward sign combined with a prescribed form of words and regarded as conferring some specific grace upon those who receive it, especially in Christianity.

Sacrifice The killing of an animal or person, the surrender of a possession, as an offering to a deity.

Scripture A sacred or authoritative book or piece of writing.

Shaman A medicine man or priest who controls the spirits, especially among the tribespeople of North America and northern Asia.

Shrine A place of worship kept holy because of its association with a sacred person or object.

Sociology The study of human societies.

Symbol Something that represents or stands for something else, usually by convention or association.

Synagogue An assembly or congregation of Jews meeting for religious observance or instruction; the building in which they meet.

Temple A building dedicated to the worship of the deity, especially in the ancient world, in India and in the East generally.

Theology The systematic study of the existence and nature of God; a particular branch of this study, for example, Christian theology.

Worship Religious devotion and respect, especially its formal expression.

CULTS
AND NEW FAITHS

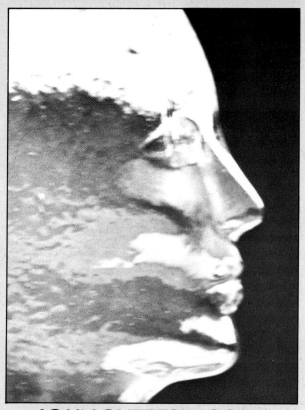

JOHN BUTTERWORTH

CULTS AND NEW FAITHS

'May I come in and discuss the Bible with you?'

'Would you like to buy a candle to help missionary work?'

'May I talk to you about your life?'

At one time or another, everyone has been approached and asked these sort of questions. And most people do not know how to react. Is this a visit from the church I went to last Christmas? Is it another charity collection? Or is it some new cult I have read about in the paper?

In the last 100 years, and especially since the 1960s, the increase in new religions, cults and faiths has been enormous. Many of the followers are in their teens or early twenties. But they also come from all ages and backgrounds. They range from the conservatively-dressed, studious Mormons to the orange-robed, shaven-headed followers of the eastern Hare Krishna movement.

But how can we tell what the movements are like? Most people used to dismiss them as small groups of cranks who were best left alone. But since the tragic mass suicide of the Jonestown People's Temple in Guyana, and TV coverage of brainwashing techniques in other cults, people have begun to realize the dangers such groups can represent.

Jesus told his followers: 'Beware of false prophets who come to you in sheep's clothing but inwardly are ravenous wolves.' As in Jesus' day, so today we have a real problem with 'false prophets'.

Who are they?

New groups which attract the label 'cults' often have certain characteristics. They frequently have a very strong, charismatic leader. Absolute obedience to the leader and his teaching is often called for. This obedience can include giving up home, job, family and possessions.

There seem to be four main categories of cult. There are the **self-improvement groups** such as Scientology, whose members are trying to discover themselves and improve their personalities. There are the **eastern groups** such as the Divine Light Mission, whose followers believe that the mystical East gives more meaning to life than the materialistic West. There are the **unification groups** such as the Moonies, who take elements of truth from many religions and claim to fulfil them all. There are the **Christian deviation groups** such as the Children of God and The Way, which seem to have been genuinely Christian to begin with but put so much emphasis on their own added teachings that they can no longer be called so.

Other new (and not-so-new) faiths cannot be labelled as cults. Baha'i, for example, is a prime example of a unification group, but is much more a young religion than a cult. Christadelphianism, Seventh-Day Adventism and Moral Re-Armament are movements which have sprung from mainstream Christianity and have their own distinctive teachings.

Why the growth in cults?

Many people, particularly the young, are thoroughly dissatisfied with society. Politics provides no answers. Science creates more problems than it solves. Mechanistic views of man and society have made man impersonal and in need of a true identity.

The future seems frightening, with the threat

of nuclear war and the running down of natural resources. At the same time family life is providing no security and the church in the West seems to be declining.

People are looking for help. And in many cases the cults seem to offer it. They have a highly organized system to believe in and become involved with. They show real interest in welcoming new members and a real enthusiasm for spreading their message.

What can be done?

By and large, members of the cults are sincere people who feel that they have discovered something important. If you speak to them on the street corner you will find most of them friendly enough—though rather persistent in their conversation. Most street-level members genuinely feel that they are right in their beliefs.

But, unfortunately, many members have found out only too late that what they have become involved with has hidden undercurrents, which they are less than happy about. It can be very hard for a member to do anything about this when he is surrounded by the pressure of a close-knit group. Can anything be done to help?

First, the facts should be made known. In some cases we do not have to look far before we see danger signs. In others pitfalls are there, but carefully hidden. Jesus said, 'You will know them by their fruit'. As a journalist and a Christian I hope that the following pages will help to show up those of them which are 'false prophets' by showing something of their 'fruit'. In short articles such as these, it has been impossible to go into great detail—and often the facts are changing very rapidly.

Second, those who are vulnerable should be helped—young people, the mentally handicapped, the lonely, the drifters, the bereaved. We should help them to see the possible dangers involved.

Most of all, the real answers should be examined, both to spiritual needs and to the problems of society. The answers of mainstream Christianity are as relevant today as ever, with the appeal of Jesus Christ for us to come to him and find new life.

KEY QUESTIONS

If you want to find out whether a group is in the mainstream of Christian teaching you can do so by asking three questions.

Who was Jesus? Christians believe that Jesus was a real historical figure and that he was both God and man. Most heresies deny at least one of these points.

How can man be saved? The Bible states: 'By grace you have been saved through faith; and this is not your own doing, it is the gift of God—not because of works lest any man should boast.' False prophets emphasize in one way or another that man can earn his way to heaven by doing the right things.

What is their authority? Christians accept the Bible as their supreme authority and as God's revelation to man. Many false prophets use additional 'revelations' which they make equal with the Bible as 'God's revelation for the present age'. Others accept the authority of the Bible—but only as interpreted by their leader.

THE CHILDREN OF GOD

"Drop out of the system and live for Jesus: Judgement is coming soon."

'We are revolutionary Christian nomads, bypassing the hopeless, unresponsive older generation and churchy people and bringing new-time religion to a New Generation,' claim the Children of God. The movement, which was begun in 1968 by David Brandt Berg, claims to have 2 million converts and 8,000 missionaries worldwide. Followers hand over all their possessions to the movement and live in colonies, in order to 'return to the truth, love, peace and beauty of our ancients ... the simple life of true happiness in God and love for our fellow man'.

Revolutionary beginnings

In 1969 David Berg claimed that he had received a prophecy from God: an earthquake would send California crashing into the sea and he, like Moses, would lead God's children through the desert.

Berg was born in 1919, the son of an evangelist couple, and for a time he was a pastor of the Christian and Missionary Alliance church. But he fell out with the leaders and became disillusioned with institutionalized religion. He moved to Huntington Beach, California, where he began working with drop-outs. One hundred and fifty of them followed 'Moses David', or 'Mo' as he was known, out of California on their journey into the desert.

For several months they wandered around witnessing, until TV evangelist Fred Jordan allowed them to stay at his 400-acre ranch in Texas. They used his ranch as the base from which to prepare the world for Jesus' Second Coming. In return they appeared on Jordan's TV show. But in 1971 Jordan evicted them after a row and they set up colonies, first in America and then throughout the world.

Very little is known about Moses David, who refuses to be interviewed. He is believed to live in Europe, probably in Italy, in self-imposed seclusion, having delegated most of the day-to-day running of the movement to trusted deputies.

Life as a Child of God

The Children of God expect a Communist takeover of the West, leading to persecution of Christians. They say the best way to prepare for

this is to live as though it has already happened. So followers live in colonies, some of which are surrounded by 'No Trespassing' signs and high cyclone fences.

To join the movement a person has to sign a form saying: 'I promise to give all my goods and income, to let you open my mail. I will obey rules and officers.' A new member goes first to a 'babe's colony'. Early in the movement's history, new members spent up to eight hours a day in Bible study and memorized hundreds of Bible verses. Today that emphasis has changed. After the babe's colony he will join another colony of about 12 people. The word 'commune' is not used, since it has connotations of sexual permissiveness. A member, who will often adopt a new biblical name, will rarely have a day off and will have no privacy, as otherwise Satan might tempt him.

The main task of the members is to sell literature on the streets. Members who achieve their quota are 'shiners', and are rewarded with a little money for their own use. Those who fail are 'shamers' and have to do extra jobs such as washing up or cleaning the toilets. Regular 'shamers' are sent to a town without a colony where they have to raise enough money to pay for their own board and keep for a month.

In its early days in America, the Children of God picked up many followers from the confused and chaotic youth culture of cities such as Los Angeles. The group offered the young disciples emotional security and a revolutionary message.

KEY BELIEFS

● They are the only true followers of God.

● The world-system, including schools, governments, churches and families, is inspired by the Devil.

● Moses David is God's prophet for today.

● No action is wrong in itself. Everything depends on attitude. If a deed is done 'in the spirit', it is right. If it is done 'in the flesh', it is wrong.

● Jesus will return to earth in 1993.

● Before then the Children of God will preach to the whole world. They will be helped in this by Colonel Gadaffi of Libya, who will make peace with Israel.

● The Battle of Armageddon will take place when Russia invades Israel. America will be drawn into the conflict and, along with Israel, be decisively beaten. A world Communist government will then be set up and will last for seven years until Jesus returns.

The changing teaching

In the last few years the Children of God, or the Family of Love as they now like to be known, has changed radically. The emphasis on the movement used to be on Jesus—now it is on Moses David. An ex-follower, whose wife was one of the movement's founder members in Huntington Beach said: 'Having a confrontation with Christ isn't the big thing any more. The key to success in COG is how effectively a person fits into the Moses David witnessing machine, producing more income and more disciples for King David.'

In the early days, followers were taught from the Bible. Now, however, the teaching is based on the MO letters. The movement's two main Bible teachers, Joab and Joel Wordsworth, have been denounced by Moses David and excommunicated. Berg has warned all members to destroy Joel's letters, threatening them with excommunication if they do not.

And the inspiration of the MO letters has become very dubious, as Moses David has become more and more involved in the occult. He claims to have a number of 'spiritual counsellors' who give him revelations, supposedly from God. They include Rasputin, the Pied Piper, Joan of Arc, Oliver Cromwell, Merlin the Magician and Martin Luther. His main counsellor is Abrahim, a supposed gypsy king who died a thousand years ago. Abrahim's messages include much that is heretical and blasphemous.

The changing practices

Even more sensational is Moses David's claim that he has sex with spirits, whom he calls goddesses. The whole movement has become increasingly sex-orientated. Moses David wrote: 'We have a sexy God and a sexy religion and a very sexy leader with a very sexy following. So if you don't like sex you had better get out while you can.' Now women followers are expected to go out onto the streets and become 'hookers for Jesus'—religious prostitutes.

In FFers Handbook (FF stands for 'flirty fish') Moses David tells women: 'There's no reason not to display the blessing of the Lord . . . Don't be afraid to wear low-cut gowns with very low necklines even to the waist or navel—no bras, see-through blouses. Show them what you've got— that's the bait . . . I want them to absolutely totally flip and fall in love with you.'

The point, says Moses David, is that 'in one night you can show what a love slave you are and how sweet and humble and unselfish you are . . . You'd better let them understand from the beginning that the reason you love them so much, that you're willing to give them everything, is because God loves them so much and expects them to give Him everything in return'.

The changing movement

In a magazine article in 1977, David Jacks, a former Children of God archbishop, explained why he had left the movement, and why he believed Berg to be a false prophet: 'I am convinced that in the early days most members really received Jesus as their personal saviour when they entered the group . . . But now the Children of God is degenerating. David Berg is getting more and more into pornography, spiritism, astrology and other far-out things—substituting this garbage for the fundamental Christian faith.'

In the early 70s, the European headquarters of the Children of God was this converted warehouse in south London. Here disciples lived in community and planned their outreach.

The main way in which Moses David communicates with his followers, most of whom have never seen him, is by the 'MO letter'. These letters contain his teachings and his latest revelations concerning future world events, which he claims to receive in a trance from his spirit guides. Some of the MO letters are sold to the public and bring in as much as $1 million profit a month.

Moses David wrote his first MO letter, *The Old Church and the New Church*, to get himself out of a tight spot. Word was getting out that he had left his wife and was living with his secretary. In the letter he explained that his wife represented the old church and his secretary the new. God was putting away the old, which was a hindrance.

Since then he has written many hundreds of letters, including the pornographic *in the beginning—Sex* and *Come on Ma! Burn your Bra*. In one letter, *God bless you and Goodbye*, he even confessed that he was a false prophet, but this was quickly followed by another letter which claimed that the previous one was a forgery.

ARE THEY THE CHILDREN OF GOD?

● The New Testament shows that the early church's 'commune' was temporary and voluntary. The Children of God say that their communes are compulsory and that members must hand over all their possessions to the movement.

● The Bible teaches that stealing is wrong. The Children of God will often 'provision' food from supermarkets.

● Followers of the movement are notorious for blasphemy and swearing.

● Members are seldom allowed to communicate with their parents and then only to ask for money. Records are kept on all parents, particularly on their earnings.

● Some parents have claimed that the movement kidnapped and brainwashed their children. In 1972, 60 parents formed the Parents Committee to Free Our Sons and Daughters from the Children of God, known as FREECOG. Shortly afterwards a Texas group, THANKCOG, was formed 'to reassure parents that these accusations aren't true'.

● The Children of God withdrew from America and Britain, saying that Moses David knew that nuclear war would wipe the countries out. Critics have said that the real reason for the departure was increased media pressure and the movement's failure to keep tax records.

CHRISTIAN SCIENCE

A church which believes in healing through prayer alone.

The Church of Christ, Scientist was founded by Mary Baker Eddy over a century ago as a church, in the words of its founding resolution, 'designed to commemorate the word and works of our Master, which should reinstate primitive Christianity and its lost element of healing'.

Most people first meet Christian Science in one of two ways. First, there are churches in towns throughout the 60 countries where the movement operates. In their Reading Rooms, the enquirer can read the church's literature. Second, the church has its own highly respected international newspaper, *The Christian Science Monitor*, which has just one religious item each day.

Mary Baker Eddy

Mary Baker was born in Bow, New Hampshire in 1821 to loving but strict Puritan parents. The first half of her life was beset by ill-health and misfortune. At twenty-two she married Major George Glover, a building contractor, who died within a year, leaving her with a baby son.

The next twenty-five years (during which she married again, and later divorced) were spent in a long and restless search for peace and healing, in which the Bible was a constant companion, while the great issues of redemption, punishment and eternal life were often in her thought. Simultaneously she explored homoeopathy and a wide range of healing methods, culminating in that of a well-known mesmeric healer, Phineas Quimby.

In 1866 she reached a decisive turning-point when she was healed of a serious injury as she studied her Bible. This experience led to her founding of Christian Science, with its method of healing through prayer alone. She began to heal others and take students, and in 1875 published

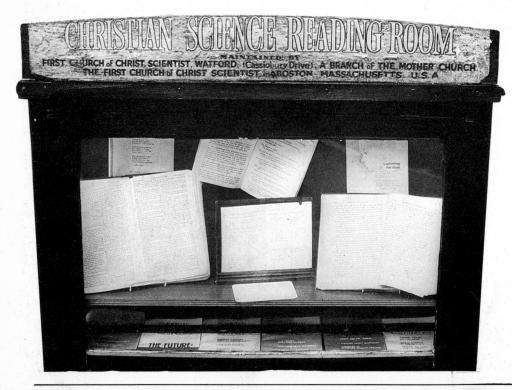

In the display boxes outside some Christian Science churches there is generally a Bible (the King James/Authorized Version), *Science and Health with Key to the Scriptures*, the *Christian Science Quarterly*, containing the weekly Bible lessons, and other periodicals published by The Christian Science Publishing Society.

A service in progress in a Christian Science church.

Each Sunday, worshippers in this church near London will hear the same message as all other Christian Scientists across the world.

The weekly Bible lesson, consisting of readings from the Bible and *Science and Health*, is studied by Christian Scientists during the week. On Sundays, this forms a 'Lesson-Sermon', read by the two Readers who conduct the service. At Wednesday evening meetings there are testimonies of healing. The Sunday School is for pupils up to twenty. The church is run by lay people and each member is expected to be actively involved.

the textbook of Christian Science, *Science and Health with Key to the Scriptures*.

Four years later the church was founded, and she found much comfort and help in Asa Gilbert Eddy, the first student to call himself publicly a Christian Scientist, whom she married in 1877. The church, and Mary Baker Eddy herself, encountered major opposition for the unorthodoxy both of its theology and of its healing ministry. But the number of churches grew rapidly in the United States and Europe.

Mrs Eddy founded *The Christian Science Monitor* in 1908, in her eighty-eighth year, and until she died in 1910 she continued to oversee the affairs of the church.

Numerically, the church peaked in the 1940s, but there has been some falling off since, though growth continues in some areas, particularly third world countries. There are now some 2,800 Christian Science churches around the globe.

KEY BELIEFS

The following are the tenets[1] to which every Christian Scientist subscribes on joining the church:

1. As adherents of Truth, we take the inspired Word of the Bible as our sufficient guide to eternal life.

2. We acknowledge and adore one supreme and infinite God. We acknowledge His Son, one Christ; the Holy Ghost or divine Comforter; and man in God's image and likeness.

3. We acknowledge God's forgiveness of sin in the destruction of sin and the spiritual understanding that casts out evil as unreal. But the belief in sin is punished so long as the belief lasts.

4. We acknowledge Jesus' atonement as the evidence of divine, efficacious Love, unfolding man's unity with God through Christ Jesus the Way-shower; and we acknowledge that man is saved through Christ, through Truth, Life, and Love as demonstrated by the Galilean Prophet in healing the sick and overcoming sin and death.

5. We acknowledge that the crucifixion of Jesus and his resurrection served to uplift faith to understand eternal Life, even the allness of Soul, Spirit, and the nothingness of matter.

6. And we solemnly promise to watch, and pray for that Mind to be in us which was also in Christ Jesus; to do unto others as we would have them do unto us; and to be merciful, just, and pure.

Although Christian Science is primarily associated with the healing of sickness, that is only one aspect of its religious ministry. *Science and Health* puts such healing in perspective by describing its purpose now as in primitive Christianity as being 'to attest the reality of the higher mission of the Christ-power to take away the sins of the world'.

[1] From *Science and Health* © The Christian Science Board of Directors, quoted by permission.

THE DIVINE LIGHT MISSION

'Maharaj Ji is here. Recognize him, obey him and adore him.'

Guru Maharaj Ji is certainly different from most gurus. He chews gum, loves ice cream and enjoys sports cars and cabin cruisers. Unlike some gurus he encourages his followers to keep their jobs, enjoy good food and make more money, though many have left their jobs to live with other devotees in 'ashrams'.

Thirteen years after his father began the Divine Light Mission in 1960, membership had soared to more than six million. Over the next few years there was a dramatic drop in numbers, but interest is rising again. Followers believe that the Guru Maharaj Ji—or 'Goom Rodgie' as they call him—is the Perfect Master for the present age, who gives 'divine light' or 'knowledge' to his followers so that they can have perfect guidance.

Activities of the religion include a 'divine airline', a publishing company which prints their newspaper *Divine Times* and their magazine *And it is Divine*, second-hand shops called Divine Sales, a New York vegetarian restaurant, a record and film company, an electronics firm, car repairs, laundry services and a food co-op.

Life of a Guru

In 1966 an eight-year-old Indian boy told the weeping mourners at his father's funeral: 'Maharaj Ji is here. Recognize him, obey him and adore him.' Immediately the boy, Shri Sant Ji, was enthroned as the new Perfect Master and took the title Guru Maharaj Ji. The mourners should not have been over-surprised at this: the boy had given his first holy discourse (or 'satsang') when he was two.

The Guru's father, Yogi Raj Paramhans Satguruder Shri Hans Ji Maharaj, founded the Divine Light Mission in 1960 and gave his son 'Knowledge' when he was six. He had begun spreading the basic ideas of the Divine Light Mission in the 1920s after he claimed to have received enlightenment through meditating on knowledge given to him by another guru, Shri Sarupanand Ji. Despite fierce opposition from orthodox Hindu sects, his movement continued to grow and when he died he had millions of disciples.

Today Guru Maharaj Ji and his three older brothers, Bal Bhagwan Ji, Shri Raja Ji and Shri Bhole Ji are all involved in the Divine Light Mission or its rival groups.

The 15-year-old Perfect Master welcomed 20,000 people to the Alexandra Palace in London in 1971.

KEY BELIEFS

● God is impersonal. He is energy. People are part of that energy.

● God is revealed through incarnations, the 'Perfect Master' for this age being Guru Maharaj Ji.

● Jesus, Buddha, Krishna and Mohammed were all Perfect Masters for their ages.

● 'Christ' is the title applied to every Perfect Master.

● Salvation comes through 'Knowledge' or enlightenment given by the Guru. This Knowledge comes not just from the mind, but from an experience of 'cosmic energy'.

● The Bible is accepted as authentic Scripture, but followers of the Divine Light Mission apply the prophecies of Jesus Christ's Second Coming to Guru Maharaj Ji. Jesus' 'coming in clouds' is said to have been fulfilled when the Guru flew into London Airport. They also believe that Christians have altered the meaning of the Bible.

● To meet 'God' one must go within oneself. Every human has a 'third eye'—the divine eye—which most people are ignorant of. This divine eye is opened by the Perfect Master who makes his followers aware of it by 'taking knowledge' or 'experiencing the light'.

● Ideas and words are unimportant—it is experience which counts.

The controversial guru

The Guru has hit the headlines with many of his exploits.

In November 1972 he was stopped by Indian customs officials in his chartered jumbo jet with a suitcase containing money, watches and jewels valued at £27,000.

Some members who have left the movement claim that they were being brainwashed. After meditating some said they lost the ability to read or do simple arithmetic. According to some former members the main leaders in the movement do little meditation: they need to retain their faculties for administration.

In 1974 the Guru married a former airline stewardess, Marolyn Johnson. This upset his family, especially when he declared that his non-Hindu wife was an incarnation of a ten-armed, tiger-riding Hindu goddess.

In April 1975 the Lord of the Universe was removed as head of the movement by his mother, Shri Mataji, for 'indulging and encouraging his devotees to eat meat, get married, have sexual relations and drink'. She installed his eldest brother Bal Bhagwan Ji as leader of a rival group. Many disciples left and the membership is reported still to be falling today. Meanwhile Guru Maharaj Ji lives quietly with his wife and two children in a mansion overlooking the Pacific in Malibu, California, and has only recently begun active campaigning again.

The Guru in India

About one and a half million people paid homage to the young Perfect Master when he first took his Knowledge to the world in 1970 by driving through Delhi in a golden chariot followed by a procession of camels, elephants and supporters. The Guru, who had left school to start his mission, dropped what his followers called a 'Peace Bomb' when he told the crowd at the India Gate in New Delhi: 'I declare that I will establish peace in this world.'

The Guru in America

Billed as 'the most significant event in the history of mankind', the Divine Light Mission in America sponsored a giant festival in November 1973 entitled *Millennium 73*. It was designed to herald the beginning of the Millennium described in Revelation chapter 20, when Guru Maharaj Ji

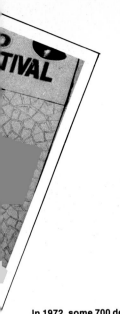

In 1972, some 700 devotees of the Divine Light Mission followed the guru to India. At the Delhi spiritual festival they stayed in tent communities.

would promise an end to human suffering and bring in 1,000 years of peace.

Entrance to the event at Houston Astrodome· was free and up to 200,000 people were expected. As the comet Kohoutek was on its way, some supporters even said visitors from outer space would be coming.

But the event turned out to be a financial flop with less then 20,000 people turning up—and not one from outer space.

The Guru in England

Pop fans at a festival at Glastonbury, England, were amazed when their concert was invaded by a white Rolls Royce. It was driven by the Perfect Master, making his first public appearance in England. He preached for five minutes to the bemused fans—before someone switched off the microphone.

GROWING IN DIVINE LIGHT

After receiving Knowledge there are four ways in which a premie can grow spiritually.

Meditation There are four types of meditation which premies are advised to practise for at least two hours a day—seeing divine light, hearing divine music (both inside one's head), tasting divine nectar and perceiving the world within oneself.

Darshan The second way is to see the Guru Maharaj Ji in person, to prostrate oneself before him and touch his feet, showing complete surrender.

Satsang The third way is spiritual discourse.

Service The fourth way is through any physical or mental activity dedicated to the Guru.

Every morning and evening before meditation, premies sing a devotional song to the Guru. Behind the ashram's altar hangs a picture of him. On the altar is usually a cup containing holy water touched by the Guru's feet, which premies drink.

GUIDE TO THE LANGUAGE OF DIVINE LIGHT

Satguru A Hindu word meaning 'one who leads from darkness to light'. It refers to the Perfect Master.

Knowledge The ultimate spiritual experience, given by the Perfect Master.

Mahatma A special disciple who passes on Knowledge from the Perfect Master to other followers.

Premie A devotee of the Guru who has become a member of the Divine Light Mission. The word is Hindi for 'lover'.

Ashram Literally a 'shelter' where premies live. Premies are expected to hand over all their possessions to the Mission; to spend their whole time serving the Mission; to obey the leader of the ashram; to sleep only five hours a day and to abstain from alcohol, drugs, tobacco, meat and sex and any food not provided by the ashram.

Premie house A community house with a less strict routine than an ashram's.

ECKANKAR

Eckankar claims to be 'the highest of all movements', the most ancient of all religious revelations to man.'

Eckankar, which teaches that by 'soul travel' man can enter the Kingdom of Heaven, was 'revived' in 1964 by an American, Paul Twitchell. He claimed to be the 971st Living Eck Master.

Since then the movement has grown rapidly and there are now more than 50,000 'chelas', or students, worldwide.

Paul Twitchell

Twitchell, believed to have been born in Paducah, Kentucky, in 1908 (though he himself gave several birthdates) had always been interested in spiritual matters.

According to him, his grandmother sent him and his sister Kay-Dee to Paris where they met an Indian guru, Sudar Singh. This has been denied by a member of his own family. In 1950 in Washington DC, he and his first wife, Camille, joined an eastern mystic group, Swami Premananda's Self-Revelation Church of Absolute Monism.

But in 1955 disaster struck—his first wife left him and he was asked to leave the church because of misconduct.

That same year, a Hindu mystic, Kirpal Singh toured the United States. He had formed his own movement, 'Ruhani Satsang'—the 'Divine Science of the Soul'—and Twitchell was initiated into the movement though still continuing to dabble in other eastern and occult systems.

Twitchell then wrote *The Tiger's Fang*, telling of his travels with Kirpal Singh through the soul planes. But his leader did not approve, and warned him not to publish. A split developed between the two mystics. Twitchell deleted all references to Singh in *The Tiger's Fang* and said that his revelations had come from a mythical 500-year-old Tibetan monk, Rebazar Tarzs. In 1971 he denied that he even knew of Kirpal Singh.

Eventually in 1964 Twitchell founded a new religion, Eckankar, a 'revived version' of 'a timeless and universal truth'. He wrote articles and gave public lectures on his philosophy and within three years his following had grown from three to several thousands.

He died from a heart attack in a hotel room in Cincinnati, Ohio, on 17 September 1971, but the movement is still continuing under his successor, Darwin Gross.

Eckankar provides 'the way to total awareness ... through the ancient science of soul travel ... the projection of the inner consciousness ... into the ecstatic states.' It is not the only group to promote astral projection—but the reality of the experience is questionable.

It was on the 'astral plane', on 22 October 1971, that Darwin Gross received the Rod of Power from the dead Paul Twitchell, and became the 972nd Living Eck Master.

KEY BELIEFS

● God is everything and everywhere. Eckankar's name for God is 'Sugmad', the everlasting ECK, the 'cosmic current'.

● It is not possible to enter the Kingdom of God except through the teachings of Eckankar.

● The Kingdom of Heaven is composed of eleven different realms. The upper six are 'heavenly'. The lower five are ruled by the devil, 'Kal Niranjan', who causes all the daily problems of the first realm, earth.

● The only way to travel through the realms to reach Sugmad is by 'soul travel'. This is achieved by submitting to the living ECK master, the 'Mahanta'.

● Man has five bodies: the physical body; the astral or emotional body; the causal body, where the recollection of the soul's past experience is kept; the mental body, including the unconscious; the soul body.

● When a person does wrong he must pay back his debt or 'karma'. This payment is made through reincarnation. The soul enters the universe as a mineral and works its way up via plant, fish, reptile and mammal incarnations to the human body. After millions of years it can reach enlightenment. If it abuses the system it will be sent back to the beginning again.

● There is a short cut to God-realization. The presence of the Living Master will burn away the debt of karma.

● There are ten initiations, one for advancing to each realm. These initiations are considered the basic 'sacrament' of Eckankar.

● There are five major forms of soul travel: imaginative projection; meditation; projection via the dream state; trances; direct projection.

GURDJIEFF

Man is spiritually asleep and can rediscover his waking state only by work, discussion, music, dancing and the discovery of his essential unchanging 'I'.

If you haven't heard of Gurdjieff it is hardly surprising. His followers are very shy of publicity. They believe that their message may be lost by being over-simplified. Hence it is difficult to become a follower because it is difficult to find out Gurdjieff's teaching.

The key to this teaching is work. One of Gurdjieff's followers, the author Colin Wilson, wrote: 'From birth until the age of 21 we grow physically and in every other sense. Changes take place inside us without our volition. Then it stops . . . and most people ossify. If growth is to continue unusual efforts must be made in order to stimulate the robot into producing "newness". This was the core of Gurdjieff's work. Its first aim was to defeat man's natural laziness, his tendency to relax and switch off.'

Although Gurdjieff died in 1949 he still has more than 5,000 followers. Several independent 'branches' follow different interpretations of his philosophy.

A spiritual traveller

George Ivanovich Gurdjieff, known to his followers as 'G', is believed to have been born near the Armenian town of Alexandropol near the Russian–Iranian border in the 1870s. As a young man he was interested in all aspects of the supernatural and even considered becoming a priest. But he became disillusioned with Christianity.

Then he travelled widely for many years, visiting many countries including Tibet. He joined an expedition to find a hidden city in the Gobi Desert and also tried to find an ancient brotherhood which he believed was established in Babylon in 2,500 BC. As well as a traveller he was a keen businessman and became involved in many projects including oilwells, fisheries, carpets and antiques.

After studying a variety of spiritual and occult schools, he believed the time was right to pass on his teaching to the rest of the world. So he arrived in Moscow just before the First World War with a million roubles and began lecturing to the intellectual classes. He gained a sizeable following and came into contact with the Russian mathematician and mystical philosopher Peter Demianovich Ouspensky who had just returned from studying religions in Egypt and India.

Ouspensky did much to spread Gurdjieff's teachings.

But the Russian Revolution came and they both left, Ouspensky going to Britain and Gurdjieff via Istanbul to France. They never saw each other again, largely because of disagreements over teaching. Ouspensky's work was methodical, organized and systematic—the product of a mathematician aiming to make clear his teaching to a wide audience. Gurdjieff's work was always fragmentary, secretive, unpredictable and anti-systematic. He published only two books, *All and Everything* and the autobiographical *Meetings with Remarkable Men*. His followers have maintained the esoteric secrecy of their founder, but the second book has now been made into a major film.

The writer Katherine Mansfield was one of Gurdjieff's followers and went to Fontainebleau in 1932 suffering from tuberculosis. Gurdjieff, who liked to dabble in medicine, told her to ignore her disease and sleep in the loft above the cowshed. Everyone was amazed at her cure—but a week later she died, aged 35.

THE GOLDEN LADDER

Gurdjieff taught that man is ruled by three centres—emotional, intellectual and physical—and most people suffer an imbalance. His aim, the 'fourth way', was to help people to achieve this balance. A person's attitude to life, rather than the lifestyle itself, must change.

Man exists on one of seven rungs of an evolutionary ladder. The ladder can be ascended not by logical knowledge, but by psychological wisdom—self-study, self-awareness, self-remembering and the discovery of the essential unchanging 'I'.

One: instinctive motor man Most people are in this category and enjoy being tossed about through life at the whim of their animal desires and instincts.

Two: emotional man Emotional man is aware of these animal desires and can at least manipulate them.

Three: intellectual man Gurdjieff particularly despised this category of those who think they know everything.

Four: transitional man He is conscious that he wants to change.

Five: integrated man For the first time man acquires some real identity.

Six: conscious man Conscious man begins to acquire super powers of a mental and physical kind.

Seven: the complete man In the final stage, man has acquired everything and is immortal.

Drawing on many mystical ideas, Gurdjieff developed his theories about man and the world. His theory of 'Reciprocal Maintenance' suggests that man both depends on and is responsible for the rest of the world. His role in the world is to improve and increase the 'psychic energy' he can release.

Gurdjieff's base for the last years of his life was the Institute for the Harmonious Development of Man at Fontainbleau, France. Here his followers were given certain tasks to test their critical faculties: work such as washing dishes, scrubbing floors and chopping wood and exercises so complicated that followers sometimes collapsed from exhaustion. Gurdjieff was also notorious for psychic and emotional brutality. He would sometimes pick on a disciple and give him a menial task such as learning by heart a long list of Tibetan words.

Though conditions were hard and food inadequate, once a week there was a feast for all. Drink flowed freely, and he gave a long series of toasts to various 'idiots'. At other times a convoy of cars filled with champagne, caviar and melons would drive into the country for a picnic. Gurdjieff would occasionally take the wheel, but he was a terrible driver and had many crashes, one of which hastened his death in 1949.

THE JEHOVAH'S WITNESSES

They have claimed to be the fastest growing religion in the world. They are well known for visiting homes, usually asking people to have a copy of their magazine.

'They' are the JWs, the Jehovah's Witnesses, the name taken from Isaiah 43:10: 'You are my witnesses, says Jehovah.' And their magazine, *The Watchtower*, has found its way into huge numbers of homes.

Because of their beliefs, Jehovah's Witnesses will not celebrate birthdays, Christmas or Easter; they will not take part in religious education at school; they will not accept blood transfusions, even in the most severe need; they refuse to do military service, to vote or to give allegiance to any country or flag.

Throughout their history this has led to persecution, particularly in Hitler's prison camps. And they are still suffering today behind the Iron Curtain and in some African countries.

Despite efforts to stamp them out, they claim to have about 2,250,000 members with 80,000 in Britain, 560,000 in the USA, 99,000 in West Germany and 64,000 in Canada.

The four leaders

'Pastor' Charles Taze Russell, born in 1852 in Pennsylvania, founded the movement. As a teenager he rebelled against his strict Calvinist background and dabbled in oriental studies. He was about to give up religion when an evangelist, Jonas Wendell, convinced him that the Bible was the word of God.

Russell gathered a group of friends together to study the Bible regularly and published their interpretations in a magazine, *Food for Thinking Christians*, later replaced by the bi-monthly *Watchtower*.

He rejected the idea of heaven and hell, but no church would agree with his views. So in 1874 he sold the haberdashery shops he had inherited from his father and founded a new religious organization, the Zion's Watch Tower, in 1879 and incorporated a Zion's Watch Tower Tract Society five years later.

Russell wrote many tracts and a six-volume series, *Studies in the Scriptures*—the main doctrine of the movement. In it he predicted the end of the age in 1914. However, the date passed and he died in October 1916.

'Judge' Joseph Franklin Rutherford of Missouri, the society's legal counsellor, succeeded Russell. In 1917 he and six other leaders were each jailed for 20 years for their anti-war talk, but he was released nine months later when public hysteria died down at the end of the war.

Until he died in 1942, aged 72, Rutherford successfully ruled the movement with an iron hand. Under his leadership the movement spread worldwide and in 1931 he named his followers 'Jehovah's Witnesses'.

'President' Nathan H. Knorr became the third leader when he was 36. Under his leadership, numbers increased more quickly than at any time in the movement's history. He emphasized education, and several schools, a short-term Bible college at South Lansing, New York, and a radio station have all opened since he took over.

The present leader is Frederick W. Franz, who has had to cope with seriously falling membership. In the past 10 years over a quarter of a million members have left the movement.

Jehovah's Witnesses are the most missionary-minded of religious groups. Every member is regarded as a minister and no one is admitted to membership until he is doing house visiting.

Ordinary members are expected to do 10 hours visiting a month and dispose of at least 12 magazines. 'Pioneers' spend at least 100 hours a month visiting and support themselves with a part-time job. 'Special pioneers' are full-time workers supported by a small allowance.

Even after their plight in Hitler's concentration camps in the Second World War, Jehovah's Witnesses have continued to be persecuted. In a court-martial in Athens in 1966, Christos Kazamis was sentenced to death for refusing to take up arms whilst on military service, because of his beliefs. But at a later trial, shown here, his sentence was changed to four-and-a-half years in prison.

KEY BELIEFS

● They alone proclaim God's truth and the only hope for the world is for everyone to join their movement.

● God is one person, Jehovah, who once existed all alone in space.

● God created Jesus, who in heaven was the archangel Michael. On earth he was a man and not divine. When God raised him from the dead he returned to heaven as a spirit.

● Jesus' death on the cross—or 'torture stake' as they prefer to call it—does not guarantee anyone eternal life. Man can accept this as a ransom for his past sins, but the only guarantee of salvation is continual striving to obey God, as revealed by the Watchtower organization.

● The Holy Spirit is the 'invisible active force that moves his servants to do his will', and is neither personal nor God.

● All other churches, and all governments, are controlled by the devil.

● The present world system will end soon with the Battle of Armageddon. Those who survive will reign with Christ for 1,000 years.

● During this time there will be neither disease nor death nor any unhappiness. Flowers and fruit will grow abundantly and wild animals will become tame.

● After 1,000 years all the dead will be raised up. Those 144,000 who reach the required standard will live in heaven; the vast majority will live on earth. Those who reject their teachings will be annihilated.

● God's kingdom on earth was established in 1914, when Christ returned to his temple and began to cleanse it. The devil was cast out of heaven and God fully established this part of his kingdom. The earthly part of his kingdom will be set up within the lifetime of those alive in 1914. Every earthquake, famine, war and catastrophe is a sign of the end which is coming soon. 'Many now living will not see death' is one of the JW's favourite themes.

Their church

Once a year Jehovah's Witnesses observe 'Memorial' (Holy Communion) claiming it should be held on the biblical anniversary of Christ's death, the 14th day of the Jewish month of Nisan. Memorial and baptism are the only formal parts of worship. The rest consists of ministry school for Bible analysis, service meetings for training in visiting, public lectures and regular Sunday study of the current issue of the *Watchtower*.

Their movement is as efficient as a commercial company. The 'Governing Body' is the all-powerful group at the head. Under them are 'Religious Servants' and beneath them are 'Zone Servants' who are responsible for the local groups known as 'Companies' which meet in the Kingdom Hall. The 'Service Director' is at the head of each company and is responsible to the

THE SIX STEPS TO BECOMING A JW

Initial visit During the first visit the Jehovah's Witness aims to introduce himself and leave some literature. Many who think the best way to get rid of him is to take some literature find that this is the surest way to guarantee another visit.

Back-call Every potential convert will receive a second visit when the JWs will try to find out his reaction to the literature. They will also try to arrange a Home Study Group.

Home Study Group The contact will be encouraged to bring friends to study some of the publications in his home. After a few weeks he will join a larger group to look at the teachings in more detail.

The Kingdom Hall After home study, the contact will be invited to the Kingdom Hall. Here he will receive VIP treatment and as he has been prepared in advance he will understand the teaching.

Visiting He will then be expected to attend mid-week lectures and learn how to go door-to-door visiting.

Baptism The final stage in becoming a Jehovah's Witness is to be baptized.

Zone Servant for running his company. He is assisted by a 'Service Committee' which is particularly concerned with visiting.

Numbers
Witnesses are highly dedicated to a movement which, to outsiders, appears to be joyless and suppressive. But their zeal in spreading their message has been tempered since 1975. Witnesses had been led to believe that the final Battle of Armageddon would happen in October 1975. Membership mushroomed and many followers left their jobs and sold their homes. But since the time came and went without incident, they had to come to terms with the fact that they had been misled. Many members left after years in the movement. Recently numbers have levelled. Witnesses are once again on the increase.

Baptism is the final step of commitment in becoming a Jehovah's Witness. At mass rallies, many hundreds of followers are baptized at the same time. In 1978, the movement took over the Twickenham rugby ground in London, and this mass baptism took place in a specially-built pool.

ARE THEY GOD'S WITNESSES?

● They quote the Bible, but their *New World Translation* is inaccurate and has never been accepted by accredited theological scholars. (For example, they translate the first verse of John's Gospel: 'Originally the Word was, and the Word was with God, and the Word was *a* god.' The 'a' before the final word is not in the original Greek. Its inclusion relegates Jesus to a secondary god.)

● Verses are taken out of context to back up their beliefs. Witnesses forbid blood transfusions and will let a member die if necessary, often quoting Leviticus 3:17, 7:26–27 and 17:10–14. But these passages are nothing to do with blood transfusions.

● Members believe that Jesus has already returned invisibly to the world. This conflicts with Revelation 1:7 which says of Jesus' second coming: 'Every eye will see him.'

● Russell said he was a competent Greek scholar and claimed that all existing Bible translations were unreliable. However, it was proved in court in Canada that he could not read Greek, though he had sworn under oath that he could.

● Another controversy was Russell's 'Miracle Wheat' sold for one dollar a pound, which was claimed to outgrow other seeds by as much as five times. He tried to sue a paper for $100,000 for labelling the claims a fake, but lost his case when government examiners could find no distinct superiority in the grain.

● In 1947 the Supreme Court of Canada ruled that Jehovah's Witnesses 'were not a religious body'.

KRISHNA CONSCIOUSNESS

'Hare Krishna, Hare Krishna, Krishna, Krishna, Hare Hare, Hare Rama, Hare Rama, Rama, Rama,' they chanted.

His Divine Grace A. C. Bhakdivedanta Swami Prabhupada at a press conference on his arrival in Britain. His teaching first took root in America, but has now spread throughout the world.

With their saffron robes, heads completely shaven except for an isolated pigtail, cloth bags round their necks containing their prayer beads and ash marks on their faces, the young men on the street corners danced and swayed to the drumbeat.

The public display over the past few years by members of the International Society for Krishna Consciousness (ISKCON) had two purposes. First, they believed that by chanting their god's name ('Hare' means Lord and Krishna is the name of their god) they could liberate their souls from the evil influence of their bodies. Second, as they chanted they publicized their teachings by selling their magazine *Back to Godhead* and raising money for the movement.

Today their publicity is less eye-catching. More often dressed in jeans and jerseys, they offer records and literature free to passers-by . . . but a donation is asked for.

They have more than 70 centres throughout the world with about 15,000 followers. There are about 10,000 in America, less than 1,000 in Britain and only four or five centres in India, the home of the movement.

One of the most famous supporters is the ex-Beatle George Harrison who has given the movement its headquarters near London and whose song about Hare Krishna, 'My Sweet Lord', reached number one in the charts.

Apart from donations the main source of income is a large factory in Los Angeles run by Hare Krishna followers who make and sell incense.

Many of the followers are former drug addicts and the group's success in getting them to kick the habit has led to praise from the mayors of New York and San Francisco.

KEY BELIEFS

● Krishna is the highest of the Hindu gods, the Lord, the Absolute Truth. He has had many incarnations.

● Jesus was not God. He was a pure devotee of Krishna, visiting from another planet.

● The Hindu Scriptures are authoritative. The Bible and the Koran are genuine Scriptures but have become distorted in translation and interpretation over the centuries.

● After death the soul is reincarnated. The way one lives this life will determine the form one will have in the next life.

● Salvation lies in purification, in complete surrender and devotion to Krishna.

● Men are superior to women.

● Any action done for Krishna cannot be bad. Krishna is above both good and evil.

KRISHNA CONSCIOUSNESS

At the movement's headquarters, Bhaktivedanta Manor, Letchmore Heath, followers attend to the statues of Hindu gods each day. Followers take on a new Indian name and a whole new way of life.

The Founder

His Divine Grace A.C. Bhaktivedanta Swami Prabhupada started his mission to the West in 1965 when he was 70. Wearing a yellow gown he sat under a tree in New York's Greenwich village chanting a mantra.

More than 30 years earlier he had been told by his guru in India to spread the message to America.

Prabhupada, born in Calcutta in 1896, did not leave India until 11 years after he retired from his job as manager of a chemical factory in 1954. He won a patron, and Sumati Moraji, the owner of India's largest shipping company, gave him a berth on a ship to America and some money to get him started.

At first he slept in a Yoga centre and he set up his own headquarters only when a follower gave him a month's rent.

He began giving classes and many joined him, particularly hippies and young intellectuals disillusioned with materialism. They became his missionaries who took his message all over the world.

In 1977 the founder died leaving the leadership in the hands of an international 12-member Governing Board Commission.

Life in the movement

Followers of Hare Krishna live in temples and must submit themselves completely to their leader, the Temple President. He in turn must ultimately answer to the governing body of 12 and carry out their orders. He must offer spiritual guidance, see that sufficient funds are obtained, ensure rules are kept, be the final authority on scriptural and ceremonial procedures and arrange members' marriages.

Around the temple are statues of deities considered to be incarnations of Krishna in material forms. These have to be dusted, dressed and fed every morning. Followers bathe the statues in a liquid of rose water, milk and a small amount of cow's urine. After the ceremony it is considered an honour to drink the liquid.

Children of Hare Krishna followers go to special schools where learning how to advance in spiritual life is as much a part of the curriculum as reading, writing and arithmetic.

BECOMING A FOLLOWER

Pre-initiation stage A person who wishes to join the movement must prove himself. He usually takes part in temple life for six months and is taught the movement's philosophy.

Initiation When a person is considered suitable for membership the temple president presides over 'harer name', an elaborate fire ceremony when a member is given a new spiritual Sanskrit name and three strands of neck beads which he must wear until he dies.

Brahmin Six months later those who are faithful members and have advanced spiritually are eligible for a second rite, the brahminical initiation. Here the follower is given a secret mantra which is to be chanted three times a day. Men also receive a sacred thread which is worn over the shoulder and across the chest.

Sannyasa Only a few members achieve the final stage, reserved for especially devoted men. They must make a life-long vow of poverty, celibacy and commitment to preach and do good works.

LIFESTYLE

Cleanliness Washing is an important feature of the movement. A follower will take many showers every day, especially every time he returns to the temple.

Sex Outside marriage, sexual relations are strictly forbidden. Intercourse is permitted between married couples only once a month for the purpose of procreation, not pleasure. Before sex the couple must chant 50 rounds on their prayer beads to purify themselves.

Food Alcohol, tobacco, tea, coffee, eggs, meat and fish are all banned. Eating is seen as an act of worship and all food is offered to Krishna and so is spiritual (prasadam).

Medicine Medicines are taken only when absolutely necessary.

Games No frivolous sports, games or gambling are allowed. Time is important. Any time not given to deepening their own devotion to Krishna should be given to spreading the devotion to others.

3 a.m.	Get up and have a shower
3–4	Personal chanting using prayer beads, or 'japa'
4–4.30	Service, with men on one side of the room and women and children on the other.
4.30–6	Individual chanting
6–7	Study hour reading the *Bhagavad Gita*, their sacred Scripture. A verse is chanted in Sanskrit, then it is explained and members ask questions
7.30	Breakfast
8–10	Clean up and do chores in the temple
10–6	On the streets raising money, with a short lunch break back at the temple
6	Meal
6.30–7	Study
7	Service
8.15	Hot milk
8.30–10	Study once any chores have been done
10–3	Sleep

MEHER BABA

'There is no doubt of my being God personified … I am the Christ … I am everything and I am beyond everything.'

The self-proclaimed Messiah from India who never said a word for 43 years attracted much interest from the media and many young people in the 1960s.

Many students and hippies became followers of Meher Baba and set up chapters of Meher Baba Centres in universities and colleges throughout America. Commitment to him is very emotional. Some followers keep photographs of him in their lockets or have posters of him above their beds.

It was back in 1921 that he gathered his first disciples (called 'manadali') and established an 'ashram' or community near Bombay. Here his disciples called him Meher Baba, which means 'compassionate father'.

After training his followers he organized a colony at Meherabad, near Ahmednagar, 70 miles north-east of Poona, India. This is still the centre for the worldwide movement which now has more than 7,000 members, its own quarterly magazine *The Awakener* and a publishing house.

The making of a saviour
Meher Baba was born Merwan Sheriar Irani, in Poona, India, to Iranian parents. One day in 1913, at the age of 19, he was riding his bicycle when he met an elderly Muslim woman, Hazrat Babajan, who was known as the great mystic of her time.

She kissed him on the forehead and 'tore away the veil which obscured my own God-realization'. He then knew that he was a saviour, the last of the great incarnations of God.

For three days he lay as though he was dead. It took nine months before he returned to normal awareness, during which time he neither ate nor slept.

Eight years later he founded his first community or 'ashram' in Bombay. He opened various hospitals and schools to help the needy. Thousands flocked to him but he suddenly closed the whole operation. His only explanation was, 'Often my external activities and commitments are only the external expressions of the internal work I am doing.'

The years of silence
Just as suddenly, when he was 31, he stopped speaking. He considered that God had laid down enough principles and said enough words—now he had to show how to live them.

From that time on he communicated only by hand signals and an alphabet board. He also wrote many books, including a five-volume work entitled *Discourse*, and *God Speaks*, which outlined the story of God and the universe.

In his *Universal Message*, Meher Baba wrote: 'When I break my silence, the impact of my love will be universal and all life in creation will know, feel and receive of it. It will help every individual to break himself free from his own bondage in his own way. I am the Divine Beloved who loves you more than you can ever love yourself. The breaking of my silence will help you to help yourself in knowing your real Self.'

But on 31 January 1969 at the age of 74, he died—or as his followers said 'dropped his body'— not having said a word for the last 43 years.

KEY BELIEFS

● Meher Baba was the final and greatest incarnation of God. The others were Zoroaster, Krishna, Rama, Buddha, Jesus and Mohammed.

● Followers must lose their identity and surrender completely to Meher Baba.

● Man's soul progresses through reincarnation. The soul begins as a stone and then moves into a metal. It continues its evolutionary journey via vegetables, insects, reptiles, fish, birds and animals. Finally the soul moves from a monkey to a human being. There are then seven planes of human existence and if a person misuses his spiritual powers as he works his way up to the fifth plane of sainthood, then he could be sent all the way back to a stone in his next incarnation. The sixth plane is the plane of illumination and the final one is Nirvana, merger into the mind of God.

'The book that I shall make people read is the book of the heart, which holds the key to the mystery of life.' Meher Baba found the way to the hearts of thousands of followers, best-known of whom is Pete Townshend of The Who.

The Meher Baba Centre

At Myrtle Beach, South Carolina, is the largest of the Meher Baba centres in America. Up to 3,000 people a year visit this shrine which contains Meher Baba's shiny blue Ford Sedan, a large meeting-hall which he used and his fully-furnished six-roomed bungalow where his robe, white underpants and locks of hair are on display. Nearby is a blood-stained pillow where his head rested after a car crash. He was involved in many crashes; according to one follower, this was to fulfil a prophecy that he would shed blood on American soil.

WAS MEHER BABA GOD?

Meher Baba claimed to be an incarnation of God, comparable with Jesus Christ. So how does he compare?

Meher Baba	Jesus Christ
Meher Baba holds out no hope for the sinner—his soul will return to stone.	Jesus offers hope and forgiveness to all.
Meher Baba died of natural causes—his body remains in the ground.	Jesus died claiming that his death provided the forgiveness of sins. He then rose from the dead to prove it.
Meher Baba died without breaking his silence—the great act which he had promised would free mankind.	Jesus completed his work on earth. On the cross he said: 'It is finished.'
Meher Baba's followers must lose their identity in him.	Surrender to Christ involves no loss of identity. On the contrary, in him believers become fully the people they are meant to be.

THE MOONIES

'Would you buy a candle to help youth work?'
'Will you give a donation to missionary work?' Many busy
shoppers when asked such questions willingly pay up.

The 'Perfect Father', Sun Myung Moon. Members of his Unification Church follow him with a deep devotion. They base their whole lives on his teaching, which they learn from his book *The Divine Principle* and from his continuing proclamations. Moon begins these speeches with the phrase 'Master speaks . . .'.

Unknowingly, shoppers raised almost £1 million in Britain alone between March 1978 and March 1979 for the Moonies, the religious group named after their leader, the Reverend Sun Myung Moon. The group has many other names, including the Holy Spirit Association for the Unification of World Christianity.

If a passer-by expresses interest he will be invited to their local centre to find out more. There he will receive the 'loving treatment'—an hour's chat over coffee before one of the leaders talks to him alone about the movement. Then he will probably be invited back for a meal and further discussion.

The argument presented runs like this: 'Everyone is eventually going to belong to the Unification Church, so why not join the Church now. Moreover, those who fight against Mr Moon will suffer'.

Those interested in joining are sent on a course

for a weekend, one, two or three weeks, where they are given intensive teaching. If they wish to join, they are encouraged to give up their job, home and possessions and live at one of the Church's centres.

The Church has been growing rapidly in numbers—many of them young people between 18 and 26—and in wealth. The Moonies claim to have more than 3 million members in more than 140 countries, although others put that figure much lower. They say there are 3,000 followers in Britain but the figure is probably more like 1,000.

Mr Moon's financial empire is said to be worth more than £35 million with a network of 80 businesses ranging from pharmaceutical firms to factories producing spare parts for military weapons.

The Church has also invested in property, including three lavish estates near New York costing more than $2 million.

The Rev Sun Myung Moon

When Sun Myung Moon was sixteen he said that Jesus appeared to him while he was praying on a mountain in North Korea and told him to restore God's perfect Kingdom on earth.

During the next nine years which included a course of study in electrical engineering in Japan, he said the Church's beliefs were revealed to him by God, Jesus, Moses and Buddha. This theology was later written up as a book, *The Divine Principle*, by one of Moon's followers, Yee Hye Wen.

In 1945 as a member of an underground Pentecostal movement he began preaching. But he upset the North Korean government and was sent to a labour camp for three years until UN forces freed him. His followers say that he was imprisoned for his anti-Communist views; his opponents claim that it was for bigamy and adultery.

When he moved to South Korea and founded the Unification Church in 1954 his wife left him. He said: 'My wife could not understand my mission.' Moon married for a second time—though there are claims that he has married at least four times.

He began building a multi-million pound network of industries and as he climbed the financial ladder the government in South Korea

began to look on him more favourably.

Moon believes that Communism is evil and is the main obstacle to the creation of the Kingdom of God on earth. He believes that the UN is a stage for the Communists, and so he has founded a number of anti-Communist groups, including the International Federation For Victory Over Communism.

He claimed that God appeared to him on 1 January 1972 telling him to prepare the world for the second coming of the Messiah.

In America he has been met by demonstrations, with some labelling him fascist because of his support for the South Korean government.

Mr Moon also tried to become involved in US politics. In 1974 he launched a 'God loves Richard M. Nixon campaign' when the Watergate scandal was just breaking. However, he remained quiet when Nixon was found guilty.

KEY BELIEFS

● The Unification Church is not a denomination but a movement to save the world.

● The *Divine Principle*, the movement's book of theology, is the latest revelation from God.

● God wanted Adam and Eve to form a 'trinity' with him and have perfect children to build his Kingdom. His desires were frustrated when Eve was sexually seduced by Satan, thereby starting a new 'trinity'—Adam, Eve and Satan.

● God therefore chose Jesus as the Second Adam, who was to create a holy family. But Jesus, a perfect man though not the Son of God, was rejected by the people and crucified before he could get married.

● God's second best for Jesus was the resurrection, which produced only a spiritual salvation. If Jesus had married and raised a family, he would have laid the foundation for man's full salvation.

● As Jesus accomplished only a partial salvation, a new Messiah is needed.

● The new Messiah, the Lord of the Second Advent, will come into the world and marry a perfect woman. They will form a 'trinity' with God and will have perfect children. Heaven will come upon earth and mankind will be brought back to God.

● The Second Coming of the Messiah will be in secret and has indeed already happened. Korea, the descendant of the ten lost tribes of biblical Israel, is to be the new Israel and the new Messiah was due to be born there around 1920. (Mr Moon was born in Korea in 1920—but he is reluctant to admit publicly that he is the Lord of the Second Advent.)

● The sins of the members of the Church and of their ancestors must be paid for by non-stop exertion. The movement stresses continual activity as the way to prevent temptation by Satan.

● Jews suffer from 'collective sin', because they crucified Christ.

● The faithful will enter the Kingdom of Heaven in families—hence the importance of marriage.

ARE THEY OF THE HOLY SPIRIT?

● They claim to be highly moralistic—yet some followers admit they practise 'heavenly deception' to raise money.

● Supporters of Mr Moon—'The Reverend' is a courtesy title—say he is the new Messiah come to save the world. Opponents, including those who have left the church, claim members are brainwashed. Some, pointing to Moon's militant anti-Communist views and support for the former South Korean dictator, Park Chung Hee, say that the movement has been used as a front for South Korean intelligence.

● Mr Moon told Americans that the Messiah would arrive in 1980–81 and that the salvation of the world depended on whether they repented within the decade. A true prophet is one whose prophecies happen, says the Bible.

● The Presbyterian Church in Korea ruled that the Unification Church was heretical because: (1) Sun Myung Moon has placed himself more than Jesus Christ as the object of their faith. (2) Their doctrine violates the morals of modern society. (3) They would destroy the Christian church by deceiving pure and sincere Christians.

LIFESTYLE

Business The movement 'wants to promote new standards in industry and business, giving quality of produce and concern for the customer'. Their network of businesses ranges from factories in Korea making tools, weapon parts and ginseng tea to a Tokyo-based company which markets honey from China.

Morals The church promotes high moral standards and aims 'to return to Christian principles in public life'. Smoking and drugs are banned. In Britain the Church supports the Viewers and Listeners Association in its campaign to clean up broadcasting.

Community life Many members live in communities spending much of their time in prayer, singing and physical exercise. Moonies always carry 'holy salt'

with them to sprinkle on their food to purify it. If they spend a night away from the community they will sprinkle the salt around their new surroundings, often opening the doors and windows to let evil spirits leave.

Worship Every Sunday morning the Moonies hold a 'pledge service' at which men wear suits and women dresses. Women sit on the left and men on the right before a table containing a bowl of flowers and a picture of Sun Myung Moon. The group bows three times to the Heavenly Father and the true parents, Mr Moon and his wife. Then everyone repeats a pledge in unison, recommitting themselves to the Unification Church. After a 20-minute prayer from one of the leaders the service finishes with everyone praying aloud together. They believe God will accept their prayer only if it is pure.

Parents' opposition

Many parents, worried that their children have been brainwashed into joining the Unification Church, have formed groups to lobby governments and to get their children out of the movement.

In Britain MP Paul Rose founded *FAIR*—The Family, Action, Information and Rescue—to help relatives, friends and ex-cult members. In America more than 1,000 families contacted the Dutchess District Attorney complaining that the Church had exercised some type of mind control over their children.

Then in February 1976 more than 300 parents and ex-cult members gathered in Washington for a 'Day of Affirmation and Protest' to demand an investigation into the Church and other groups. Senator Robert Dole of Kansas was presented with the 14,000-name petition.

For parents who go to the courts to get their children back, costs become enormous and some have had to mortgage their homes to find the money. Many parents have found other methods. Some have hired people to remove their children forcibly from the Church and to de-programme them to overcome their brainwashing.

The world's biggest wedding service. Sun Myung Moon married 791 couples at a mass ceremony in Seoul, South Korea, in October 1970.

Members of the Unification Church submit a list of five potential marriage partners to their leaders, who then make the final choice.

Sex before marriage is forbidden and marriage partners are not allowed to consummate their marriage for three years so that their offspring's blood will be 'pure'.

Divorce is allowed only if a partner leaves the Unification Church.

THE MORMONS

'May we come in and discuss the Bible with you?' ask two well-groomed young men on the doorstep. For many people, that is the first introduction to the Mormons.

According to the Church of Jesus Christ of Latter-Day Saints there are at present 30,000 young Mormon missionaries working to try to add to their 5 million followers throughout the world. They claim to make 180,000 converts a year in the 90 countries where they are working.

Mormon families consider it a privilege to let their sons go abroad for two years of missionary service, paying their own way as they go door-to-door visiting.

The headquarters of the church is Salt Lake City in Utah, a state where 60 per cent of the people are Mormons. Because of Mormonism the state has an excellent reputation for its work in public health, education and social services. And the people are renowned for their honesty, cheerfulness and hard work.

Joseph Smith

But despite the sincerity and real faith and devotion of today's Mormons, the origin of the movement remains very dubious. Joseph Smith

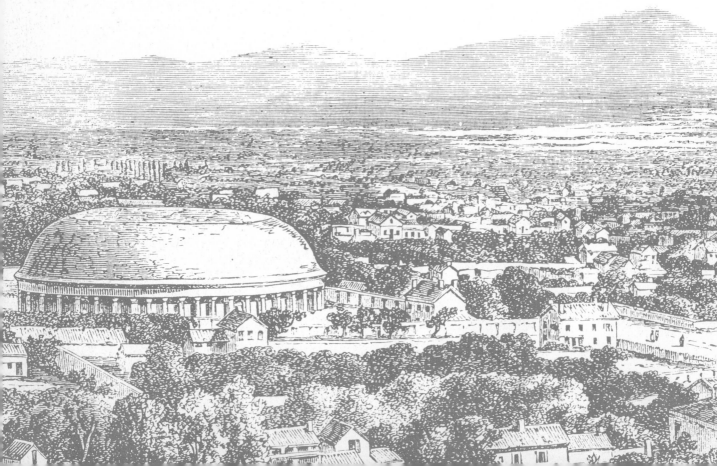

was born in Sharon, Vermont, in 1805. When he was 14 he said God appeared to him and told him not to join any of the churches as 'all their creeds were abomination'.

Three years later an angel, Moroni, told him to go to the hill Cumorah, near Palmyra, New York, where he would find a book written on gold plates telling the history of the early Americans and the complete gospel.

Although the writing was said to be in 'reformed Egyptian' the angel told him he would be able to translate it with the aid of the 'Urim and Thummim' found nearby. He claims to have found the plates and the means of translation but Moroni told him not to touch them for four years. Joseph Smith obeyed.

It was not until 1827 that he began dictating from behind a screen to three scribes what is now known as *The Book of Mormon*. Moroni then took the gold plates back from Joseph Smith.

On 6 April 1830 as the book was being published, Smith and five supporters founded the Church of Jesus Christ of Latter-Day Saints at Fayette, New York State. Although he soon had many followers he faced much ridicule and opposition forced him to keep moving around.

When some of his closest friends left and began to expose Smith and his alleged immorality in a newspaper, Smith as Mayor obtained an order from the Nauvoo city council for the printing offices to be destroyed.

He appealed to the state governor but Joseph Smith, his brother and two others were arrested and remanded in custody until his trial. But it never took place—a mob stormed the prison at Carthage and Smith died in a gunfight in 1844.

Salt Lake City is the 'promised land' of the Mormons. When persecution of the first Mormons came to a head in 1844 with the murder of Joseph Smith, his successor, Brigham Young, led hundreds of Mormons on a flight to the west. When they reached the Great Salt Lake, they began to plough the land and plant crops.

Others followed and together they built a great city and a nation of their own out of the desert.

Their faith and industry were rewarded when Utah was admitted to the union of the United States in 1895.

In the middle of the city is the Genealogical Society, where Mormons can explore their ancestry in order to baptize their dead forbears.

THE MORMONS

KEY BELIEFS

● All mankind will be resurrected. Only Mormons will find a place in the third (highest) heaven.

● *The Book of Mormon* has equal authority with the Bible.

● God the Eternal Father was once a mortal man, who became God.

● A person will be judged by works.

● Redemption from personal sins can only be obtained through obedience to the (Mormon) gospel and a life of good works.

● According to many former Mormon leaders Jesus and God the Father were polygamously married.

● The Mormon Church is the Kingdom of God upon the earth.

● Baptism is essential to return into the presence of God. Proxy baptisms for the dead are therefore practised.

● The marriage relationship can continue into the next life. Mormons marry in the Temple for time and all eternity. (Plural marriage was suspended in 1890.)

● Before Jesus returns to earth to reign for 1,000 years Mormons will be gathered together and the Jews will return to Jerusalem.

● At the end of the 1,000 years there will be a second resurrection and all will be judged. Those worthy of the highest grade of salvation will live on the new earth, the others being put elsewhere. The third of the spirit world who rebelled before creation and a small number of humans guilty of the worst sins will spend eternity in hell.

The Book of Mormon says...

The Book of Mormon teaches many things about the history of America. According to the book, an Israelite, Lehi, and his family and friends escaped from Jerusalem in 586 BC, built a boat and started sailing east round the world. With the aid of a compass they landed in America and from Lehi's family sprang two nations of people who became the ancestors of the American Indians. For 1,000 years they recorded their history on plates in an unknown language. Before they were wiped out in AD 421 the last survivor, Moroni, buried the plates in a hillside.

After his resurrection Jesus visited America and founded a new church because his hopes in the Old World had been dashed. Jesus will return to earth and establish his Kingdom in America.

LIFESTYLE

True Mormons live very carefully according to a high moral code.

● They give a tenth of their income to the church.

● They fast once a month. They will eat meat only in moderation.

● They will not smoke, nor drink alcohol, or coffee or tea, even though the artificial stimulant in these is minimal.

● Families hold a weekly 'Family Home Evening' where they sing, pray, play games and discuss family relationships.

● They support 'Youth and recreational programmes' drawing young people to the faith.

Mission is a key part of Mormons' activity. Many young Mormons spend two years as unpaid missionaries, working long hours in systematic door-to-door visiting.

The world's most famous young Mormon missionaries—the seven members of the pop group, the Osmonds. The seven, Marie, Jimmy, Donny, Jay, Merril, Wayne and Alan are all members of the Mormon Church and were brought up in Utah, USA. Their seven gold records have boosted the Mormon image and led to some of their fans becoming Mormons.

ARE THEY LATTER-DAY SAINTS?

● *The Book of Mormon* covers from 600 BC to AD 400—yet it contains Bible passages in the language of the Authorized/King James Bible, translated in AD 1611.

● A Mormon leader claimed the way *The Book of Mormon* was translated ruled out any possibility of error. 3,913 changes have been made to the book since 1830.

● Mormons claim that the truth of *The Book of Mormon* can be supported by the archaeology of America. W. Duncan Strong of New York's Columbia University said, 'I do not believe there is a single thing of value concerning the pre-history of the American

Indian in *The Book of Mormon* and I believe the great majority of American archaeologists would agree with me.'

● Mormons claim Professor Charles Anthon of Columbia University vouched for the genuineness of the plates. The professor said in a letter to a friend: 'The whole story about my having pronounced the Mormonite inscription to be "reformed hieroglyphs" is perfectly false.'

● In the preface to *The Book of Mormon*, Oliver Cowdery, David Whitmer and Martin Harris claim an angel showed them the plates and engravings. All three

witnesses later said they had seen them with 'the eye of faith' and renounced Mormonism.

● Was *The Book of Mormon* from God or not? Between 1809 and 1812 a Solomon Spaulding wrote an imaginary history of two civilizations coming to America. He died and the manuscript was left in the printer's office. A compositor at the office, Sidney Rigdon, met Joseph Smith and became a Mormon. Later Mrs Spaulding, the widow of Solomon said *The Book of Mormon* was her husband's work—an allegation hotly denied by the Mormons.

● Though Mormonism today is

highly moral, its original leaders were rather less so. In 1834, 62 of his neighbours signed a petition saying Smith and his father were 'entirely destitute of moral character and addicted to vicious habits'. Later Joseph Smith was found guilty of forging money. Brigham Young left 17 wives, 56 children and a fortune of £400,000. He was utterly ruthless with disillusioned members who tried to leave Salt Lake City soon after the long march and some who tried to escape were killed on his orders.

THE PEOPLE'S TEMPLE

*'All my life I have endured the pain of poverty and suffered
many disappointments and heartaches common to mankind.
For that reason I try to make others happy and secure.'*

Jim Jones, leader of the People's Temple Church, regularly ordered his followers to drink an unknown liquid and syringe some into their children's mouths, telling them death would follow in 45 minutes. When the time had passed he told them the 'white night ritual' was to test their loyalty to the cause.

On 18 November 1978, 913 members including Jones and 260 children drank the liquid at their jungle settlement in Jonestown, Guyana, South America. However, this time it was laced with cyanide. The death of all 913 took less than five minutes.

Who was Jim Jones—'Dad' to his followers—and how could he have such control over them?

Jim Jones was once a respected social leader, with carefully developed political alliances. By the end he was a paranoid dictator, surviving on alternate stimulants and tranquillizers.

Jim Jones

James Warren Jones was born on 13 May 1931, in Indiana in the tiny mid-western town of Lynn (main industry, coffin making).

He preached his first sermon to a group of children when he was 12. Two years later his parents separated and he lived with his mother until he married a local nurse when he was 18.

Jones studied at Indiana University but gave up after a year to spend his time preaching. He obtained a degree at night school and became a pastor at a Methodist Church. But he left after a disagreement over doctrine.

He then founded his own church and he came up with what must be the most novel way yet to raise money to buy a church building—he began selling South American spider monkeys door-to-door.

In a shrewd move he affiliated his People's Temple Church with the Disciples of Christ. This allowed him to say he was an officially ordained minister of a 1.4-million-member Christian denomination.

He believed in practical Christianity and opened a soup kitchen for down-and-outs and two nursing homes for the elderly and sick. He also adopted a Korean and two coloured children.

After attending a spiritualist meeting in 1950 he began to believe in reincarnation and to denounce the Bible as an idol.

Still God's heir on earth, as he called himself, he began attracting more and more people to his temple to see 'miracle' healings—all of which were fakes.

In 1964 he prophesied that the world would be engulfed in thermonuclear war on 15 July 1967. Many gave up everything to follow him from Indiana to Northern California where he assured them they would be safe.

Ten years later, his first prophecy forgotten, he said persecution was about to begin and many fled with him to a refuge in the Amazon jungle which the movement had bought for $1 million.

Investigations begin

Those who left the People's Temple claimed the movement allowed bizarre sexual activities, brainwashing of members, and ritualistic beating of children. Informing on other members was encouraged, and there were interrogation

WHY DID IT HAPPEN?

What led to this mass death? Mel White in his book *Deceived* suggests the following factors.

● Jones created a brilliant illusion of respectability, by public relations, flattery, intimidation and favours. He had dined with the First Lady, Mrs Rosalyn Carter, flown with Vice-President Walter Mondale in his private jet and had been appointed the first full-time director of a human rights commission by the Mayor of Indianapolis.

● He undermined the authority of both the Bible and the church. He outlined various 'errors and contradictions' in the Bible which a theologian would see through but which could disturb an ordinary Christian.

● Temple members were kept in a state of exhaustion, psychological isolation and poverty. Defection was difficult in America, almost impossible in Guyana.

● Members feared Jones and were kept in sexual bondage. Break-up of partnerships was encouraged. Jones expected and encouraged sexual preference for himself from both men and women.

sessions and threats of reprisals for defecting. Some who did leave died mysteriously soon afterwards.

Hardly anyone took much notice of these stories except US Congressman Leo Ryan. He was eventually given an invitation to visit the jungle headquarters and on 17 November 1978, he and some journalists, lawyers and relatives set off in a chartered plane.

Smiling and dancing hosts and hostesses looked after their visitors very well during their stay. Everything seemed to be going well until a grandmother begged Ryan to get her out and then 20 others followed her.

One of Jones's aides tried to stab Ryan but he was pulled away and the congressman and his group escaped towards their aircraft.

But before they could get away seven of them were shot dead—three journalists, three defectors and Ryan.

White night

'Alert, alert, alert' screamed the loudspeakers just after 5 p.m. Jones's followers hurriedly gathered round him in a huge semi-circle.

'Dad' told them Ryan's plane would be shot down and that 'they' would come parachuting into the settlement for revenge. His congregation knew 'they' referred to the CIA, fascists or mercenaries.

'If we can't live in peace, then let us die in peace,' shouted Jones as his followers cheered. When they were silent he said: 'Take the potion like they used to in ancient Greece. It is a revolutionary act . . . There is no way we can survive.'

A huge vat was brought in as at every 'white night rehearsal'. Hardly anyone faltered as they stepped forward for their drink.

Jones's empty throne overlooks the carnage of the 'white night'. Beneath the throne, a voice-activated tape-recorder took down all that happened on that appalling night.

SCIENTOLOGY

'We are the heralds of a New Age. Scientology is a passport to this new time.'

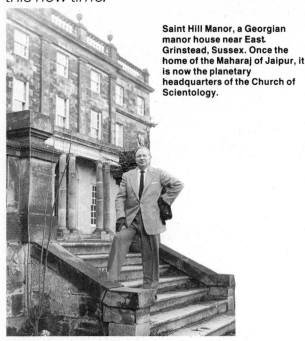

Saint Hill Manor, a Georgian manor house near East Grinstead, Sussex. Once the home of the Maharaj of Jaipur, it is now the planetary headquarters of the Church of Scientology.

Founded in the early 1950s, the Church of Scientology is one of the most controversial of modern faiths. It claims to increase a person's intellectual ability and knowledge of himself.

The church, which has about 2 million members, has been in the newspapers many times. It claims to have been the target for a long-running Nazi conspiracy by the CIA, the FBI, the US Inland Revenue Service and the psychiatric profession, known as the 'Tenyaka Memorial'.

The church has about 65 full-time researchers working to substantiate this claim. In the course of their investigations, they have uncovered many stories which have embarrassed governments. These include drug abuse in prisons, the use of dangerous chemicals as weedkillers, and British involvement in American mind-blowing experiments.

L. Ron Hubbard
Lafayette Ron Hubbard was born in Nebraska in 1911. He claims that after serving in the US Navy for five years in World War II, he was crippled, blinded and had twice been declared dead by doctors. His restoration to health, he says, was by the principles of 'Dianetics'.

After the war, Hubbard became a well-known science-fiction writer and began developing his theory. In 1950 his 435-page book *Dianetics: The Modern Science of Mental Health* became an overnight best-seller. The book was a sort of do-it-

yourself manual to mental health. Hubbard went on to set up dianetic organizations around America, but bankruptcy proceedings and criticisms from medical experts closed the institutes.

'Scientology', extrapolated from the earlier Dianetic research was, however, recognized as a religion—its freedom guaranteed under the American constitution. Since then it has grown worldwide.

The religion of Scientology
Scientologists hold services every Sunday, with robed ministers leading worship and prayers. The sermon is usually a taped lecture by Ron Hubbard. Scientology also has its own rites of baptism, marriage and funerals.

Hubbard himself claims (allegorically) to have visited heaven on two occasions. On his first visit he found 'the gates . . . well done, well built. An avenue of statues of saints leads up to them. The gate pillars are surmounted by marble angels. The entering grounds are very well kept, laid out like the Bush Gardens in Pasadena, so often seen in movies'. But on his second visits, eons later, the place had deteriorated.

Scientology hits the headlines
Scientology has been in the news many times.

In 1963 the US Food and Drug Administration raided the movement's headquarters in

Ron Hubbard occasionally lectures to his followers. On the desk is one of the E-meters which is used to measure stress and anxiety.

THE NATURE OF MAN

Scientology teaches that man consists of four parts.

A thetan (pronounced 'thaytan') This is the immortal spirit, which is capable of reincarnation. It is in complete control of the total person and is capable of showing enormous powers. Thetans created the universe, but over millions of years became ensnared in their creation and forgot their true status. It is through Scientology that a thetan becomes aware once again of its potential.

A physical body The thetan enters the physical body at conception.

The analytic mind (conscious) Under normal circumstances this causes the person to act normally.

The reactive mind (subconscious) Injury, shock or pain can cause the analytic mind to switch off. When this happens the reactive mind takes over, recording unpleasant experiences, 'engrams', which occasionally reassert themselves later in life as 'aberrations'—neuroses and other psychological disorders.
When a thetan enters a body it brings with it all the engrams from its millions of years of evolution.

THE WAY TO BE SAVED

According to Hubbard the basis of life is to survive. Scientology provides the means to do this.

A clear To be a clear is the aim of all Scientologists. Those who 'reach clear' will obtain IQs of more than 135, creative vitality, deep relaxation and revitalized memory. There are seven grades to reach clear, achieved through a series of progressive courses. There are then a further eight grades—Operating Thetan 1–8.

Auditor or private counsellor A pre-clear's first step to becoming a clear is through sessions with an auditor in which the pre-clear talks through the experiences of his life. The aim is that the pre-clear should confront and overcome the sensitive areas within him.

E-meter or electropsychometer To help the auditor the pre-clear holds an E-meter, a kind of lie detector which monitors stress.

Washington and a prosecution followed. Ten years later the case was dismissed.

In 1967 the British Minister of Health, Mr Kenneth Robinson, attacked Scientology in the House of Commons. He said: 'It alienates members of families from each other and attributes squalid and disgraceful motives to all who oppose it; its authoritarian principles and practice are a potential menace to the personality and well-being of those so deluded as to become its followers; above all its methods can be a serious danger to the health of those who submit to them.' For thirteen years foreign Scientologists were banned from entering Britain to work or study at Scientology establishments.

Also in 1967 the US Court of Claims ruled that Scientology failed to qualify as a group 'organized and operated entirely for religious purposes'. It then lost its tax-exemption status. The ruling has since been reversed.

In 1977 the FBI seized documents from the movement's American headquarters. Among other things, these revealed the extraordinary activities of their 'internal intelligence organization'. The organization had harassed a critical author, Paulette Cooper, including suing her 14 times, putting her name on pornographic mailing lists and framing her on a charge of bombing.

SCIENTOLOGY AND CHRISTIANITY

Scientology	Christianity
Man is basically good. The cause of all his problems lies in past experiences.	Man is made in the image of God, but has gone his own way rather than God's and so has a bias towards evil.
With the aid of Scientology alone, all man's problems can be put right.	Because of his state of sinfulness, man cannot know God except through Christ, who died for his sin.
Salvation can come only through the counselling sessions of Scientology, which have to be paid for.	Salvation is a free gift from God, offered to all.
Scientology enables man to be more aware of himself and God.	The way to God is by Jesus Christ alone.

THE WAY

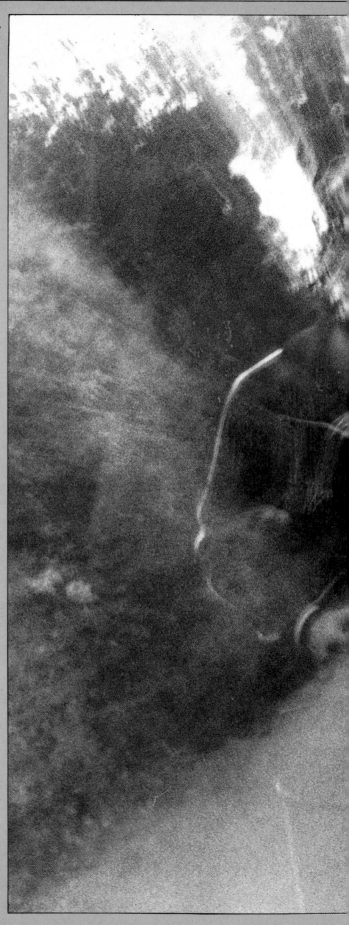

'I have read every commentary in existence. I commit every one of them to Gehenna.'

'You can have whatever you want. Every problem you ever had can be overcome when you are fully and accurately instructed' claims the poster around the colleges and universities.

The way to achieve this is to pay $100 and 'join the most amazing class in the world'—The Power for Abundant Living. One course in the USA consists of listening to 33 hours of tapes over a three-week period, and at any one time more than 1,000 Americans are following it.

The initial Bible course promises that 'right' believing will keep away sickness, ensure prosperity and even protect soldiers from enemy bullets.

The course was developed by Victor Paul Wierwille, the founder of The Way International, a Bible research and teaching organization. Wierwille, said by his followers to be the greatest teacher since Paul, claims to have rediscovered the 'true' teachings of the original apostles, which he has since taught to his 23,000 followers in 37 countries.

The start of the Way
Victor Wierwille was born in 1916. He holds a master's degree and a doctorate in theology from an alleged 'degree mill', Pike's Peak Theological Seminary and for a time was a minister in the Evangelical and Reformed Church. But it was in 1942 that he claimed that God spoke to him with a message which provided the answer to his long search for 'the key to powerful, victorious living'.

He claimed that God promised to 'teach me the word as it had not been known since the first century, if I would teach it to others'.

He began his teaching in 1953 and his years of Bible study and his alleged experiences were enough to convince followers that his teaching was right. The teaching puts strong emphasis on the inerrancy of the Bible, so long as it is 'rightly divided'—which Wierwille alone can do. His spoken and written teaching is absolutely authoritative.

His family farm near New Knoxville, Ohio, is the international headquarters of the movement, whose magazine *The Way* now has a circulation of 10,000.

Their Way
The Way's organization is described in the terms

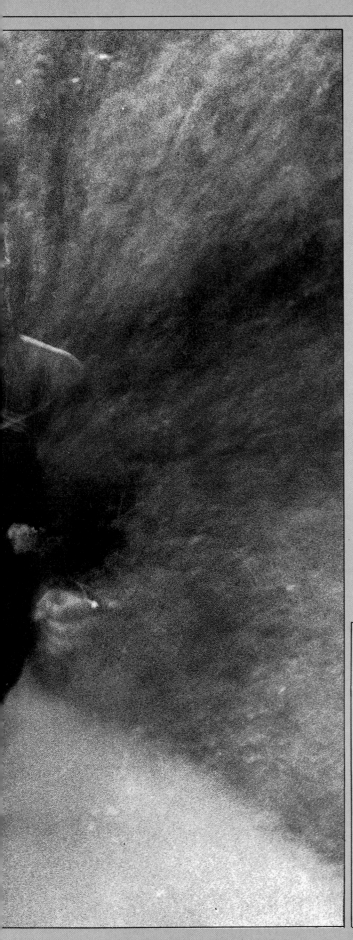

Fitness is vital for followers of the Way. At The Way College, in Emporia, Kansas, exercises form a regular part of daily activity.
But more unusual was a course run for all the students in 1978—the use of military weapons. A pamphlet circulated at the time said that the movement was willing to 'take to the streets with rifles if religious freedom is threatened'.

of a tree. A *twig* is a fellowship group; several fellowships make up a *branch* or city unit; each state unit is a *limb*; limb leaders report back to Regional Directors who report in turn to the International Co-ordinator in Ohio headquarters.

After a new member has taken the foundation class of the Power for Abundant Living there then follows the Intermediate Class and the Advanced Class.

The next stage is to become a WOW Ambassador (Word over the World). Ambassadors take up a part-time job and spend a minimum of eight hours a day witnessing, helping set up local fellowships and running Power for Abundant Living courses.

Finally WOW Ambassadors are encouraged to enrol in The Way Corps, a full-time three-year leadership training programme.

Time

Marie Leonetti was a member of The Way for 22 months before she left the movement. In her story in *Youth Brainwashing and the Extreme Cults* by Ronald Enroth, she said each member of The Way Corps had to keep a record of how he or she spent every minute of the day. They were each given a 'Redeemed Time Analysis' form containing a column entitled 'How I spent my time' and another one 'How I can improve'. There was space opposite every hour from 5 a.m. until midnight.

IS IT THE WAY TO GOD?

The Way believes	The Christian Church believes
The Bible is not the Word of God but only contains the word of God.	'All Scripture is inspired by God' (2 Timothy 3:16).
Jesus is not God. He was a Judean man conceived by God, whose perfect life made him the perfect sacrifice for man.	'In the beginning was the Word (Jesus), and the Word was with God and the Word was God' (John 1:1).
Jesus was crucified with four thieves on a Wednesday.	'And with him they crucified two robbers' (Mark 15:27). This happened on Good Friday.
The Holy Spirit is not personal but merely a 'power from on high'.	'But the Counsellor, the Holy Spirit, whom the Father will send in my name, he will teach you all things' (John 14:26).
The Old Testament and the Gospels are of no use for Christians today. Only the New Testament epistles are.	'All Scripture is inspired by God and profitable for teaching, for reproof, for correcting and for training in righteousness' (2 Timothy 3:16).

THE WORLDWIDE CHURCH OF GOD

A free glossy, monthly magazine with the title 'The Plain Truth' introduces many people to one of the most efficiently run religious organizations of today.

The founder of the Worldwide Church of God is Herbert W. Armstrong, a former sales and advertising executive, who says that just as Jesus chose the highly-educated Paul to take the gospel to the Gentiles, so God has chosen him to spread the gospel in the last days.

Herbert W. Armstrong

As a teenager, Herbert W. Armstrong said he wanted to be rich, famous and learned. By the time he was 40 he had failed with three business ventures.

And Armstrong, born in Des Moines, Iowa, in 1892, was not much more successful with religion after his 'conversion' in 1927 through his wife.

After earlier links with the Quakers and Methodism he became an ordained minister in the Church of God (Seventh Day). But he was asked to leave because of his sensational writings on prophecy and his criticism of other ministers.

When he was 41 he started his own denomination. He began giving lectures on the biblical formula for success and prosperity, which he himself was beginning to enjoy.

He began broadcasting from a local radio station and printing a paper to give to interested listeners. The movement expanded rapidly and in 1968 the Radio Church of God became the Worldwide Church of God. At its peak in 1973, 3.2 million copies of *The Plain Truth* were distributed, and *The World Tomorrow* was broadcast on more than 400 radio and TV stations. More recently, *Quest* magazine has been distributed in America and Great Britain. With its glossy production and its aim of 'the pursuit of excellence' it has reached many readers.

Is it the Plain Truth?

Since 1973, controversies have hit the Worldwide Church of God. In 1972 Garner Ted Armstrong, the founder's son and heir, was relieved of his duties with the radio and as vice-president of the organization and vice-chancellor of the three-college campus. He went on indefinite leave of absence 'for purely personal reasons'. He returned four months later but only to his radio work. Rumours of sexual misdemeanours began circulating.

In February 1974 six ministers resigned from the church over Garner Armstrong's alleged

Armstrong's message is a mixture of religion and personal development. This illustration is part of an advertisement for his booklet *The Seven Laws of Success.*

Members of the church are called to be ambassadors of the message.

The emphasis is on witnessing to others, not trying to convert them. One way is by education and so Armstrong has set up his own radio programmes and three 'ambassador colleges' in America, Australia and England.

sexual misconduct. In all, 29 ministers and 2,000 members joined a rival church, The Associated Church of God. Garner Armstrong has now left the movement. Further splits have since taken place.

A 92-page exposé, which had taken two years to prepare, was published in 1977 by six ex-students

According to *Plain Truth*, the prophet Jeremiah escorted the last king of Judah's daughter to Ireland in 569 BC and carried with him the stone which Jacob had used as a pillow when he had the dream of a ladder between heaven and earth (Genesis 28). Today that stone, says the magazine, is under the Coronation Chair in Westminster Abbey—the Stone of Scone.

PROPHECY

Prophecy is an important part of Armstrong's message, which includes the following teaching.

● The Romans successfully stamped out the preaching of the gospel in AD 69 when Jerusalem fell. A counterfeit gospel was preached until the true church appeared again on the first Sunday of 1934. This was the day when *The World Tomorrow* began broadcasting and *The Plain Truth* was first published.

● The 'ten lost tribes of Israel' wandered across Europe after being freed from their captivity in Assyria. They were the forefathers of the British people. Proof of this, says Armstrong, is the word 'Saxon', which is derived from 'Isaac's son'. Similarly 'Denmark' comes from 'Dan's Mark'.

● The return of the Jews to Israel indicates that the temple will soon be rebuilt as prophesied in the Old Testament. It has been claimed that a young Australian who tried to burn down Jerusalem's Al Aksa Mosque so that the temple could be rebuilt was a member of the Church.

KEY BELIEFS

● God is a family, a team made up of resurrected believers.

● The purpose of life is that God is reproducing himself in us. At the resurrection we shall be changed instantly from mortal to immortal. We shall then be like God, part of his family.

● Before Jesus was conceived by Mary he was not the Son of God.

● Everyone can get to heaven, but only if they keep all the commandments, as interpreted by Armstrong.

● When Jesus returns to earth he will offer salvation to everyone. Those who died without learning about Christ will be given a second chance as they will be resurrected during a 100-year period after Jesus' 1,000-year reign on earth.

● The Holy Spirit is not personal—but 'a divine, spiritual love'.

● Sickness is the penalty for sin. Healing is forgiveness. God is the only real physician.

● The 'end of the age' will come soon, with wars, famines and disasters. Christ will bring these to an end and set up his kingdom. The 12 tribes of Israel will be reunited and will keep all God's laws, as an example to the rest of the world.

LIFESTYLE

Members of the Worldwide Church of God live according to strict rules.

● They must keep to the Old Testament laws and calendar of feasts. New Testament festivals such as Easter and Whitsuntide are considered as pagan. Christmas parties and birthdays are not celebrated.

● At all the major Jewish festivals special offerings are made to the church. These, on top of regular offerings, bring their giving to over 20 per cent of their income.

● They must join a congregation, which will meet in a hall. A typical service will include a sermon, hymn-singing, Bible teaching and reports on the group's work.

● They must be baptized as adults.

● They must take the Lord's Supper once a year, at Passover.

● They must eat food according to the strict Jewish laws.

● They must keep Saturday as the Sabbath.

of the Ambassador College. Their complaints against the Worldwide Church of God included financial irregularities, exploitation of members, opulence and false prophecies. (Armstrong prophesied three dates for Christ's return to earth, all of which have passed.)

BAHA'I

Leo Tolstoy described it as 'the highest and purest form of religious teaching'. Historian Arnold Toynbee has predicted that it will be 'the world religion of the future'.

In 1960 in America there were just 10,000 followers of the Baha'i Faith, a religion one century old. Within 10 years that figure had soared to 100,000 and today Baha'i is one of the world's fastest-growing religious groups.

Baha'is believe that a wealthy Iranian, Baha'u'llah was the manifestation of God for this day and age. Baha'i teaches that all religions are basically one and the same. It emphasizes the oneness of mankind, peace, universal justice and racial harmony.

The forerunner

The origin of Baha'i dates back to 23 May 1844. Mulla Husayn was a young visitor to the Iranian town of Shiraz. He was a member of the devout Muslim Shaykhi sect, who believed that a divine messenger was about to be sent into the world.

In Shiraz, Husayn met a young Iranian, who took him home. 'How will you recognize the messenger?' asked his host, Siyyid Ali-Muhammad.

'He will be between 20 and 30, medium height, won't smoke, will have no physical defects, will possess great knowledge and be descended from Fatimih, the daughter of Muhammad.'

'I am he,' replied the host: from that time on he was known as the Bab, the gate.

Since then every year on 23 May, Baha'is have celebrated the Anniversary of the Declaration of the Bab, when God showed himself to his people through this forerunner, who heralded their coming great Messiah.

The founder

The Bab spent three of the next six years in prison, before being shot in Tabriz in 1850. During that time, 10,000 of his followers were martyred and many thousands more were imprisoned.

One of these was a wealthy nobleman, Mirza Husayn Ali. Whilst he was in jail, he claimed that in a vision, God called him to announce to the world the coming of the Promised One. Four years earlier, he had assumed a new name, Baha'u'llah, 'the glory and splendour of God'. On his release he was exiled to Baghdad where he began to reveal the Baha'i scriptures. But he did not announce publicly that he was the Promised One until 1863. Baha'u'llah's half-brother had tried to start a

In 1850 the Bab was executed in Tabriz. The execution was surrounded by apparently miraculous events. Years later, Baha'u'llah arranged for the remains of the Bab's body to be brought to Haifa. The beautiful Shrine of the Bab has now become a central point of the Baha'i world.

Baha'u'llah spent much of his life in exile or in prison. At Acre he was held in this prison for nine years. Finally the authorities recognized his innocence and allowed him to leave the prison and live in comfort in the city.

Abdul Baha was one of Baha'u'llah's closest companions. He helped his father in much of his work, and was finally appointed his successor. He achieved much in organizing the new faith of Baha'i.

religious war to oust him from power, and now the Turkish government decided to exile them both.

The interpreter
Baha'u'llah was sent to Constantinople and then to Adrianople. In 1868 he began writing to world leaders with his ideas. The same year he was exiled once more.

Baha'u'llah spent the rest of his life in Acre, near Haifa in Palestine, where he was allowed to live freely and in comfort. After his death in 1892 his son, Abbas Effendi, was appointed to control the movement and took the title Abdul Baha, 'the servant of Baha'. Today Haifa is the administrative centre of the faith.

KEY TEACHING

The Oneness of God God is one and there is one God for all the world.

The oneness of religion All the great religions came originally from God revealed through his messengers. They are all fulfilled in the Baha'i faith.

The oneness of man Everyone belongs to the same human family. 'The earth is but one country and mankind its citizens' (Baha'u'llah).

Equality All prejudices of colour, nation, creed and class are destructive and must be abandoned.

Education All children must have the chance of education.

Equality of the sexes Man and woman are equal. They are the 'two wings' of humanity. 'Unless both wings are strong and impelled by some common force, the bird (of humanity) cannot fly heavenward.'

Unity of truth Both religion and science are aspects of truth and cannot contradict each other.

A world auxiliary language To help communication and to eliminate misunderstanding every child should be taught, as well as his own language, one other language—the same for all the world.

A world Parliament Elected representatives from every country should have the power to enforce peace where necessary.

These children are learning the
history of Baha'i by acting it out.

Lifestyle

Baha'i has no clergy and no religious ritual.
Worship of God is by prayer, spiritual reading and
the dedication of daily life. Work, too, is seen as a
religious offering when performed in a spirit of
service.

Followers of the faith live according to the laws
of their countries. They may try to get unjust laws
altered, but must not become involved in political
dissension. One unique part of Baha'i's lifestyle is
their calendar, which has 19 months, each of 19
days.

The supreme legislative and governing body of
the faith is the Universal House of Justice at the
Baha'i World Centre in Haifa, Israel. Local,
national and international administrative bodies,
the 'Spiritual Assemblies', are elected by the
followers and answerable to God alone.

In personal life, followers have a high moral
code. They will not gamble, gossip, take drugs or
drink alcohol. And they consider marriage to be a
life-long spiritual and physical union.

Meetings and conventions are an important way for Bahai's to learn more about their faith.

In 1978 more than 500 Baha'i delegates came from all over the world to an international convention in Haifa.

BAHA'I AND CHRISTIANITY

Baha'i claims to be the fulfilment of Christianity, but in several points the two differ.

Baha'i teaches that there have been a number of manifestations of God to man. Each manifestation brought the fullest revelation which the people of their time could understand.

Jesus' message was appropriate for his time, and he died in order that men might live. Baha'u'llah was essentially the same manifestation as Jesus. Since he came later, his message was fuller, revealing that all religions have a common origin. He was imprisoned in order that men might be free.

Christian believe that this contradicts the Bible's teaching that Jesus was the unique Son of God. Christians also doubt the idea that mankind's spiritual awareness is increasing. Baha'i teaches that error is in need of guidance, darkness needs light, and falsehood is the lack of truthfulness. It admits the fact of evil, but does not supply the same answer as Christianity. The Bible states bluntly that 'all have sinned and fall short of the glory of God,' and teaches that there is salvation in no one other than Jesus.

So to the Christian, Baha'i is seen as unnecessary. Through his death and resurrection Jesus provides the radical solution to man's need today. 'Christ offered one sacrifice for sins, an offering that is effective for ever' (Hebrews 10:12).

In New Delhi a new Baha'i House of Worship is being built in the shape of a lotus flower. No rituals or ceremonies take place in the Houses of Worship. They are places for quiet contemplation, as Baha'is believe that every person is responsible for their own spiritual development. Every House of Worship has nine sides, since to Baha'is the number nine symbolizes 'open to all'.

FREEMASONRY

It is an all-male friendly society 'founded on the purest principles of piety and virtue,' yet even today it is banned in a quarter of the world.

Der Steynmetz.

Ich bin ein Steinmetz lange zeit/
Mit stangn/Winckelmäß vñ Richtscheit/
Ich auffricht Steinheuser wolbsinn/
Mit Keller/gewelb/Bad vnd Brünn/
Mit Gibelmauwrn von Quaderstein/
Auch Schlösser vnd Thürnen ich meyn/
Setz ich auff festen starcken grundt/
Cadmus erstlich die Kunst erfund.
Z   Der

In the Middle Ages, skilled stonemasons travelled throughout Europe to work on many huge building projects. Their 'trades unions' were the origins of Freemasonry.

As time went by, Freemasonry stopped being a society for masons alone. Symbols and mystical ideas were borrowed from Ancient Egyptian mythology and the movement became a social society.
   The ceremony shows an apprentice being admitted into a French Freemasons' Lodge.

Freemasonry is the largest international secret society in the world, with more than 6,000,000 members. It is known for its strange initiation ceremony and its secret signs and handshakes by which members recognize each other. It is claimed that 'no outsider reading the printed rituals can grasp the spirit of Masonry. What at first appears to be childish games can within the atmosphere of the lodge (where Freemasons meet) form a unique bond between men.'

It is an all-male friendly society for mutual help in times of need. Its principles are explained as 'brotherly love, relief and truth'. In theory any believer in God, Christian, Jewish, Muslim, Hindu or Buddhist can become a Freemason.

Members have suffered imprisonment and persecution because Masonry is claimed to be anti-patriotic and anti-Christian. Even today Freemasonry is banned in Russia, China, Hungary, Spain and Portugal. Many of the major Christian bodies including the Salvation Army and the Roman Catholic and Greek Orthodox churches forbid their members to become masons. But in the Church of England and the Free Churches there is no ban and leading members of these churches have held high office in Freemasonry.

In many ways, Freemasonry acts as a businessman's guild. There is strong emphasis on giving to charities—some of which, such as Masonic hospitals and schools, are of great help to Masons. And in the past Masonry has been the passport to success in the world of finance, law and, surprisingly, licensed victualling!

Some of the signs and symbols of Freemasonry.

How it began

During the Middle Ages all crafts had their secret skills and passwords in order that their members could keep the limited amount of work available to themselves and stop other people cashing in.

One group of craftsmen were the freemasons who travelled freely from country to country helping build cathedrals and churches. Near their sites and temporary homes they built 'lodges' where they could spend their leisure hours together.

As cathedral building began to decline so freemasons began accepting honorary members to boost their numbers.

During the seventeenth century working masons began to drop the 'free' prefix, while 'speculative' members took the title 'free and accepted' and began adopting the rites and trappings of ancient religious orders.

In 1717 the first Grand Lodge was founded in England. In 1725 a group of English noblemen staying in Paris founded a lodge there and soon Freemasonry spread throughout Europe.

One important member was Count Cagliostro (1743–95) who claimed to make gold, cause miracle cures, prolong sexual powers and extend life to 5,557 years. He dominated the Lyon Lodge and created his own brand of 'Egyptian Masonry' which included women's lodges presided over by a 'Queen of Sheba'.

Persecution

Freemasonry met much opposition and many members were imprisoned. In 1737 Louis XV of France issued an edict forbidding all loyal subjects to have anything to do with the movement, while in 1738 Pope Clement XII issued a Papal bull forbidding Catholics from joining Freemasonry with the threat of excommunication. He said they were 'depraved and perverted' and most 'suspect of heresy'.

Since then Freemasons have been blamed for the French Revolution, the First World War, Germany's runaway inflation of 1924 and the Spanish Civil War. But since the Second World War when Freemasons fought in the resistance movements, the anti-patriotism jibe and the attacks by the church have become much less frequent.

FREEMASONRY

To be a Freemason one has to be an adult male believing in the existence of a supreme being and the immortality of the soul— and be able to pay the subscription. Members cannot ask to join; hints are usually dropped that they would be welcome if they wished to join.

The actual initiation ceremony is very dramatic and full of symbolism.

Stage one. The candidate takes off his jacket and tie and removes any money or metal items to show he has entered the Freemasons 'poor and penniless'. His left trouser leg is then rolled up to his knee, his shirt is opened to expose his left breast and his right shoe is removed and replaced by a slipper. He is blindfolded to show 'his state of darkness' and a running noose or 'cable-tow' is placed round his neck.

Stage two. He is led to the lodge threshold where his way is barred by the Inner Guard who holds a pointed dagger to his bare chest.

Stage three. He is then led to the Worshipful Master, the chief officer of the lodge. Kneeling before him he answers a series of ritual questions before swearing an oath of secrecy.

Should he divulge any of the Masonic secrets he accepts the penalties of 'having my throat cut across, my tongue torn out by the root, and buried in the sand', although this is seen as symbolic. Or he may be 'branded as a wilfully perjured individual void of all moral worth and totally unfit to be received into this worshipful Lodge'.

Stage four. The candidate has now entered into the light of masonry. The blindfold and the noose are removed and he is given the step, the sign, the grip and the word of an entered Apprentice Freemason. He is also presented with the following objects: a 24-inch gauge representing the 24 hours of the day to be spent in work, prayer and refreshment, a gavel or hammer representing the force of conscience and a chisel showing the advantage of education. Finally he is encouraged to obey the laws of Freemasonry, the Bible and the state.

When the ceremony is over the candidate has 'worked the first degree' and within a few months may attain the two 'Craft' degrees of Fellow-Craft and Master Mason.

CAN A CHRISTIAN BE A FREEMASON?

Freemasonry claims to be acceptable to all religions. But its teachings include many points which Christians are hard put to agree with.

● The 'lost name of God' is the underlying object in all Masonic Ritual. In the initiation ceremony the candidate is introduced to God as the 'GAOTU', the Grand Architect of the Universe. As a fellow craft member he is taught a further name JHVH—short for Jehovah. As a Master Mason he learns there is far more about the mystic name which is revealed in the Royal Arch Degree. The mystic name is discovered to be a combination of Jewish and Middle-Eastern names of God, which is never pronounced except by three Royal Arch masons each saying one syllable.

● Freemasons have many gods who are considered equal to Jesus.

● Masonic literature denies that Jesus is the only saviour of the world.

● Freemasons reject Christ's death on the cross as God's sole remedy for sin.

● Salvation depends on works, not faith in God.

● The sacred books of many religions, such as the Vedas and Koran, are regarded equally as revelations from God.

● At the initiation ceremony the candidate has to confess he is in darkness reaching for the light. A Christian believes he has found the true light; Jesus said: 'I am the light of the world' (John 8:12).

MORAL RE-ARMAMENT

When man listens, God speaks; when man obeys, God acts; when God acts, nations change.

Moral Re-Armament looks forward to a God-controlled world. Followers believe they can change the world by changing individuals through 'soul surgery'.

Founded by an American, Frank N.D. Buchman, around 1920, it has been known by different names, first for a brief period as A First Century Movement, then as The Oxford Group, and since 1938 as Moral Re-Armament. With the threat of war and the talk of re-armament against Germany as the theme of the time, Buchman said that what the world needed was moral re-armament.

Frank Buchman

Buchman was born in Pennsburg, Pennsylvania, in 1878 and ordained a Lutheran pastor in 1902.

On a visit to Keswick, in England, he heard a woman preaching about the way Jesus' death on the cross had changed her life. At the time Buchman was very depressed, having just resigned after a disagreement with six trustees of a boys' hostel.

Hearing the woman led to a radical conversion for Buchman. He wrote a letter of apology to the six trustees and the relationships were mended. On his return to America he became YMCA Secretary at Penn State College. He began to develop the principles of Moral Re-Armament, finding that religion was not essentially a matter of intellect or emotions but of the will.

Two Anglican clergy invited him to Oxford and Cambridge to talk to the students and in 1921 he formed The Oxford Group, largely consisting of students. The movement spread rapidly to

The basic message of Moral Re-Armament is simple.

One way in which Moral Re-Armament puts over its ideas to the world is through films and plays. The Westminster Theatre in London is owned by the movement.

Another important work is the organization of houseparties, where people can relax and enjoy each other's company and share their personal testimonies and the confession of their sins. The first such houseparty was in 1918 in Kuling, China.

THE PRINCIPLES OF MORAL RE-ARMAMENT

Moral Re-Armament has no creed and instead of members it draws sponsors. To bring about a change in their life sponsors go through five stages, the five Cs.

Conviction: realizing their sins.
Contrition: being sorry.
Confession: saying sorry.

Conversion: living a new life.
Continuance: continuing to live that new life.

Once a member's life has been changed he should strive for the four absolutes in his life,

absolute honesty
absolute purity

absolute unselfishness
absolute love.

These virtues are to be attained by the four principles:

Sharing The confession of sins and temptations is used as a witness to help others recognize and acknowledge their own sins.
Surrendering Past, present and future life is surrendered to God's keeping and direction.

Restitution This involves paying back to all whom one has wronged directly or indirectly.
Guidance This means listening to, accepting, relying on God's guidance and carrying it out in everything one does or says, great or small.

Holland in 1927, South Africa in 1928, Canada in 1932 and Scandinavia in 1938. By the time Buchman died in 1961 the movement was worldwide.

The movement has no specific membership—men and women are loosely associated with it. They strive to live according to the 'four absolutes', to listen to God frequently in times of quiet during the day and to follow what God tells them.

Christians and Moral Re-Armament

Though many Christians have been involved in the movement, Moral Re-Armament is not exclusively Christian. Indeed, it embraces people of all faiths.

The strong points of Moral Re-Armament include the importance placed on changed lives and on witnessing to others, and the obvious effort which has been put into solving political and industrial problems. Many politicians and industrial leaders have spoken together on the independent and friendly platform of Moral Re-Armament. In the years after the Second World War the movement was active in helping the reconciliation between France and Germany.

The movement has been criticized for tending to concentrate on the influential 'up-and-outs' rather than the down-and-outs. Its emphasis on man's own ability to change himself could be seen as devaluing God's role in salvation. Christians believe that man can do nothing to save himself, but must look to God alone in Christ if he is to be saved. And guidance for the Christian life comes not from within oneself but from the Word of God, the Bible.

THE RASTAFARIANS

They are the 'cult of the outcasts', the modern-day Israelites in captivity in 'Babylon'—the Jamaican state, the West and all organized institutions.

'Love Jah and live. Hate him and die' says the graffiti. It is written by tne Rastamen who believe that Ras Tafari, later crowned Haile Selassie of Ethiopia, is the new Messiah for the black people of the world. 'Jah' is their word for God.

There are more than 7,000 Rastafarians in Jamaica, the home of the movement, and many more in areas of the big cities of England and America where the 'cult of the outcasts' is growing rapidly.

Rastafarians are unmistakable with their hair in long braids, called 'dreadlocks', worn with a woollen hat in the Ethiopian colours of red, black, green and gold.

As they refuse to give up smoking marijuana or to cut their hair (they quote verses from the Bible to back up their arguments), Rastamen have great difficulty in getting jobs and many remain unemployed. Rastamen say they are peaceful, but fringe followers of the cult have sometimes given the faith a violent image.

Followers of Rastafarianism or Ethiopianism deliberately speak a patois to confuse outsiders.

LIFESTYLE

Drink Many Rastafarians refuse to drink because they say that white men enslaved black men by getting them drunk and putting them on slave ships.

Drugs They often take pot (known as 'ganja', 'weed of wisdom' or the 'holy herb') to help them meditate either on their own or in groups. Ganja is seen as a medical, mental and spiritual food. After smoking, they share and debate the understanding reached during meditation in an act called 'reasoning'.

Food Only Ital (natural) food is eaten. Canned or chemical food or food from scavengers such as pigs and shellfish is never eaten.

Marriage This is looked upon as part of the establishment and therefore sinful. Sexual permissiveness is banned, yet a couple need stay together only as long as they want to.

Morals Rastafarians are highly moralistic—deceit, evil thoughts, lying and stealing are all forbidden.

They have no organized church and no place of worship. But many followers will carry a picture of Haile Selassie wherever they go. Some, too, have a red, black, green and gold shed in their garden as a sort of shrine.

Jamaican reggae star Bob Marley, who died recently, has been the single most important figure in spreading Rastafarian ideology. He has attracted many new members to the movement through his successful concert tours and astronomical record sales in England and America.

Since Marley and his group, the Wailers, many other Rasta-based reggae bands have followed, putting their message over in music.

Roots

Few in the 1920s took much notice of the Jamaican, Marcus Mosiah Garvey, who founded the ill-fated Universal Negro Improvement Association to encourage his countrymen to return to their rightful homeland, Africa.

Even those interested soon forgot his prophecy that a black king would be crowned in Africa who would call negroes home. Garvey retreated humiliated to England where he died in 1940.

But when Ras (Prince) Tafari, who said he was a direct descendant of King Solomon, was crowned Emperor Haile Selassie in 1930, the sceptics began to take notice, particularly when the numerous titles at his crowning ceremony included 'Conquering Lion of Judah', 'King of Kings' and 'Lord of Lords'.

Jamaicans began to search the Bible. Some believed that the Book of Revelation was an allegory about them and their suffering and that Haile Selassie was the Living God. To back their case they quoted such verses as Revelation 19:16, 'On his robe and on his thigh he has a name inscribed, King of Kings and Lords of Lords.' Garvey was now recognized as a hero and the father of black nationalism.

For the blacks who had been moving from island to island in the West Indies in search of a home and work, enduring economic depression and race riots, the idea of an African destiny was very appealing.

Garvey had said that they would leave the West Indies by 1960. In 1959 and on a number of other occasions, up to 15,000 people turned up at Kingston, Jamaica, having been persuaded to buy bogus tickets to the homeland. Not surprisingly the ships they were expecting never turned up.

Some followers then decided to try to improve their lot by getting involved in Jamaican politics. When in the 1970s Premier Michael Manley presented himself as 'Joshua leading the people to the Promised Land' and carrying a rod given him by Haile Selassie, he won his elections easily.

Earlier, in April 1966, their 'Messiah' Haile Selassie himself had visited Jamaica and been given a huge reception. Many refused to believe the news of his death in 1975.

The royal line of Ethiopia is said to be descended from the son of King Solomon and the Queen of Sheba. In 1930, the heir to the throne, Ras Tafari, was crowned Emperor Haile Selassie, and received honours and representations from all over the world. The event provided a vital focus for the aspirations of the black people of the West Indies.

The Jamaican, Mosiah Marcus Garvey, founder of the Universal Negro Improvement Association.

KEY BELIEFS

Many Rastafarians are unclear about the basic beliefs of their religion; some are even unsure who Ras Tafari was. But the central beliefs are as follows:

● God, Jesus, the Israelites and the early Christians were all black. They accuse orthodox Christians of misrepresenting Jesus as a blue-eyed European.

● God became man—not as Jesus but as Haile Selassie, who is still alive and living in another dimension.

● They are the true Jews.

● The Bible was written by and for black people.

● White men are devils.

● Black men will be free only when they are back in Africa.

● Some believe in reincarnation and a few claim to remember their journeys in the slave ships. Others believe that Queen Elizabeth I has been reincarnated as the present Queen of England and that the Duke of Edinburgh is a reincarnation of Philip of Spain.

TRANSCENDENTAL MEDITATION

The Rolling Stones, Mia Farrow, the US army—all of them have investigated the claim of the Maharishi, that his teaching is the ultimate solution to all the problems in the world.

An unknown Indian guru achieved world fame overnight when the Beatles went to see him in 1967. One of them, George, had met the Maharishi Mahesh Yogi when he was studying Indian music and his enthusiasm convinced John, Paul and Ringo to go to a remote corner of Wales to study Transcendental Meditation with the Maharishi.

He says that his system, TM, is not a religion or a philosophy but 'a natural, easy and scientifically verified technique'. There is no dogma to be believed nor need anyone change his or her religion.

More than two and a half million people throughout the world practise TM, including some Christian clergy. Even the US Army has expressed interest in TM.

The practice of TM

The basic technique of TM is simple. Each follower is given a 'mantra', a secret phrase or syllable to fit their personality. Followers are expected to meditate on their mantra for 20 minutes, morning and evening, repeating it over and over again under their breath. Regular meditation, it is claimed, will make them feel more energetic and less tense.

The giving of the mantra takes place in a ceremony called the 'puja'. This is described as a simple Indian ceremony of gratitude for the long tradition of TM. It is performed in Sanskrit and no translation is available to those being initiated.

The Maharishi

Maharishi (meaning Great Sage) Mahesh (his family name) Yogi (one who has achieved union with God) was born Mahesh Prasad Warma in north central India in 1911.

After studying physics at Allahabad University

he graduated when he was 31 and worked in a factory for five years where he began dabbling in yoga in his spare time.

At the end of the Second World War he retreated to the Himalayas to seek enlightenment for 13 years with his guru, Swami Brahmananda Saraswati (Guru Dev). Just before he died Guru Dev told Mahesh Yogi to evolve a single form of meditation for everyone. For two years he stayed in the Himalayas before revealing his ideas to the world in 1959 when he was 48.

He started in Madras but got little response. He then came to London after announcing a nine-year plan to spread his message via the International Meditation Society. The movement was known at this stage as the Spiritual Regeneration Movement. It later changed its name to the Science of Creative Intelligence.

For a while he created little impact in London. But then the Beatles went to see him and suddenly this small Indian in a simple white loincloth and beads, with rubber-thonged sandals and an ever-present flower in his hand, hit the headlines.

But the novelty soon wore off and the Maharishi flew home saying: 'I know I have failed. My mission is over.' He vowed never to return to the West.

But his mission was not over. From his 15-acre, 58-room air-conditioned ashram in Rishikesh, India, he evolved a new plan, aiming to set up 350 teacher training centres which would become universities of TM.

Mentmore Towers in Buckinghamshire, England, the former home of Lord Rosebery and the Rothschilds which the TM movement bought in 1977 for only £248,000.

Maharishi Mahesh Yogi aims to create a 'world government' to administer the 'age of enlightenment' and Mentmore Towers is his 'capital' in Britain.

Here 80 young bachelors look after the house and its 83 acres of land.

Although Mentmore Towers was stripped of its treasures by Sotheby's 'sale of the century' the movement has restocked it with valuable antiques, hung 700 metres of velvet at the windows and even lined the walls with silk.

Since TM began spreading from its headquarters by Lake Lucerne in Switzerland in the early 1970s the movement has bought several mansions in England.

TRANSCENDENTAL MEDITATION

At Mentmore Towers, Lord Rosebery's billiard room has been turned into the Flying Room. With about 70 people aiming to reach heights of up to five feet, a plan has been drawn up to stop anyone bumping into another flyer. The plan divides the room into a parking area, a central reservation, a freeway and a platform area and warns members not to park on the freeway or around the platform. Before TM followers start flying they tick off their names and are reminded of 'flight safety procedures'.

The technique, called the TM-Sidhi programme, is supposed to improve the quality of life not only in the practitioner, but also of the whole community. When sufficient numbers practise TM-Sidhi they 'radiate an influence powerful enough to affect the trends of the whole society'. They believe this will reduce crime rate, accidents and sickness over a wide area.

Is it the way to Creative Intelligence?

There has been opposition to TM in both the East and the West. Some Hindu gurus say the Maharishi has misinterpreted their holy book, the *Bhagavad Gita*. Other yoga and eastern religious authorities dislike his idea of 'instant Nirvana' and his commercialism—would-be followers have to give a week's pay for their courses. Again others reject his linking of TM and materialism.

Some members of TM have left the movement saying they had never learnt to fly despite promises that they would. Instead of peace and tranquillity, their attempts to fly have given them severe mental and physical problems. Meditators of other traditions, such as Christian monks, have long known of these dangers and warned against them. According to some meditators the technique does not solve problems, it merely blurs them. They also say that TM encourages a self-centred approach to life which has harmed their personal relationships.

American psychologist Leon Otis reported that 'a substantial minority' of people meditating for at least 18 months developed anxiety, depression, physical and mental tension and other adverse effects.

IS TM A RELIGION?

● At the puja ceremony no translation of the Sanskrit is given. But the words are in fact a call to Hindu gods asking for help and offering them sacrifices. In particular, Guru Dev is identified as a divine incarnation.

● A mantra is chosen according to a 6,000-year-old tradition, say followers of TM. Actually there are only 16 mantras and the present tradition goes back only to 1973. All the mantras are the names of, or close to the names of, Hindu gods.

● Maharishi is a Hindu bhakti monk and evolved his technique while studying the Hindu Vedic Scriptures.

● Transcendental consciousness is only the first stage of TM. There are four more stages of consciousness ending with 'God consciousness', 'union with God', and 'Brahma consciousness'.

● TM is undoubtedly Hindu in its teachings. Even their basic textbook *The Science of Being and the Art of Living* says TM is the real 'eternal truth' at the base of all religions. Like Hinduism it teaches that God is impersonal; life is a cycle of rebirths; man can become perfect; sin can be overcome through meditation; Jesus Christ was a prophet and not the saviour of the world.

● After a two-year legal battle a federal court in New Jersey ruled that TM is religious by nature. This ruling meant that TM would no longer be taught in state public schools.

GLOSSARY

Many of the ideas of the new faiths take words from existing faiths and give them a different meaning.

In the West, many of the words have been taken from Christianity. So this list not only explains some of the recurring themes of the new faiths, but also brings out the original meaning of the words and their Christian usage.

GOD

Almost all the cults and new faiths have a belief in God, 'Ultimate Reality', 'Universal Truth' or some similar idea.

God Christians believe that there is one God who created and sustains all things. God is not an idea or a force; he is personal. He is characterized by holiness and love. He is separate from his creation. He is one. And he makes himself known to mankind as three different 'persons'; as the Father, as Jesus Christ the 'Son', and as the Holy Spirit.

Jesus Christ A real man who lived in history, Jesus claimed to have come to introduce a whole new world order, which will one day be complete. Many faiths consider him to be a good teacher, a prophet or one of many incarnations of God. Christians believe that Jesus is God himself. By his death for human sin and resurrection to new life, Jesus inaugurated the new age. (See too *The Future*.)

Incarnation God becoming man. Faiths of Eastern origin believe that throughout history, and today, there have been many incarnations. Christians believe that there is one God who became man once, in the person of Jesus Christ.

Holy Spirit The Hebrew word means 'breath' or 'life'. Many faiths have a belief in a 'life-force' of some sort. Christians believe that the Holy Spirit is personal, the very life of God. When someone first believes in Jesus, he receives the Holy Spirit, who then gives him the power to live out the life of Jesus.

Messiah 'Annointed one', the deliverer awaited by the Jews. The term has also been applied to many people who have claimed to reveal God in a special way and to bring salvation to mankind. Christians believe that Jesus is the one and only Messiah, sent by God. ('Christ' is Greek for 'Messiah'.)

HUMANKIND

Underlying the teaching of every faith is a particular belief about the nature of mankind. The beliefs vary widely, and often provide a key to understanding the rest of the movement's teaching.

Origins Most faiths believe that mankind was made by God. Some believe that the creation and the creator are one and the same. Some believe that the creator is no longer concerned with his creation. Christians believe that each person is made in the 'image' of God, with personality, creativity, love and infinite value.

Good and evil Some faiths believe that there is no such thing as evil. Others believe that at heart people are good—and given the right opportunities each person will become good. Christians believe that God created mankind perfect and in fellowship with himself. But mankind chose the way of independence from God. Separation from God was the inevitable result of this deliberate disobedience, 'the fall'. Pain, death and other evils followed.

Enlightenment Any fresh, inspiring understanding of life could be termed 'enlightenment'. Some groups teach that this is the one real need of mankind Christians believe that more is needed.

Salvation Literally 'being saved'. Many groups believe that it is possible for an individual to be saved by good deeds, enlightenment, or even by marriage. Christians believe that Jesus Christ is the only one who can 'save' us from evil, and from being separated from God. For his death paid the price of man's rebellion.

Resurrection 'Rising again' from death. Resurrection involves the body (or a 'new body'), not just the soul. The resurrection of Jesus (the 'best attested fact of history') proved his claim to inaugurate the new age.

EVIL

There are two basic approaches to the problem of evil. One is to say that people can separate into good. themselves from evil. The other is to say that evil can be transformed

Sin All faiths recognize that man has a tendency towards wrong. Christianity makes a distinctive analysis of this. It points to sin as rebellion against God. It recognizes the reality of sin and evil, and provides an answer in the death and resurrection of Jesus.

Evil spirits The existence of a world of spirits is acknowledged by the majority of faiths. These spirits can be good or evil. Evil spirits can affect individuals and events, but Christians believe that Jesus Christ has power over them.

The devil Satan, the chief of evil spirits, is the personification of evil.

Disease and death Some cults teach that disease and illness are 'spiritual' and not 'physical'. Others teach that illness and death are a judgement for disbelief. Christians believe that they are real, inevitable results of mankind's rebellion against God.

Karma Eastern groups believe that each evil action that a person commits builds up 'bad karma' for them. This can only be purged away by good actions or by reincarnation.

REVELATION

Answers to 'ultimate questions' are not easily found. So where can we look for them? Some cults depend on the teaching of their leader; some on personal experience; most on a mixture of the two.

Prophecy Many new faiths emphasize strongly certain prophecies about the future. The prophets in the Bible proclaimed God's standards for their own time. The 'apocalyptic' books in the Bible are full of imagery which has to be understood in context.

Scriptures Most religions, and many new faiths, have 'sacred writings' which include the basics of their beliefs. Christians believe that the Bible is, in a special way, the Word of God. Many cults of Western origin have re-interpreted parts of the Bible, or added to it, to back up their own teaching.

Mystical experience Followers of all religions down the centuries have known of visions, dreams and other mystical experiences. Christians believe that these are expressions of faith, not the way to faith. Some mystical techniques, such as soul-travel and consulting spirits, are potentially dangerous.

Self-development Groups which believe that the answer to our needs lies within each person teach that 'enlightenment' comes from within. But Jesus taught that 'evil is within us'. So Christians believe that we need new life from God, not just development of 'self'.

HOW TO LIVE

The follower of a faith takes part in certain 'religious' activities.

Prayer Almost all faiths encourage prayer. Christians believe that only God can answer prayer: to pray to another human being, or to a man-made object, is pointless.

Meditation In many religious traditions, especially Eastern ones, meditation is commonly used. This often involves the repetition of a phrase or 'mantra'.

Worship The whole-hearted expression of love, devotion and submission to another person or to God.

Miracles A number of faiths exercise miraculous powers, such as healing and prophecy. When a group places major emphasis on these, there is danger of fraudulent tricks, and of 'counterfeit miracles' performed by evil spirits. Some leaders who wish to impress their followers have used tricks, or paranormal forces which are not fully understood. The miracles of Jesus were a demonstration of the 'new age'. They showed his power for good over sickness and death, and over the forces of nature.

Mission Most groups make special efforts to win new members. Some groups teach that it is through sharing in this outreach that their followers can be saved.

Faiths give their followers guidelines for living.

Community In many religious groups some of the followers live together in special communities. Some modern cults insist that all their followers should live like this. So membership can mean separation from home, family and everything outside the group. Christians are encouraged to live as members of their family, their local community, and the 'new community', the church.

Authority Most groups have a structure of leadership. Some groups give total authority to their leaders, even over such matters as clothes, possessions, time and marriage. Christians believe that each individual is responsible to God. Leaders are to be 'servants of the community'.

Marriage Some groups have taught that the way to salvation is to abstain from sex and from marriage; others, that salvation comes from having a 'perfect marriage'. Christians believe that for the majority of people, marriage is a gift from God, to be enjoyed for mutual help and the creation of family life. But it is not the way to salvation.

THE FUTURE

The question of what will happen at the end of time has been the subject of much speculation.

Second coming of Christ The Bible teaches that Jesus will one day return to earth. No one can know when. All will see his coming, and he will complete his work, setting up the 'new heaven and new earth'. Many cults have set a date on this 'second coming'; when the date has passed, they have been forced to re-interpret either their own prophecy, or the Bible.

Millennium A thousand years. Used in the symbolism of the Bible to speak of Christ's reign of 1,000 years, which some equate with the 'new heaven and new earth'.

Battle of Armageddon Used in the symbolism of the Bible to speak of the final battle between God and evil: 'Armageddon', the 'hill of Megiddo', had been the scene of many battles in the past. Ultimately God will conquer and destroy evil, suffering and death.

Life after death All religious groups have some teaching on what happens after death. Eastern groups believe in reincarnation— the soul is reborn in a new body many times, until it is ultimately absorbed in the divine. Western groups believe in continued life, but in a new sort of reality. Christians believe, not just in the 'immortality of the soul' (a Greek idea), but in the resurrection of the body.

Heaven and hell What happens after death is clearly unknowable unless it is revealed from outside. Christians base their belief on the teaching of the Bible. After death comes judgement: those who have put their faith in Jesus will enjoy God's presence for ever. Those who have not will be separated from him for ever.

MYSTERIES

JOHN ALLAN

INTRODUCING MYSTERIES

Skulls that scream . . . heavy tables rising in the air . . . strange craft in the skies . . . people who suddenly burst into flames. The subject matter of this book is exciting and exotic. It is also vast. All that we can do here is to draw the main outlines of the paranormal, to give the briefest of introductions to a subject which is frequently complex, baffling and very contradictory.

And please remember, as you read, that in this area there are more dubious and fraudulent claims per square inch than in almost any other subject. There are several reasons for being cautious.

Deliberate faking

The nineteenth-century fascination with spirit messages began on 31 March 1848, when three young girls—Kate, Margaret and Leah Fox—discovered they were receiving mysterious communications, in rapping noises, from a 'spirit' who claimed to be a murdered pedlar. Or were they?

In 1888 Margaret Fox publicly admitted that it had been 'all fraud, hypocrisy and delusion'. Was this a genuine confession, or was she just an embittered widow, envious of the fame of her successful sister Leah? One thing is sure: since 1848, there has been no lack of fraudulent mediums who have faked 'supernatural' noises and apparitions in order to make money.

Inaccurate reporting

Erich von Däniken's theory that human beings were 'created' by astronauts has won him 35 million readers. Few of them realize that his six books are simply a tissue of inaccuracies and factual distortions.

When a theory is attractive, people are often careless about facts. In 1915 Arthur Machen wrote a story 'entirely without foundation' about angel troops who had rescued British soldiers in the retreat from Mons. To his horror, the story was accepted as true, and several 'witnesses' of the angels came forward. The legend still lingers today.

Auto-suggestion

When it suits their wishes, people are often prone to believe what appears to happen rather than what does. And this can produce real effects.

Australian 'clever men', for example, perform psychic 'operations' on the bodies of sick believers. Ronald Rose once asked one of them if it wasn't just clever conjuring. 'Smiling, he agreed, but immediately stressed the psychological point of view: "They bin get better all the same."'

A mixture of causes

The famous Cock Lane ghost in Smithfield, London, in 1759 was probably a genuine paranormal occurrence. But no one would believe this when Elizabeth, the daughter of the house, was detected counterfeiting rapping noises with a piece of board. However, Elizabeth had been told that unless the ghost manifested itself that night, her family would be sent to prison; and so probably she simply decided to lend a helping hand. She could certainly not have counterfeited some of the other manifestations. In this way paranormal phenomena, genuine in origin, can become entangled with purely human effects.

Demonic deception

The Bible teaches that there is a deceptive, dangerous spirit world which human beings should make no attempt to contact, which distorts reality and can ruin lives.

Many paranormal researchers have become aware of the reality of something evil behind the phenomena which they investigate. G.K. Chesterton commented, after experimenting with a ouija board, 'The only thing I will say with complete confidence, about that mystic and invisible power, is that it tells lies.'

The paranormal is real; there is too much evidence to dismiss it as wishful thinking. But it is not necessarily nice; and never straightforward.

Investigating mysteries

We are living at a time in history when science seems to be demonstrating, over and over again, how little we know about reality. Quantum physics, DNA, genetic codes, quasars—all of these revolutionary new ideas 'represent not only additions to *what man knows* but changes in *the way he knows*'. This claim is made by Professor Harold Schilling, an American physicist. He continues, 'Men's minds and hearts are being liberated from inhibiting attitudes and conceptions . . . they are now able to explore realms and dimensions of reality from which they had been blocked until recently.'

Is there a supernatural? Are there paranormal powers and agencies of which science has so far failed to take account? This book will show that there are many areas in which there is some evidence that we still have massive discoveries to make. But there is evidence, too, of real perils and deceptions, and it is hoped that the book will serve as a warning as well as an explanation. I write this book from my position as a committed Christian. And I hope that by the end you will see that such a standpoint is not a blinkered one; rather it offers our only hope of understanding the world of the paranormal in a sane and safe way.

JOHN ALLAN

TIME AND SPACE

Einstein's theories have fundamentally changed our understanding of time and space. Do they also provide the key to some extraordinary mysteries?

Nobody believed Sister Mary when she told her superiors about her work in converting the Jumano Indians to Christianity. It was hardly surprising. The Indians were in Central America—and her convent was in Spain.

But then Father Alonzo de Benavides returned from Mexico in 1630, bringing stories of a mysterious 'lady in blue' who had visited several areas to evangelize before him. He brought with him a chalice which the lady had left behind; and it was recognized as coming from Mary's convent. When she was questioned on obscure points of Indian lore and Mexican geography, her knowledge proved phenomenal. Yet she had never left Spain for a second.

Materializations and teleporting

Can a person be in two places simultaneously? The pupils of nineteenth-century teacher Emilie Sagée certainly thought so. On one occasion, when Emilie was writing on the blackboard, her double appeared beside her. At another time she 'materialized' in a classroom when the real Emilie was clearly visible outside in the garden. Two of the girls who touched the apparition said it felt 'like muslin'; another boldly walked through her.

Telepathy is a possible explanation of some cases like this. Sometimes apparitions can be projected telepathically into the minds of other people, and their minds will then be stimulated to produce a recognizable image of the 'agent'. It has been shown that this image will act naturally and usually obey physical laws (such as producing reflections in a mirror), sometimes communicating verbally.

But this does not explain Sister Mary's very solid chalice. Fanciful elaboration? Perhaps; 1630 was a long time ago.

But there may be other explanations. Albert Einstein held that motion affected time and distance. For example, a spaceship travelling at half the speed of light would be only 85 per cent of its length when at rest, and the clock on board

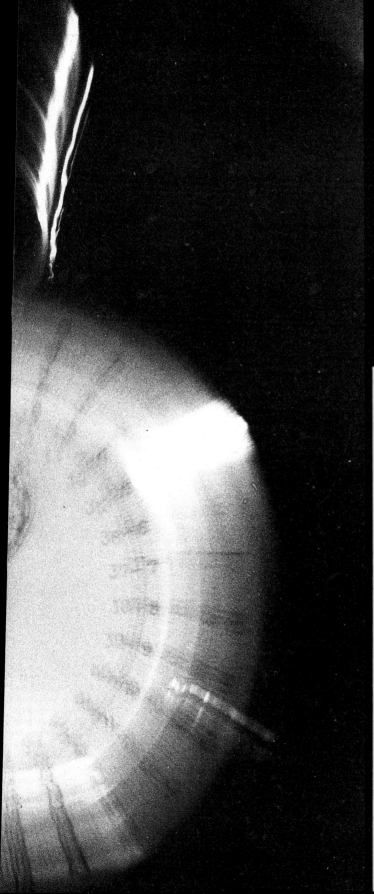

would be running at only 85 per cent of its normal rate. He saw space–time as a unity, rather than two entities, 'space' and 'time', which suggests that it might have more flexible qualities than we have imagined.

Perhaps, occasionally, it is possible for time and space to become compressed in such a way that the normal rules no longer apply. That might explain why a honeymoon couple in Brazil felt drowsy as they drove in Rio Grande do Sul, fell asleep—and woke up in Mexico!

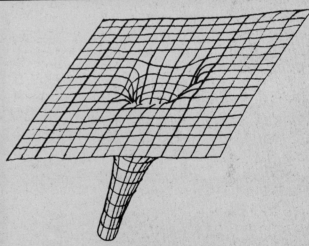

BLACK HOLES

The normal laws of time and space are dramatically flouted by 'black holes'. These form in space when a star burns up all of its internal energy and collapses in on itself, with a stronger and stronger gravitational pull, until it becomes infinitesimally small. It soaks up all light, allowing none to escape, and so becomes invisible; it sucks nearby objects into itself, crushing them to nothing, and inside its 'event horizon' (sucking distance) time operates differently. Some scientists suggest that travellers drawn into a black hole will emerge on the other side, through a 'white hole', into another dimension; this is unproven.

Professor John Taylor's bestseller *Black Holes: The End of the Universe?* argues that the discovery of black holes shatters all of our religious conceptions. His argument is based on a series of naive assumptions and misunderstandings of basic Christian teaching (for example, about soul and mind, Satan and the Fall, the personality of God, salvation and immortality). Interestingly, his colleague R.L.F. Boyd—Head of the Mullard Space Science Laboratory, concerned in the discovery of black holes—is an unabashedly convinced Christian.

DEFYING SCIENCE

In Singapore in 1861 an earthquake was followed by a deluge of rain. After the rain, the streets were full of fish. Where had they come from?

Do showers of frogs fall out of the sky? Can rain be black, or yellow, or red? How can we explain metal objects found inside lumps of coal, or the gopher turtle who flopped out of the clouds into a small Mississippi village?

Charles Fort's third book, *Lo!*, was published in 1931. It described many strange events, but suggested no explanations. Fort said, 'I shall find out for myself, and anyone who cares to, may find out with me.'

Fort and Forteana

Questions like these fascinated the peculiar brain of Charles Hoy Fort. A penniless journalist from a wealthy New York family, Fort devoted his life to collecting facts which would not fit into nineteenth-century science. He wrote seven unreadable books, but is mainly remembered for his third, *The Book of the Damned* (1919), which pieces together a weird array of facts 'damned' by scientists who could not explain them.

Although not much recognized in his lifetime, Fort has many modern-day admirers, and a Fortean Society still catalogues in its *Fortean Times* strange information from around the world. Fort had no theory about why these odd occurrences took place (although he suggested several); he simply wanted to expose the smugness of scientific orthodoxy. Recently *The*

Book of the Damned has begun selling widely again. 'Forteana'—the kind of phenomena which delighted Fort—have continued unabated throughout this century. In January 1969 in Maryland, hundreds of dead ducks dropped on to the streets; in June 1954, hundreds of little frogs bounced off the heads of pedestrians in crowded streets in Birmingham.

Strange abilities continue to be shown by unlikely people; Ted Serios, for example, a simple-minded alcoholic hotel worker from Chicago, has developed the ability to produce identifiable pictures ('thoughtographs') on a piece of photographic film, simply by staring into the camera lens. As he places a 'gismo'—a cardboard tube—against the lens first, there have been allegations of fakery, but Serios has performed his feats under stringent test conditions.

No one knows what ball lightning is. A small bright globule generally follows an erratic course, sometimes passing through walls, or even aeroplanes in flight, before exploding.

Spontaneous combustion

One of the most gruesome phenomena investigated by Fort was 'spontaneous

On 5 December 1966 the gasman called on Dr John Irving Bentley, a semi-invalid who lived on his own in Pennsylvania, USA. When he got no reply to his calls, he searched the house and found this gruesome sight; a mysterious fire had totally consumed Dr Bentley, but damaged nothing around him.

WHAT IS THE WORLD?

Some people think that the miracles recounted in the Bible contravene natural laws, and therefore cannot be true. But this is to misunderstand what natural laws are.

The word 'law' can mean two things: first, a *prescription* for human conduct (for instance, 'You must not steal or you will be sent to prison'); second, a *description* of what seems to be happening in nature or scientific experiments. 'Natural laws' are descriptions of what we observe taking place around us, not prescriptions for what *must* happen! When we see something occurring which seems to conflict with the natural laws we understand (for instance, an aeroplane in the sky, which

conflicts with the laws of gravity) it does not mean *either* that the law of gravity does not work *or* that our senses are deceiving us; it simply means that there are other natural laws at work which we may not know about (in this case, the laws of aerodynamics).

Hence the Bible's miracles need not be suspensions of natural laws (although if God is really the all-powerful Creator, there is no reason why they shouldn't be). Both miracles and Forteana could *also* simply be applications of natural principles we do not yet understand. Indeed, the Bible stresses that the universe does not operate randomly, but is created and sustained in an ordered way by God.

combustion'. Mrs Mary Carpenter was on a boating holiday in East Anglia, in the summer of 1938, when suddenly she burst into flames and was reduced to ashes in front of her husband and children. They were unharmed, and so was the boat. There was no flame from which she could have caught fire.

She was one of about two dozen known cases of 'spontaneous combustion' in the last hundred years. Strangely, the surroundings of 'combustion' cases are usually unaffected by the flames; in 1922 Mrs Euphemia Johnson's calcined bones were found lying in a heap inside her undamaged clothes. The explanation may be something to do with the effect of magnetic disturbances upon the body (many cases happen within a weak magnetic field) or the electrical discharge of the human body itself.

THE UNKNOWN EARTH

Lines of power. Dragon paths. Did our ancestors understand the world we live in better than we do?

On 30 June 1921, an English brewer named Alfred Watkins was riding across the hills of Herefordshire. As he looked down on the countryside below, he suddenly realized that the little churches, the hilltops and the ancient monuments seemed to fall into a pattern. It was as though there had once been a system of straight lines and tracks connecting them.

Leys

Watkins expanded his ideas into a book. He claimed that the tracks, which he called 'ley lines', were a system of ancient trade routes running right across Britain. Not many archaeologists were convinced, but later Wilhelm Teudt found identical tracks—'heilige Linien'—in Germany, and Xavier Guichard claimed to trace an amazing geodetic system running right across Europe and linking up hundreds of towns with names sounding like 'Alesia' (Versailles, Alessio, Calais, Elsendorf). In the locality of each one, he claimed, one could find landscaped hills and a man-made well.

It seems impossible that leys were trade routes. But dowsers such as Guy Underwood have suggested that the connection with water is important. Megalithic sites (see *Ancient Engineering*) seem at times to contain a mysterious energy, not unlike electromagnetism, and it is possible that the leys were channels for flows of this energy. Underwood suggests that the underground springs at ancient sites have something to do with the 'geodetic force' which he has discovered there. Certainly both Stonehenge and Avebury may be criss-crossed by a labyrinthine network of underground streams, and Welsh dowser Bill Lewis claims to sense a spiral force around ancient standing stones, derived from the streams which cross one another directly under the stone.

Was there once an age when men lived closer to the earth than today, and so knew of strange forces running through the earth which are presently unknown to science? In China it is still common to site new buildings carefully according to the laws of *feng-shui*, an intricate code for fitting buildings into landscapes in harmony with the 'earth force', observing 'dragon paths' which, like leys, run across the land. Most scientists still doubt that 'geodetic force' has any reality; but no really satisfactory testing has yet been done.

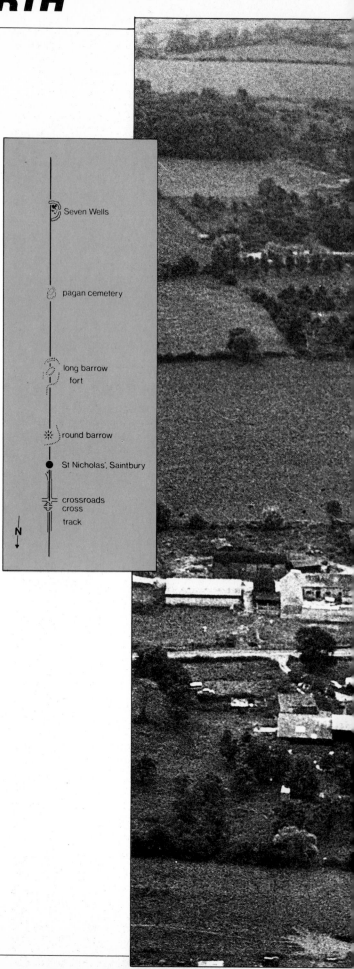

Seven Wells

pagan cemetery

long barrow
fort

round barrow

St Nicholas', Saintbury

crossroads
cross

track

N

A typical alignment of man-made sites is the so-called Saintbury ley in the west of England. In a three-and-a-half-mile straight line lie an old cross, a road, a church and four ancient earthworks.

Geometric earth?

Three Russian scientists of the sixties—scholars of history, engineering and electronics—combined to write a paper for the USSR Academy of Sciences, entitled *Is the Earth a Huge Crystal?* They believe it is possible to trace a lattice-work pattern, a 'matrix of cosmic energy', running across the earth's face, dividing it into twelve pentagonal slabs.

They claim that the idea explains the siting of ancient civilizations, the occurrence of hurricanes, volcanoes, and magnetic anomalies. Western scientists are less convinced; they point out that the supposed 'lines' are drawn so vaguely that anything could be read into them; and that if it is true that the continents have shifted position, the 'crystalline' symmetry would have disappeared long ago.

A HOLLOW EARTH?

When Charles Fort (see *Defying Science*) theorized in his book *Y* that the earth could perhaps be hollow, no one paid any attention. But recently the idea has surfaced again, notably in the books of Brinsley Le Poer Trench, one of Britain's foremost UFO experts and a member of the House of Lords. Trench believes that:

● We are being watched from the skies by a friendly race of space visitors.

● We are also being threatened from within by another evil race.

● This race lives inside the hollow earth and reaches the surface via a crater at the North Pole.

● Photographs of the earth from space often show a strange indentation over the Pole—the crater lip.

Quite apart from the fact that to Trench, Jesus is merely an 'initiate', not the Son of God, there seems to be overwhelming evidence against his point of view.

TAPPING NATURAL FORCES

Metal detectors are a useful tool in looking for buried treasure.
But many claim that a piece of hazel twig would do just as well.

Where does water come from? There is something like 1,370 million cubic kilometres of it in the oceans of the world—far too much simply to have dropped from the sky as rain. Scientists are beginning to think that somehow water is formed somewhere deep within the earth—at the rate of 100 cubic metres per year.

Finding underground water

Whether or not this is true, it is something which 'dowsers' have always believed. Dowsing is the art of tracking down underground sources of water with the help of a forked twig—preferably of peach, hazel, willow or witch-hazel, but whalebone or wire can do instead. Dowsing has been practised for centuries, and often works when orthodox geology fails. But no one knows how it works. Is it simply a response to natural laws we have yet to discover, or is some supernatural force involved?

If it is a purely natural process, it is hard to explain why it works when the fork is held above a map of an area, as well as in the area itself. And certainly an interest in dowsing has led some gifted, sensitive practitioners into an unhealthy fascination with other 'supernatural' practices. But many dowsers are practical, unspeculative people more concerned with employing their gift

usefully than with occult study. Perhaps they are simply more sensitive than others to a kind of radiation signal emitted by the stream. But then again it is possible to dowse for other things besides water; dowsing can become a kind of clairvoyance.

Beyond water

Dowsers claim that some underground water— 'black streams'—can trigger off arthritis and cancer in human beings. Dr Herbert Douglas of Vermont was sceptical about this. But when he tested the beds, chairs and couches of 55 arthritic patients, he found that without exception they were placed above the intersection of underground streams. Twenty-five of the patients agreed to move to a different bed—and each of them either improved condition or was completely cured.

Dowsing becomes dangerous when the practitioner moves from exploring real, if mysterious, phenomena in the physical world, to making unwarranted assumptions about the supernatural. Tom Lethbridge, for example, who dowsed with a pendulum, came to believe that beyond a certain length the pendulum registered vibrations from another 'dimension'—the world beyond death. There are no grounds for this idea.

THE FINDHORN COMMUNITY

At Findhorn in the North of Scotland there is a 'New Age community' which boasts unusual agricultural achievements. On fairly unpromising soil the community members have grown plants of staggering size in spectacular profusion. They attribute their success to the fact that they have attuned themselves to the energies and forces of nature, and are guided by communications from Devas (the spirits of plants) and Nature Spirits (elves, gnomes and fairies, including the god Pan, all of whom are 'servants of God and function according to His will only'). Spirit messages and visions are important.

Some outsiders attribute their successes to collective ESP, and dismiss the 'spirits' as delusions; but in view of the way in which the 'spirit' messages have drawn the community from a broadly Christian base deeper and deeper into pagan nature-worship, it is possible that demonic forces are also at work.

DISAPPEARANCES

A few days' journey from Japan, nine ships disappeared without trace in four years. A government ship was sent to investigate. It disappeared.

It was 7 November 1872, when Captain David Moorhouse of the *Dei Gratia* spotted another ship behaving erratically just ahead. They were in the Atlantic, some 600 miles/950 km west of Gibraltar. It looked as if no one was steering the other ship. With a shock, he realized she was the *Mary Celeste*—a ship with a 'jinx' reputation, commanded by his friend Benjamin Briggs. Fearing the worst for Briggs, Moorhouse hurriedly sent across a boarding party. They found—nothing.

From that moment on, the *Mary Celeste* was destined to become the best-known mystery ship of all time. Where were the Briggs family and the crew of eight? There were no signs of violence. Oliver Deveau, leader of the boarding party, later testified, 'There seemed to be everything left behind in the cabins as if left in a great hurry, but everything in its place.'

What happened? We may never know; none of the many theories quite fit the facts. All we can say is that many theories cannot be disproved. There is certainly no case for suspecting intervention by astronauts or flying saucers. Strange things happen at sea, and paranormal causes should never be invoked until natural ones have been ruled out.

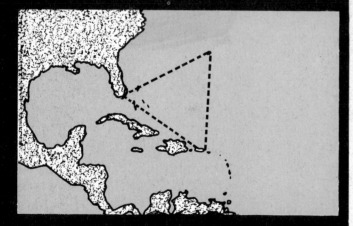

The Bermuda Triangle
Most people have heard of the 'Bermuda Triangle', first described by Vincent Gaddis in 1964. 'This relatively limited area,' he claimed, 'is the scene of disappearances that total far beyond the laws of chance.'

Unfortunately, the US Coastguard Service announce that very few ships do disappear in the

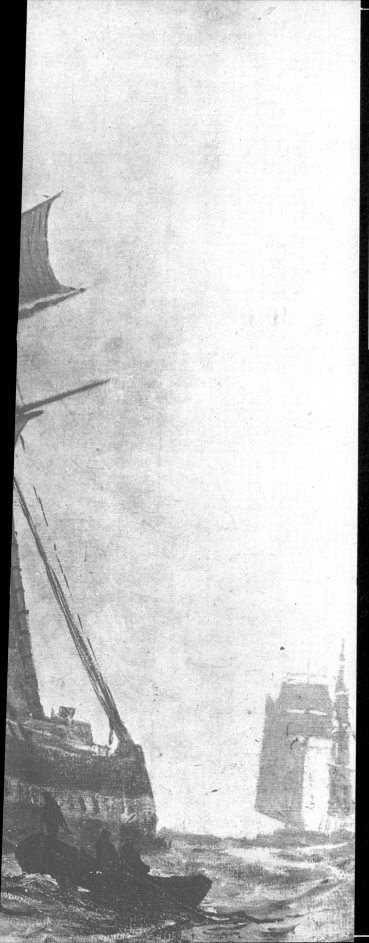

MANIPULATING DISAPPEARANCES

Why do things (and people) disappear? One suggestion is that gravitational or magnetic forces can be tampered with artificially. Maurice Jessup claimed in 1955 that the US Navy had actually done this 12 years earlier—rendering a destroyer and its crew invisible, and 'teleporting' them from Philadelphia to the area of Newport News.

Although the experiment was a success, according to Jessup, the crew suffered terribly; some died and others went insane. The 'Philadelphia Experiment' has become a well-known legend, but unfortunately it seems never to have happened. Jessup was relying on shoddy information.

It may not be impossible, in principle, for something like this to happen; but we cannot say. It has never been done, and we know too little about magnetic properties to attempt it.

Triangle. In 1975, for instance, of 21 ships lost without trace off the American coastline, only four were in the Triangle. There is also a question as to where the Triangle *is*; if the corners of it are Florida, Bermuda and Puerto Rico, then most of the tragedies claimed for it actually happened outside.

Lawrence Kusche of Arizona State University has shown definitively that most of the legendary Triangle mysteries can be explained quite simply The best one can say is that this area of the world is prone to sudden freak storms, and magnetic irregularities, which can sometimes lead to inexplicable disasters.

The Marie Celeste case is one of the world's best-known mysteries.

MYSTERIES OF THE BODY

From time to time, as medical knowledge increases, doctors are forced to take seriously ideas that had been dismissed as old wives' tales.

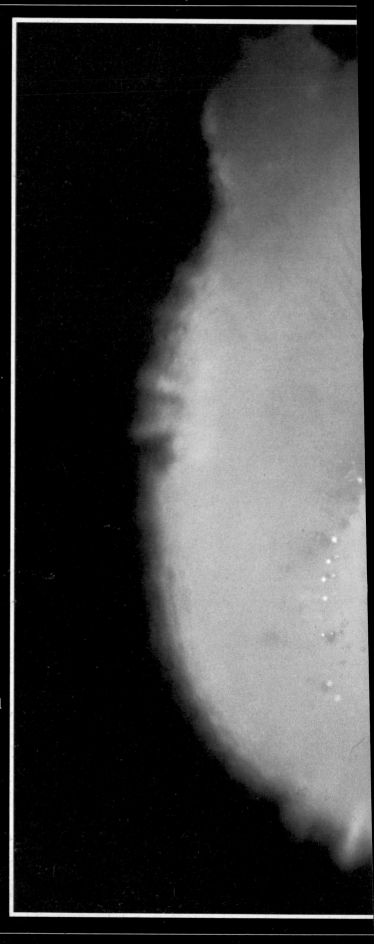

In 1939 Soviet doctor Semyon Kirlian made a strange discovery. When he placed his hand between two electrodes containing a photographic plate, and turned on the current, he found that he had produced a photograph—not just of his hand, but also of a strange glowing aura around it.

Experiments showed that leaves, and other people's hands, produced the same results. The colour and type of aura seemed to vary depending on whether or not the person was well, sick, or mentally disturbed. Was this a new discovery about the human body? Are we all surrounded by a Kirlian aura?

Earlier, in 1911, Walter J. Kilner of St Thomas's Hospital had discovered that he could see an 'envelope of energy' surrounding human bodies when he looked at them through a solution of dicyanin diluted in alcohol. This envelope, he claimed, consisted of three layers— an outer and inner aura, and the 'etheric double'—which radiated for 12 inches/30 cm from the body and changed in size and colour when the person was sick or hypnotized.

A useful study?
Disciples of Kilner have since discovered a type of glass reportedly producing the same results as dicyanin, and 'Kirlian goggles' are now available for sale. Scientists are sceptical; it is possible that the 'auras' (which not everyone can see) are produced simply by suggestion. Kirlian photography is equally unproven. Some results could have been examples of 'Lichtenburg figures', a well-known electrical phenomenon which has nothing to do with the human aura. Professor William Tiller has shown since that there were many potential sources of uncontrolled error in Kirlian's research equipment, and that when the equipment was stringently controlled there were no differences between the auras of different types.

Kirlian's advocates point out that Tiller is now admitting that 'some of the conclusions ... may have been premature', and that his work was based only on the fingertips, not the whole hand. But their case is far from proven.

Acupuncture
For centuries the Chinese have taught that the body is crossed by lines of force, the junctions of

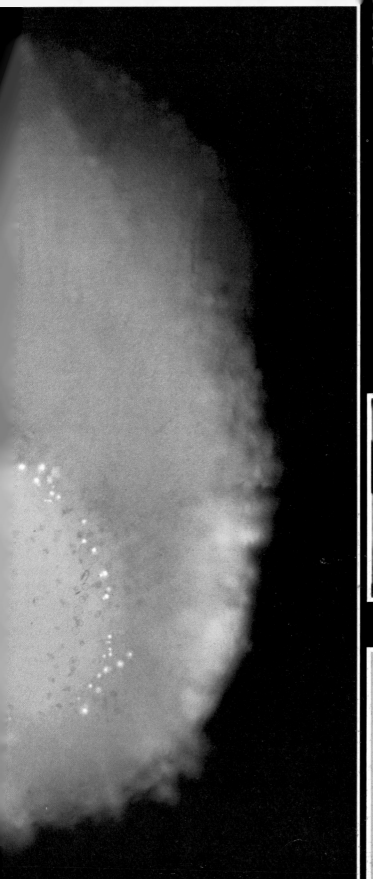

which control bodily health. This is the basis for acupuncture, the science of inserting vibrating needles at the junction points in order to induce anaesthesia or even a cure. Recently a Christian doctor, Meg Patterson, has introduced electro-acupuncture to Britain as a seemingly effective cure for drug addictions; however, she has found that a slight electrical charge—without the insertion of needles—has an equal effect. The scientific validity of acupuncture has yet to be properly examined in the West, but undeniably it has achieved interesting results, and is used regularly in medicine and surgery in the East.

There is much we have yet to discover about our bodies; perhaps, just perhaps, some of these experimental techniques may point the way forward. But we need more evidence.

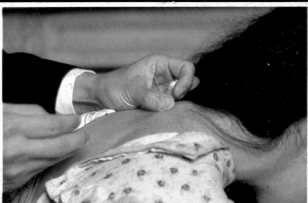

Acupuncture has been practised for centuries in China, but it is only recently that it has been used in the West.

WHAT IS MANKIND?

The expression and development of bodily powers is often seen as a path to spiritual enlightenment. But the Bible's view is that more than personal development is needed.

● Some religions, such as Hinduism, teach that there is no distinction between the physical and spiritual aspects of man. Therefore, bodily practices such as meditation, yoga exercises or chanting can help us realize God within ourselves.

● Other points of view, deriving from Platonic philosophy, hold that the body is unspiritual and therefore evil. The only way to realize God is to loathe and mistreat the body.

● Christians have at times been influenced by both these views. But the Bible's emphasis is rather different. God created man. All that God created is good. Therefore man's body is good. But man is more than body—he is also spirit. And only when made spiritually alive by contact with Jesus Christ does he become capable of appreciating and knowing God.

HEALING

All over the world, alternative medicine is practised. What powers enable people to heal the sick?

On 7 October every year, the *Liverpool Echo* carries a special notice. It is a message of gratitude from Mrs Sheila Speirs to the man who gave her back her health; and she intends to insert it every year until she dies. The man concerned is not a doctor, but an ex-blacksmith from Liverpool called John Cain.

Cain has been a full-time healer since 1972. He is one of around 8,000 spiritual healers in the British Isles, 2,500 of whom belong to a body known as the National Federation of Spiritual Healers. This body is gradually attracting more attention and interest from the medical profession.

In Brazil, spirit healing has always been more respectable. There has been a 600-bed Spirit Hospital there since 1926. In Britain, the Medical Association claims that no one has conclusively shown that spiritual healers do any good. But in 1977 the General Medical Council permitted doctors to refer patients to healers provided they kept control of the case. Before this, any doctor doing so would have been struck off the register.

What happens?

Spirit healers work in a variety of ways. Cain often lays hands on clients, but has also found that the very sight of his picture can trigger off healing. Once he instructed a lady by telephone to place her hands on a sick nephew's head; working as Cain's proxy, she was able to cure the boy.

Healing seems to involve a transfer of energy from one person to the other. Harry Edwards, the famous psychic healer, used to close his eyes to attune himself and feel the power flowing through him, before he would do anything. But exactly what the energy *is*, it would be hard to say.

It is also hard to establish when a genuine cure has taken place; all sorts of factors can be at work. 'Spontaneous remission', for example (when a disease abates of its own accord) can happen unpredictably for no apparent reason. Wrong diagnosis is another possibility which can account for an unexpected change in a patient's condition.

How does it happen?

Though some healing can be explained away, there seem to be real successes. Why? Many healers believe that their powers come from spirit guides with medical skills. Matthew Manning

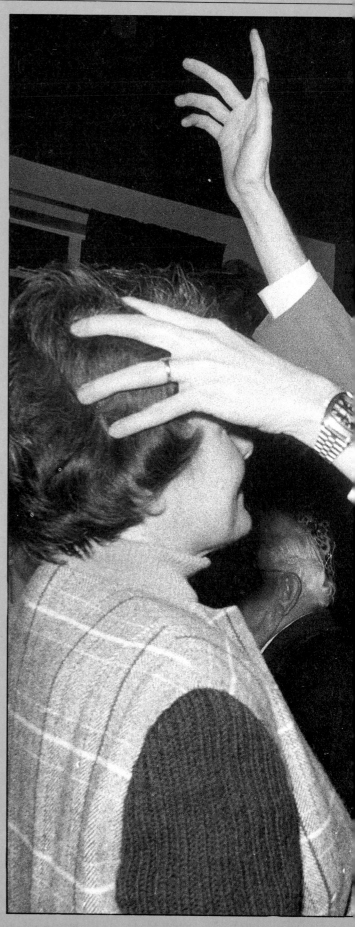

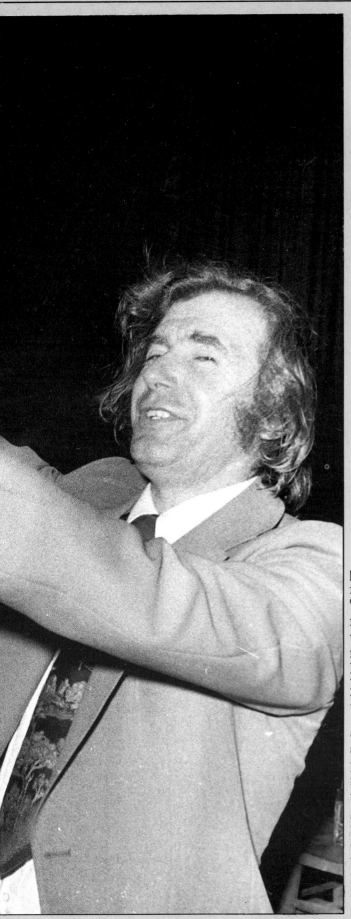

One of Britain's best-known healers is Trevor Dearing. A Christian minister, he received the power to heal at the time of a personal spiritual renewal. His work is now entirely devoted to exercising what he sees as an important gift from God.

produces by automatic writing diagnoses from a nineteenth-century doctor who calls himself Thomas Penn; these diagnoses have often proved fantastically correct. On the other hand, some of them have merely fulfilled the subconscious fantasies of the patient, clearly because Manning has picked up telepathic messages from them. Manning himself is very sceptical about whether his powers prove survival after death.

'Gifts of healings' are mentioned in the Bible as a spiritual attribute given by the Holy Spirit to some Christians. But that does not rule out the possibility that some people, too, may have natural gifts of healing which science cannot at this moment explain. The danger is that their gifts may lead them into wrong ideas about the nature of the supernatural world; few are as objective as Manning. There is also the possibility that Satan can produce 'counterfeit gifts' for purposes of deceit; Jesus warned that any of his miracles was liable to be copied by the powers of evil.

Spirit surgery

In Brazil and the Philippines, there are spirit healers who claim to open up bodies with their bare hands, remove diseased matter, and then cause the wound to heal over instantly, leaving no scar. At times this is mere conjuring; the growths supposedly removed have proved to be decayed chicken livers. Jim Jones, fanatical leader of the mass-suicide 'People's Temple' cult, used to produce such 'miracle cures' by sleight of hand.

The British scientist Lyall Watson, who has watched spirit healers in action, is convinced that some are 'capable of controlled materializations'. In other words, the objects removed do not come from within the patient's body, but simply appear at the healer's fingertips.

What must be said is that whenever exhaustive tests have been done, there has always been plenty of evidence of fraud. 'Spirit cures' are often psychosomatic, brought about by the patient's faith in the healer, not by the healer's actions themselves.

Types of healing

There are probably four types of 'miraculous' healing which need to be distinguished. *Spirit healing* is practised by witch doctors and shamans, who place themselves at the use of spirit powers in general, without any clear idea of which spirits are using them. *Spiritual healing* involves the summoning of certain known spirits to provide the power required. Harry Edwards, for instance, used to call on the power of Louis Pasteur. *Psychic healing* is manifested quietly and unspectacularly by a few people who claim to have had the ability since birth. Seemingly, there is no spirit involvement. *Christian 'gifts of healing'* are given by the Holy Spirit to some Christians.

All four types can work. The only question is: what precisely is the supernatural agency which is supplying the mysterious power to heal?

HOLISTIC HEALTH

'Holism' or 'holistic health' is the name given to the movement (centred on America) which is promoting in hospitals and universities the viability of 'non-traditional means of treatment' in healing disease. This includes psychic surgery, bio-energetic therapy, radionics, laying on of hands, and 'soul therapy'.

Some of these techniques are arguably effective, but there are two problems: first, little thought is given to *how* they work, and so we may not be aware of *all* their effects; second, holism often involves unjustified religious stances. 'Holistic Health is a point of view about the Universe,' according to one spokesman; '. . . the creative intention . . . leads each person to . . . seek a personal knowledge of the inner vision and spirit of the Higher Self (God within).'

By contrast, Christians believe that God is external to us, and can be personally known only by someone who enters into a relationship with him through Jesus Christ.

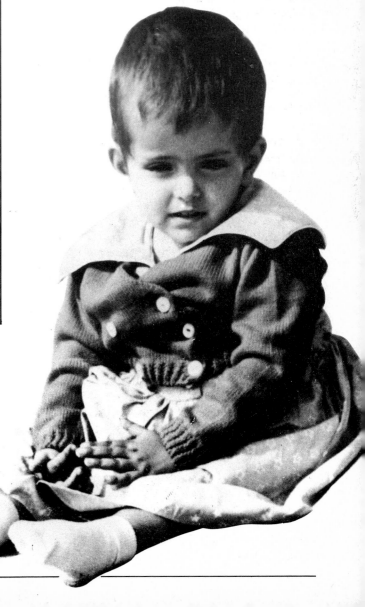

YOGA

'Yoga' is the Hindu word which signifies a spiritual discipline by which men may reach union with God. Thus it covers a wide range of religious practices. What most Westerners know as 'yoga' is one branch of the subject—'hatha yoga'—involving physical posture exercises to achieve psychic power.

. Most Western yoga practitioners do it merely as a form of healthful exercise, but Stephen Annett comments, 'It should be borne in mind that physical improvement in health is really incidental to the original aims of hatha yoga.' Its purpose is to prepare the mind for spiritual enlightenment, and most organizations teaching yoga include a degree of the basic Hindu philosophy underlying it as part of the course. How inextricably linked the two aspects are is open to debate. Some Indian Christians, for example, believe that yoga can be helpful to Christians; others suspect its Hindu roots and fear occult involvements.

The traditional medicine of Africa is still carried out today, alongside the orthodox medical work of hospitals and clinics. In Ghana, Kojo Goku makes a very successful living as a 'witch-doctor'. Here he is attempting to cure a paralysed man by rubbing him with a chicken, which he will then kill.

The ability to heal may be a function of the brain which is not normally released. At the age of two, Linda Martel underwent serious brain surgery. Miraculously she survived, and was then able to cure headaches, coughs and even paralysed limbs merely by touch.

IMPOSSIBLE FEATS

Stories of beds of nails or firewalking were once dismissed as mere travellers' tales. But not any more.

Many of the records in the *Guinness Book of Records* are constantly being challenged. But few people want to take on the two set by 'Komar' (Vernon Craig) of Wooster, Ohio. On 7 March 1975, Komar walked for 25 feet/7.5 m over blazing coals of elm wood at a measured temperature of 1183°F/640°C; and on 23 July four years earlier, he had completed 25 hours and 20 minutes on a bed of needle-sharp six-inch nails, spaced two inches apart from each other.

How did he do it? Dr Norman Shealy undertook numerous tests on him, and is reported to have found that Komar did *not* possess congenital analgesis (the medical condition which permits no physical awareness of pain). He was just as likely to suffer as anyone else. How are such feats possible?

Mayne Reid Coe, who trained himself to walk through fire and lick red-hot steel bars, believed that perspiration drops on the body might form a barrier between the heat and the performer's limbs. This may indeed be a factor, but it is certainly not enough to explain very long fire-walks, such as Komar's, nor to explain why the fire-walker's *clothing* does not catch fire either.

Harry Price, the noted psychic researcher, undertook some fire-walking experiments in 1935, and concluded that the secret lay in the fact that each foot touched the embers for less than half a second—not long enough to burn. But some Hindu fire-walks have been slow, dignified affairs; and again there is the question of the performer's clothing.

A spiritual power?

Probably the true explanation is that most fire-walkers go into a trance which induces anaesthesia. This would explain also the self-scarification rites carried out by the medium, or *dang-ki*, in the spiritist cults of Singapore. The *dang-ki* thrusts skewers through his cheeks and neck, and sits on a chair of sharp knives, to demonstrate the powers of his *shen* (possessing spirit) in protecting him from injury. It has been noticed that the *dang-ki*'s body becomes abnormally cold at the moment he is possessed by his *shen*.

Similar explanations may hold for the remarkable physical powers which can be produced by study of Eastern martial arts, which are closely bound up with spiritual exercises. The same applies to *tumo*, the Tibetan lama's art of body-heat projection, which protects him (despite his scanty clothing) against the rigours of Tibetan winters.

Stan Gooch believes that primitive peoples are better at these skills than Westerners because of 'a difference in the precise structure of the nervous system'. This may be so, but the phenomena can look very like demon possession too, and a degree of spirit influence should not be automatically discounted.

TODAY'S SUPER-POWERS

At least two present-day cults claim super-powers for their practitioners. TM (Transcendental Meditation), is a 'non-religious' meditation technique, which claims to increase people's personal vitality. Advanced students of TM can undergo the TM-Siddhi course, which promises skills such as levitation (the ability to rise a few feet from the ground while meditating), invisibility and clairvoyance.

Although pictures exist of meditators levitating, the movement is extremely reluctant to allow outsiders to witness it happening. Some observers theorize that the phenomenon may be more like a sudden hop in the air than a dignified floating upwards, and so may be produced by involuntary jerks of the muscles, a frequent occurrence among meditators. Invisibility can be a mentally-induced phenomenon (if I *want* my hand to disappear, my brain may tell me eventually that it has done). On the other hand ex-meditation teacher R.D. Scott claims in his book *Transcendental Misconceptions* that demonic influence can be a factor in TM too.

Another group, Scientology, believes that its graduates— 'clears'—possess psychokinetic, clairvoyant and teleporting powers (see *Glossary*). Public demonstrations—now discontinued—have been remarkably unimpressive.

THE WAY TO ENLIGHTENMENT ?

There is plenty of evidence that our bodies and minds may possess powers which we have not yet learnt to use. And it is right that we should explore our potential to the full; but wrong to expect that by doing so we will necessarily find all the answers we are looking for or even find the personal fulfilment we desire.

According to the Bible, man is made in the image of God, and made good. But that image has been ruined by the rebellion of human beings against their creator. Hence it is important to realize that exploring the nature of man will bring us face to face not only with our potential, but also with our fallen, sinful self. God is not 'within', the Bible teaches. Because of sin he is 'outside' our lives. Salvation must involve allowing him to restore both our relationship with himself and our true human nature.

Is it possible to defy gravity? In the 'Indian rope trick', the magician, or *sadhu*, makes a pliable rope rise in the air and become rigid enough for a boy to climb up. It certainly looks genuine, though Western magicians perform similar feats merely by sophisticated trickery.

At Kataragama in Sri Lanka, a fire-walking ceremony is held annually. Participants prepare themselves spiritually beforehand, and are completely unharmed by their slow barefoot walk over the red-hot embers.

MENTAL MYSTERIES

How does the mind work? As more studies are made, more complexity is found. And there are bizarre effects which seem to defy understanding.

Oliver Fox had always dreamed vividly—ever since his long spells of illness as a child. And in his teens, as an engineering student at Southampton, he discovered that he had a strange ability: to dream of a place, then pull himself physically into it until he felt a 'click' and arrived actually in the place he had dreamed about. In his 'dream body', that is; for his physical body was still lying in bed at home. He could walk around and observe his surroundings for a while, then—with another 'click'—reunite with his physical self.

Was this merely an illusion? He decided to put it to the test by projecting himself into an examination room the night before an exam, in order to look at the question paper. He memorized two questions; and both—one an extremely unusual question—came up in the 'real' paper next day.

Astral travel?
From experiences such as this, occult thinkers have derived the theory of 'astral projection'—the idea that each of us has a second body which can leave the sleeping physical body to take itself to other places as a fully conscious, thinking entity. In projection, emotions can be felt, intellectual decisions made, and sensory stimuli experienced. The 'astral body' rises out of the physical body through the head (Fox at first had headaches

J. B. RHINE

The study of the mind's extra-sensory perceptive abilities was first put on a scientific footing by Dr Joseph Banks Rhine, who coined such terms as 'ESP', 'parapsychology' and 'psi'. This pioneering North Carolina psychologist set standards of invincible integrity which are an example to all subsequent parapsychologists. In 1974, after 47 years of work, he realized that his right-hand man had been faking results, announced the fact publicly, and began immediately to develop a new method of analysis.

His initial work, between 1929 and 1934, seemed to afford staggering results, but as time passed and he tightened up his experimental controls the results proved more elusive.

'It is shocking but true,' he wrote, 'that we know the atom today better than we know the mind that knows the atom.'

J.B. Rhine (right), with his most successful subject, Hubert Pearce. In card-guessing tests, Peace consistently scored high above the statistical odds. Typically of ESP subjects, Pearce's extraordinary powers lasted for only a few years.

'A complete consecutive series of drawings transmitted by telepathy from Mr Guthrie to Miss E. without contact during the Liverpool experiment ... When No. 6 was being transmitted, Miss E. said almost directly, "Are you thinking of the bottom of the sea, with shells and fishes?" and then, "Is it a snail or a fish?"—then drew as above.' (From the *Proceedings of the Society for Psychical Research, Volume II*).

Originals

when projecting) and is connected to it by a 'silver cord' which lengthens as the second body moves away. At death, the cord breaks, and the bodies separate.

Astral projection has become the basis of a modern cult, Eckankar, but its 'reality' is impossible to prove. Remarkably convincing experiences can take place in dreams, and it is curious how many pioneers of astral travel had at one time or another suffered long periods of illness and been frustrated by the immobility of their physical bodies. It has been shown that drugs such as mescalin can produce very similar effects. Any information picked up (such as the examination questions) could arguably have telepathic causes. At Stanford Research Institute in California some work has already been done on 'remote viewing'—the psychic ability to perceive scenes and events many miles away.

Many people have attempted to link the 'silver cord' of astral projection with a reference in the Bible's book of Ecclesiastes. However, the passage there refers merely to a cord suspending a golden oil-bowl from a ceiling. The theory of an astral body is foreign to the Bible. It is not to be identified with the 'soul', which Christians see as much more than just a bit of ghostly stuff floating within the body (see *Life after Life*).

Copies

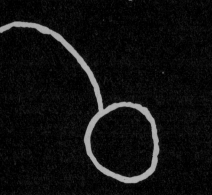

MINDFORCE

Can the power of the mind bend a fork? Raise a table?
Produce what seem to be the effects of a ghost?

Psychokinesis

One of the most controversial figures of the early seventies was a young Israeli psychic named Uri Geller. He shot to fame because of his ability to bend forks and rings simply by stroking them; to stop watches and clocks with the power of thought; and to reproduce pictures which were sealed inside an envelope. Was he an example of remarkable psychokinesis ('PK' for short—see *Glossary*), or simply a fraud? Conjuror James Randi points out that Uri is an ex-night-club illusionist who has been tested only by scientists, never by professional fakers; and he offers to reproduce all of Uri's 'paranormal' feats by trickery alone.

Medical researcher Itzhak Bentov explains Geller's feats as the activity of 'low-level poltergeists', and certainly some of the phenomena seem very similar. John White, one of Uri's earliest scientific testers, now believes that Uri has been duped and used by powers of evil in the universe. Uri's former mentor, Andrija Puharich, claimed that Uri was a channel for communications from 'the Nine', mysterious governors of this universe, and that he had been contacted by space beings from Hoova, a planet 16,000 times the size of earth with an advanced civilization whose life-span was a million years.

The extravagance of these claims has done Geller's reputation no good, and recently he has disavowed it. 'Concerning what Andrija believes . . . that's totally up to him . . . It could be a pure energy force, a pure intelligence pattern. It could be anything. It doesn't have to take the form of a being.' Certainly the Hoovids' 'revelations' through Uri have always been disappointingly tame or bafflingly inscrutable. And it seems unlikely that they would have singled out someone like Uri, whose personal intelligence is not great and whom Puharich admits is an 'unabashed egomaniac'.

A real force

But the powers of 'psychokinesis' which Geller claims are not unique. A Russian housewife, Nina Kulagina, has demonstrated the ability to move small objects (matchsticks, pens and compass needles) simply by concentrating her mind. Felicia Parise and Ingo Swann in New York possess similar powers. And whether or not Geller

Uri Geller on television in Denmark. As usual, his broadcast affected clocks and watches in viewers' homes.

is a fraud, during his TV appearances clocks stop, forks bend and keys snap in the homes of viewers—clear evidence that *someone's* mind is exerting unusual energies.

The experiments of J.B. Rhine (see *Mental Mysteries*) suggest that our minds may be able to influence the fall of a dice, or the results of card guessing, much more than is usually assumed. Paranormal researchers now tend to regard ESP (see *Glossary*) and psychokinesis as dual aspects of one mysterious ability called 'psi'. Psi may well exist, as a spiritually neutral force. It remains to be shown that it could ever be harnessed for practical uses.

During seances (see *Contacting the Dead*), mediums often produce extraordinary physical effects. Here the medium Jack Webber is causing a table to levitate. Whether the power is coming from his mind or from some other source is not clear—nor is the cause of the marks at the bottom of this infra-red photograph.

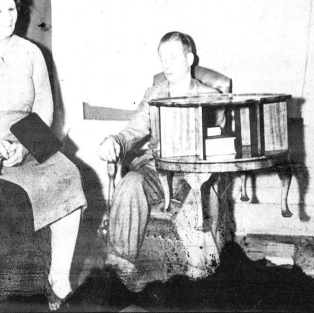

OBJECTS ON THE MOVE

Can an object suddenly dematerialize and reappear somewhere else? This is the claim of believers in 'apports'—which are articles (a button, a book, a loaf, a glass of wine, even a 39-inch snake or a four-foot-high plant) which suddenly appear in a room having apparently travelled instantaneously from another place.

Sometimes people appear to have been 'apported'; the Victorian medium Mrs Guppy, an extremely bulky lady, is said to have landed with a bump on the table in someone else's seance, holding an accounts book and a pen. Three theories are common.

● All reports are fraudulent. Apports rarely or never appear in test conditions, so this conclusion is just possible.

● There is a fourth dimension, a higher form of space into which objects can temporarily be lifted.

● A medium's mind can influence the molecular structure of objects. René Sudre has put forward this theory as an explanation of temporary dematerialization.

Any of these theories may be valid; there is certainly no need to invoke the spirit world for an answer.

When the great preacher John Wesley was a boy of 13, his home was invaded by 'Old Jeffrey'. This was the Wesley family's name for their pet 'ghost', who first manifested himself in strange knocking noises and dismal groans early in 1715. Soon other sounds were intermittently heard: footsteps on the stairs, the rustle of a gown, the sound of a rocking cradle. Family prayers were frequently interrupted by the noises.

The Wesleys grew accustomed to 'Old Jeffrey', and the youngest daughter, Kezzy, played a game of chasing 'him' from room to room. Then suddenly, two months after the first noises, 'Old Jeffrey' disappeared, and has never been back.

Was the Wesley family being haunted by some dead intelligence? Most ghost hunters would agree that it was not. 'Jeffrey' was a poltergeist; the German word means 'noisy spirit', and 'ghosts' of this type have produced a terrifying range of phenomena to disturb ordinary households—including messages written on walls, eerie voices, apports, physical blows, levitation, strange lights, furniture movements, disappearances of household items, even haircuts with invisible scissors.

Where does the power come from?

But few researchers today believe that spirits are responsible for producing poltergeists. There seem to be more obvious physical reasons. The Wesley episode, for example, was investigated by the scientist Joseph Priestley, and he observed that John's nineteen-year-old sister Hetty seemed to be the cause of the trouble. 'The disturbances were centred around Hetty's bed,' he reported, 'and were marked by Hetty's trembling in her sleep.'

Studies have shown that frequently in the house where a poltergeist manifests, there is a teenager passing through the sexual awakening of adolescence. It seems that the latent sexual energy is the cause of the trouble. Certainly poltergeists are all the more violent when sexual development is disturbed (as in the famous cases of Betsy Bell, who was probably molested by her father as a child, and Esther Cox, a victim of attempted rape), or when the person concerned has psychic abilities. Austrian medium Frieda Weisl possessed such violent sexual energies that objects would jump off the fireplace as she made love.

Power with a character

Despite their seemingly human origins, poltergeists appear to like attention. Phenomena will obligingly increase when encouraged—Kezzy Wesley was probably innocently responsible for multiplying 'Old Jeffrey's' efforts. In the Betsy

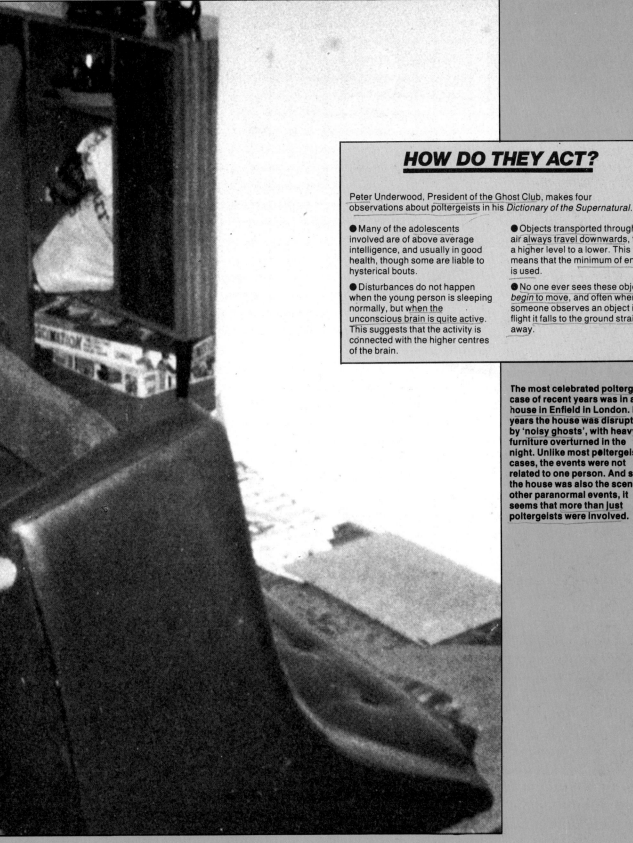

HOW DO THEY ACT?

Peter Underwood, President of the Ghost Club, makes four observations about poltergeists in his *Dictionary of the Supernatural*.

● Many of the adolescents involved are of above average intelligence, and usually in good health, though some are liable to hysterical bouts.

● Disturbances do not happen when the young person is sleeping normally, but when the unconscious brain is quite active. This suggests that the activity is connected with the higher centres of the brain.

● Objects transported through the air always travel downwards, from a higher level to a lower. This means that the minimum of energy is used.

● No one ever sees these objects *begin* to move, and often when someone observes an object in flight it falls to the ground straight away.

The most celebrated poltergeist case of recent years was in a house in Enfield in London. For years the house was disrupted by 'noisy ghosts', with heavy furniture overturned in the night. Unlike most poltergeist cases, the events were not related to one person. And since the house was also the scene of other paranormal events, it seems that more than just poltergeists were involved.

Bell case, an investigating committee of neighbours did more harm than good by encouraging the 'spirit' to perform certain tricks.

Failed attempts at exorcism, or seances held in houses dogged by poltergeists, can also result in stepped-up activity. But the sudden disappearance of the 'ghost' usually takes place as soon as the unknowing adolescent cause of the problem grows up a little bit more.

SEEING THE FUTURE

Tea leaves, yarrow sticks, animals' entrails. All these objects have been used in trying to find out what will happen tomorrow.

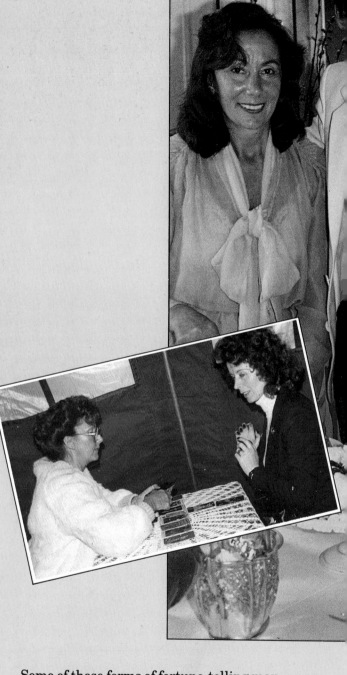

Did you read your horoscope this morning? Two-thirds of the British nation did—along with 53 per cent of the French, and 63 per cent of Germans. In America, 30,000 people each month buy a 'personalized' horoscope turned out by an IBM computer, but nonetheless there is plenty of work for 10,000 full-time and 175,000 part-time astrologers. Forecasting the future is a growth industry.

Astrology

Peter Sellers was one of many prominent people who has believed in astrology. 'The simple rules of astrology definitely work out in real life,' he insisted. 'I feel sure the planets must have some influence on our lives.' When the Beatles set up their recording company, Apple, they hired a professional astrologer to advise them. Even psychology professor Hans Eysenck has admitted that the stars may affect a person's choice of career.

Western astrology began when it was noticed that the sun seemed to move round the earth in a regular yearly path, spending about the same length of time in the vicinity of each of twelve groups of stars. These constellations of stars divided the heavens up into 'houses' (see diagram), and one's destiny was supposed to be dictated by which 'house' the sun was in—and which planets were in the same 'house'—when one was born. Serious astrologers insist on knowing the exact *moment* of birth before casting a horoscope; the date is not enough.

Many methods

Astrology is only one of many forms of forecasting which are gaining new popularity today. Recently the sophisticated woman's magazine *Cosmopolitan* produced a supplement explaining in detail to its 'liberated' readers how to read tea-leaves and coffee grounds, how to lay out tarot cards, and how to read palms.

Tarot cards contain pictures with various occult meanings, and when laid out in a certain order are claimed to spell out messages about the future. Closely similar is the ancient 'I Ching' method of throwing down yarrow sticks—or nowadays coins—and reading messages from the patterns formed.

Some of these forms of fortune-telling may merely be devices to enable people to tell themselves what they have already subconsciously decided. What one sees in a tea-cup, for example, or reads into the tarot message, will be shaped decisively by one's preoccupations and temperament. Gazing at a crystal ball ('scrying') is probably a form of automatism in

Once a partner in a firm of chartered surveyors, Ilyn Miller is now a high-society clairvoyant. She gives brandy-glass readings and 'tea and telepathy' afternoons as well as the more usual tarot readings. Ilyn sees her abilities as a gift which should be used to benefit other people.

ASTROLOGY

Astrology is completely unscientific.

● The planets are supposed to influence our lives—all except for Pluto and Neptune, which are ignored; they had not been discovered when astrological rules were formulated.

● A *thirteenth* constellation, Ophiucus, is never mentioned.

● The sun does not spend an equal amount of time in each 'house'; its stays vary between six days in Scorpio and 47 in Virgo!

● The 'constellations' are not really natural groupings of stars; they only appear to be when viewed from earth. In fact, two stars in Orion are closer to earth than they are to one of their partners in the constellation!

● Most importantly, over the years the heavens have shifted. Thus despite the fact that astrologers still insist that someone born in early October is a Libra, a quick look at the sky shows that the sun is actually in Scorpio!

SCIENTIFIC FORTUNE-TELLING

In the 1960s the Rand Corporation of America developed a forecasting method called DELPHI in order to enable business firms to predict future trends accurately on the basis of advice by experts. Nothing occult was involved; DELPHI was a simple psychological tool.

But in 1979 a forecasting consultant named Francis Kinsman evolved a variant of the method, which he called TAROT, for gaining a picture of the world's future from the statements of astrologers, numerologists (see *Glossary*), clairvoyants, mediums

and sensitives. As a result he published a report, *Future Tense*, which predicted world-wide economic collapse for 1982, a spate of earthquakes, a new Russian leader, and a Far East war in the late 1980s between Russia and China. Other events of the eighties were to be a 'bloodbath' in Africa, the collapse of the EEC, and the abdication of the Queen of England. TAROT represents a bizarre attempt to fuse a reliable method with uncommonly unreliable sources of data.

which the subconscious mind sends messages, in picture form, to the conscious self. And this explains the eagerness with which devotees tenaciously defend the reliability of their chosen method, often in the teeth of the evidence. But we do not know all the forces involved; it seems undeniable that a fascination with future-gazing can bring perilous spiritual consequences.

SEEING THE FUTURE

Michel de Nostredame (1503–66) was already a well-known pioneering doctor when in 1555 he published his book *Centuries*. But within a few years this one cryptic book was to win him a massive, controversial reputation of a quite different kind.

'Nostradamus' was an astrologer, and *Centuries* contained a collection of inscrutable stanzas gathered in hundreds (hence 'centuries'), which purported to predict the future. Nostradamus' modern followers claim that he predicted accurately the Plague, the Great Fire of London, the French Revolution, Napoleon, the death of Pope John Paul I, and two World Wars.

In 1975, young British psychic Matthew Manning foresaw two disasters in dreams: the Boeing 747 crash at New York's Kennedy Airport and the Moorgate tube disaster in London. He suggested that 'great human anguish and pain ... generates energy that has the power to move backwards in time ... and can be "audible" before it occurs'.

JEANE DIXON

Jeane Dixon, an American society lady, has become perhaps the best-known 'prophet' of the twentieth century. She accurately predicted the assassinations of John F. Kennedy and Martin Luther King; and caused a sensation by predicting, on a visit to the Ambassador Hotel in Los Angeles, that Robert Kennedy would die violently in the same building. He did. However, she has made many mistakes. World War III did not begin in 1958, nor the Vietnam War end in 1966; Jackie Kennedy did remarry.

Mrs Dixon claims that her mistakes are caused by the fact that some 'revelations' can be turned aside if the person concerned knows what is predicted, while some are just 'telepathic vibrations'—strong signals of human intention, which can go wrong if the person concerned later changes his mind. This leaves her a wide margin for error. American researchers calculate that Mrs Dixon's 'score' of accurate prophecies has dropped sharply since 1970.

Nostradamus' accuracy is impossible to assess. His work is just too obscure, and some stanzas could refer either to trivial events of French court life or major international disasters. Certainly one quatrain refers to 'Hister'—Hitler?—a 'child of Germany'. But *both* sides in World War II were able to interpret Nostradamus as prophesying victory for them!

Premonitions

Sometimes ordinary people, too, have unusual precognition ('knowledge of future events'). Nine-year-old Eryl Mai Jones, for example, told her mother in October 1966 that she had dreamed of going to school and finding that 'something black had come down all over it'. Next day Eryl and 139 others died when half-a-million tons of coal waste slithered on to their Aberfan village school.

London psychiatrist Dr John Barker discovered 60 seemingly authentic premonitions of the Aberfan disaster. There were similar 'waves' of premonitions before the *Titanic* sinking and the R-101 airship crash; so can impending doom be sensed? An American mathematician, William Cox, surveyed train crashes over several years and calculated that whenever a train crashed there were *invariably* fewer people on it than might have been expected. When a crash is coming, people change their bookings, decide not to travel, or choose an alternative route. The odds against his findings were over 100 to 1.

Lyall Watson explains this phenomenon as 'life's receptivity to very subtle stimuli that tell us that the future has already started'—on a par with the danger instinct in animals. Certainly animals show a high level of precognitive ability; in laboratory tests, mice were able to predict choices made by a random number generator, at odds of 1,000 to 1 against chance.

Laboratory tests on humans, however, have been largely disappointing. Whether or not precognition exists, it seems it cannot be controlled at will.

San Francisco in California, USA, has suffered many violent earthquakes. In 1906, 700 people died and 250,000 were made homeless. Today, the city has two 'premonitions bureaux' so that members of the public can report their premonitions of future disasters.

WHAT DO WE WANT TO KNOW?

It is not difficult to see *why* people want to know the future. In an uncertain world, where the rate of change is constantly speeding up and 'future shock' is forever exposing us to unpleasant surprises, it gives us a sense of power and security to feel that we are forewarned.

But exactly *which facts* do we need to know for our own good? 'Unless man were to be like God and know everything,' wrote John Buchan, 'it is better that he should know nothing.' The Bible's attitude is quite clear. Partial revelations of future events may be quite useless and irrelevant; but the Creator himself is prepared to guide us directly if we depend on him.

JINXES AND CURSES

When five people have all had accidents in the same car, can it be coincidence?

At 19,000 tons, the *Great Eastern* was the largest ship in the world. But it seemed also to be the most deadly. While it was being built, a riveter and his boy apprentice mysteriously disappeared. When it was ready for launching, it became stuck in the slipway and took three months to free. After the launching, its builder collapsed on deck with a stroke. He was dead within a week.

But this was just a start. One of the funnels exploded; five firemen died, and another was crushed by the paddle wheel; the captain drowned; a man was lost overboard; the paddle wheel claimed another victim. The ship's mounting catalogue of disasters gave her such a bad reputation that she started losing money heavily, and only 15 years after launching was abandoned to rust at Milford Haven.

Coincidence or reality?

Are there such things as 'jinxes' or 'curses' which hang around certain objects or people, luring them to destruction? There are thousands of stories supplying evidence, but we must remember that two or three cases of misfortune can seem like an incredible sequence to the people concerned, yet actually be mere coincidence. Also, once an object is thought of as evil, all kinds of other 'evidence' will suddenly accumulate—much of it circumstantial or wishful thinking.

Yet some cases are well-documented, suggesting that not all curse stories are tall tales. The Lockheed Constellation aircraft AHEM-4 caused four years of disasters before crashing with no survivors in 1949. The car in which Archduke Ferdinand was assassinated had seven subsequent owners who suffered serious (usually fatal) accidents. The Porsche in which James Dean died in 1955 was similarly ill-fated.

Sometimes distinguished families claim their own ancestral curses. The Bowes-Lyons, Earls of Strathmore, inherit the 'Horror' of Glamis. No one outside the family knows what the affliction is, but the heir of Strathmore is told the secret by his father, tradition has it, on his twenty-first birthday. Females are not told. A former Lord Strathmore remarked to a friend, 'If you could know of it, you would thank God you were not me.'

The Alexandra Palace in London was destroyed by fire in 1980. There have been many theories about the cause of the fire—this group of psychical researchers believed that leys were to blame (see *The Unknown Earth*). But local inhabitants recall that an old gypsy laid a curse on the palace at the time it was built.

Warnings of disaster

In Ireland, the banshee, or *bansidhe* (from the Gaelic word for 'fairy woman') is a weird spirit creature whose blood-chilling wail is supposed to presage a human death. Banshees are really guardian spirits rather than harbingers of doom, but their cry always spells disaster. The banshee wailed for ancient Irish heroes, such as Brian Boru and Finn MacCool, but was also reported in County Cork in 1922 when Irish revolutionary fighter Michael Collins died in an ambush, and in 1963 when the Irish-American President John F. Kennedy was assassinated.

Other nations have similar traditions, and some accounts are fairly convincing. Sheila St Clair suggests that the banshee is 'part of an inherited memory . . . stamped on our racial consciousness' suddenly released by the mind 'as a kind of subliminal "four-minute warning" so that we may prepare ourselves for that tragedy'.

HOW DO CURSES WORK?

Extra-sensory forces
Traditionally, curses can be placed on other people by methods such as spells, sticking pins into wax images and reciting incantations. Possibly the intense concentration involved can bring some psychic power to bear on the victim's mind.

The power of suggestion Often in a primitive tribe, a man who knows he has been cursed will simply lie down and die—not necessarily because of the curse, but because he is convinced that he will die anyway.

'Psychic tape-recording' Peter Underwood believes that 'somehow, thought or feeling can imprint itself on an object or person in such a way as to be picked up by other people; if the thought is malevolent, then the effect can be unpleasant.'

Supernatural activity Colin Wilson has shown that some stories of cursings suggest active malice by a real, personal disincarnate entity. Christians would recognize this as an 'evil spirit'. Certainly the power of curses is unpredictable and dangerous; those who try to capture it usually find that it has captured them. Christians believe that the powers of evil have been conquered by Christ's death, and that this victory over evil can be exercised by Christians today.

The cult of voodoo thrives in the Caribbean. Images such as this doll are used both to attract the power of spirits and to focus evil power on other people as a curse.

WICCA AND MAGICK

Witches have never had it so good.
Today, their craft is legal – and profitable.

The occultist Aleister Crowley attracted many followers. Here he is seen performing a ceremony in one of his occult groups. In 1920 he founded a secret society in Sicily, but within two years he had been expelled by the other members.

This elaborate ceremony on a snow-covered moor may be nothing more than a publicity exercise. But it is certain that witches' covens meet regularly throughout the world thirteen times a year.

Today in London an ex-priest and psychic called Alex Sanders is openly involved in initiating new witches and supervising several covens. Sybil Leek, perhaps the first millionairess witch in the world, has made a fortune from books, television appearances and syndicated articles.

This marks quite a change in the public attitude to witches. Between the fifteenth and eighteenth centuries in Western Europe, it was serious business. While a few 'witch finders', such as the notorious Matthew Hopkins, grew rich from detecting it, thousands of others—many of them undoubtedly innocent—died by fire or water.

Why witchcraft?

Who were the witches? Their opponents said they were in league with the devil; there seems little evidence of that. Historians now believe that the witchcraft 'craze' had its origins in the medieval church's fascination with demons; being a witch, or fantasizing about being one, was a secret way of thumbing one's nose at the 'establishment', which included a very wealthy and powerful church. Keith Thomas, in his book *Religion and the Decline of Magic*, suggests that it offered 'a way of bettering one's condition when all else had failed ... a substitute for impotence, a remedy for anxiety and despair'.

Earlier this century, however, one distinguished scholar, Margaret Murray, claimed that witchcraft in Europe had been a systematic religion, the true 'Old Religion' which had always

SATANISM

Since Anton LaVey began his First Church of Satan in1966, several organizations have sprung up around the world dedicated to the worship of Satan. They generally do not think of Satan so much as a personal figure (which is the way he is presented in the Bible), but as an abstract principle of evil, 'a dark, hidden force that was responsible for the workings of earthly affairs for which science and religion had no explanation and no control'.

Satanic weddings and funerals are held, but so, too, are lust rituals and destruction rituals. One researcher, Burton Wolfe, comments, 'Satanism is a blatantly selfish, brutal religion. It is based on the belief that man is inherently a selfish, violent creature, that life is a Darwinian struggle for survival of the fittest...'

Satanists are relatively open about their activities, by contrast with the other main group who worship Satan—devotees of black magic. The main ceremony of black magic is the Black Mass, a ceremony of worship of the devil which is an obscene parody of the Roman Catholic rite; occasionally in history it has been attended by human sacrifice and perhaps even cannibalism. Satan is worshipped as a power-conferring alternative deity to the God of the Bible.

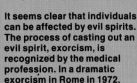

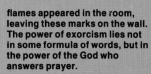

It seems clear that individuals can be affected by evil spirits. The process of casting out an evil spirit, exorcism, is recognized by the medical profession. In a dramatic exorcism in Rome in 1972, flames appeared in the room, leaving these marks on the wall. The power of exorcism lies not in some formula of words, but in the power of the God who answers prayer.

existed secretly as an alternative to Christianity. Although now discredited, her views were widely accepted for a long time. She even wrote the article on witchcraft for the 1929 *Encyclopaedia Britannica*. Eventually Gerald Gardner, a student of the occult, began to found covens of witches to 'revive' the 'Old Religion'. His attempts bore fruit; today covens exist throughout the world. The name his followers give to their faith is 'wicca'.

What is it like?

Witches distinguish between *black magic*, which involves devil worship and the practice of evil, and *white magic*, which is used for good purposes. But even white magic involves claiming for oneself godlike powers over other human lives, and it can be used with a chilling lack of morality. Explaining some dubious deeds of her own, Sybil Leek claims that 'evil may be justified if it is for the greater good of the whole'.

In view of this, it is not surprising that the Bible opposes witchcraft of any kind. Present-day 'wicca' is founded insecurely on Murray's exploded historical research, hazardous moral practices, and promises of limited spiritual powers which are a pale shadow of the power of the living God.

WICCA

'Wicca' beliefs are much closer to Eastern religions than to Christianity. Witches believe in a Supreme Being who, says Hans Holzer, is not a person but merely 'a great principle, a spiritual force'. Sybil Leek explains, 'From this Supreme Being comes life, and by a process of many incarnations, ascending a spiral of spiritual development, we are drawn back into the life force.' The Supreme Being is worshipped in the figure of a Mother Goddess, and sometimes also a male horned god.

The witch Madge Worthington predicts that wicca 'will supersede Christianity—certainly by the end of the century, if not before'. There are no signs that this is happening.

MAGICK

Not all magic is worked by witches. Today's 'magick' (the spelling often used to distinguish it from conjuring tricks) derives from the secret practices of early twentieth-century occult groups, such as the Order of the Golden Dawn, and figures such as Aleister Crowley, self-styled 'wickedest man in the world'.

A large occult body in America, the Rosicrucians (split into two main rival groups) perpetuates magick teachings. It claims to be non-religious, but its teachings involve assumptions about the nature of the universe which conflict with Christianity. Modern magick groups derive their views from ancient traditions of the cabbala and alchemy.

Magick has existed in every age, and requires two anti-Christian assumptions: first, that certain objects or activities contain inherent spiritual power; second, that we can and should employ this power to affect others.

PYRAMIDS

Only one of the seven wonders of the world survives – the pyramids of ancient Egypt. And their mystery is as fascinating today as ever.

No-one would dispute that the Great Pyramid of Cheops is one of the wonders of the world. The 90 million cubic feet of stone in it (covering an area of about 14 acres/5.6 hectares) would build 30 Empire State Buildings, or all the churches, chapels and cathedrals in England. The two and a half million blocks of limestone are fitted together so tightly that the gaps between them are minute. The sides are aligned exactly to face north, south, east and west. But what is the whole thing for?

A fortress tomb?

Most modern Egyptologists believe that it was simply a fortress-tomb for the Pharaoh Khufu, or Cheops. They point out that this seems to have been the purpose of each of the 40 major pyramids built along the Nile, and that the Great Pyramid contains an imposing sarcophagus, obviously built into the pyramid as an integral feature (the doors are too narrow for it to be moved in or out). Unfortunately, nobody has ever found any bodies in any of the pyramids!

Were the bodies removed by grave robbers? Possible, but unlikely; grave robbers usually stole the rich burial trappings and left the bodies behind. Did the priests remove the bodies to foil robbers? That seems more likely. Or are the bodies still there, but in as yet undiscovered secret chambers? If so, the sarcophagi so far discovered would simply be decoys.

The Great Pyramid of Cheops, at Giza in Egypt.

A store of knowledge?

Another possibility, suggested by the careful mathematical construction of the Great Pyramid is that the primary purpose of the whole building project was to embody certain geometric, astronomical and occult data. It has been claimed that the Pyramid reveals the precise circumference of the earth, the mean length of the earth's orbit around the sun, the specific density of the earth, the speed of light, and the weight of this planet.

It is hard to tell how much of this is wishful thinking. Using the same processes, one could extract exactly the same figure for the earth's density from the Eiffel Tower! And since about 33 ft/10 m are missing from the top of the pyramid, we can only guess about its exact dimensions and weight. It is claimed that the perimeter of the pyramid indicates the length of the solar year, when measured in special 'pyramid inches'; but if so, the pyramid builders must have believed that each year contained 362.76 days!

Last century 'pyramidologists' claimed to read predictions about the future in the dimensions of the pyramid. Since this involved the Second Coming of Christ in 1881, 1936 or 1953 (depending on one's interpretation), and the completion of God's final judgement for 20 August 1953, 'pyramidiocy' is now firmly discredited.

PYRAMID POWER

In the early 1930s Antoine Bovis was on holiday in Egypt when he became fascinated to find that small animals which had wandered into the pyramids and died had not decomposed. Their bodies had been perfectly mummified. After experiments he came to believe that fruit and vegetables could be kept fresh longer under a cardboard model of a pyramid. He was ridiculed, but some years later a Czech radio technician named Karl Drbal patented a pyramid-shaped object which he declared would sharpen razor blades. It is now claimed by believers that pyramids can improve the taste of food, enhance plant growth, aid meditation, assist restful sleep, induce clairvoyance, and even halt ageing.

Experiments with a Gauss meter suggest that the pyramid shape may indeed induce magnetism, and the force field created may in some circumstances provoke electromagnetic dehydration. But since similar magnetic fields do not produce similar results, other energies may be at work. It remains to be seen whether this is a genuine scientific discovery or an occult curiosity.

ANCIENT ENGINEERING

'All that can be learn'd from them,' said Daniel Defoe, 'is that there they are.'

For centuries there has been no explanation for the scores of standing stones which form gaunt circles all over the British Isles. Some of them (especially Avebury, in Wiltshire, and Stonehenge) are clearly major ancient monuments.

Who built them, and why?

Recent research at Stonehenge demonstrates that its builders knew a great deal about astronomy and geometry. 'A veritable Newton or Einstein must have been at work,' comments astronomer Sir Fred Hoyle. Without any system of writing, the builders were able to construct, teach and retain a knowledge of mathematics scarcely inferior to Egyptian knowledge of the same

period. And even today we have no good idea how the major stones were erected into place.

Facts such as these have tempted people such as the writer Tom Lethbridge, and less intelligently Erich von Däniken, to speculate that the construction may have owed something to ancient astronaut visitors. Lethbridge theorized that the stones might have been giant markers for the guidance of aircraft or spaceships. There is no evidence for this view, and much against it: the site clearly had other functions; it is hard to see what use the markers in their present locations could have been to aircraft; and there are strong arguments against contacts with alien spacemen (see *Close Encounters*).

Cosmic proportions

John Michell claims that Stonehenge was based on the same set of 'cosmic proportions' as Glastonbury Abbey, Chartres Cathedral, the Pyramids, and Solomon's Temple. These figures, he says, derive from the data given about the New

Jerusalem in the Book of Revelation, but to find them one must read the Bible 'properly'—in other words, in terms of the secret, occult wisdom of Gnostic gematria (see *Glossary*), the mysticism of the early Christians.

Michell's theory is so much romantic moonshine. For one thing, the Gnostics were not early Christian leaders, but interloping heretics, rejected vigorously as sub-Christian by Jesus' first followers. Revelation is not a Gnostic book. Furthermore, Michell's calculations do not add up. He has to assume that the builders of Stonehenge thought in terms of two different measuring systems—cubits and feet—simultaneously; he changes some of the actual data in Revelation to 'commensurable proportions' to make it fit. Finally, he has to *guess* one of the most critical figures on which the entire calculation depends.

Colin Wilson says that Stonehenge and other sites were 'apparently intended to be giant accumulators of magic power'. There may be indications of this in the associations with leys and underground streams (see *Tapping Natural Forces*). But all we can say with confidence is that the sites were used both for ritual purposes and as astronomical observatories. Which may be all that there is to know.

GLASTONBURY

The town of Glastonbury is situated on leys which also pass through Avebury and Stonehenge, and strange legends have long been associated with it. From 1191, it has been proclaimed the burial place of the mystical British king Arthur and his wife Guinevere. A strong local tradition asserts that Joseph of Arimathea came to Glastonbury after Christ's crucifixion and built the first church there.

In 1964 an occultist named Mrs Maltwood announced that she had discovered Glastonbury Tor to be surrounded by a 'temple of the stars', a zodiac formed out of natural features such as fields, banks, rivers and earthworks. Earlier this century, the 'Glastonbury Scripts'—examples of automatic writing (see *Glossary*) obtained by the Abbey's Director of Excavations, Frederick Bligh Bond—claimed that secret gnostic techniques had been used in the construction of the Abbey. All of this points to some strong local occult connections, although the specific legends may be unfounded.

At midsummer every year, ceremonies are still held at Stonehenge, England, by people who believe that the site has religious significance.

REINCARNATION

Hindus and Buddhists believe that after death, the soul moves to a new body. Today an increasing number of people in the West share this belief.

In 1935, the Deva family in India grew worried about the strange behaviour of their daughter Shanti. She had begun to talk incessantly about a place called Muttra where, she said, she had lived in a previous life. Her name had been Ludgi. She had been the mother of three children, and had died in giving birth to the third.

Her stories were dismissed as fanciful knowledge—until by accident they discovered that a woman called Ludgi had died in precisely those circumstances at Muttra. Taken to Muttra, Shanti lapsed into the local dialect without ever having learned it; recognized her 'husband' and the two older children; and described her former home before she had seen it.

A world-wide belief

Stories such as this are often claimed to prove reincarnation, the idea that after death human beings are born again as babies to live another life. Reincarnation features in several world religions (Hinduism, Buddhism, Sikhism, Jainism, some Islamic sects and Christian heresies) as well as present-day cults such as Scientology and Theosophy. Opinion polls show a steady rise in the number of people accepting the belief.

Two of the main sources of evidence for the idea are *déjà vu* experiences and 'hypnotic regression'. *Déjà vu* is what happens when a person has the curious feeling that he has visited a certain place before, or has witnessed a certain event before.

LIFE AND DEATH

What does the Bible say about life after death?

● There will be a day of judgement when all the dead will stand before God. They will be judged according to whether or not they believed in Jesus Christ. Those who trusted him to forgive their sins will enter God's kingdom. Unbelievers will go into eternal punishment.

● Jesus claimed that his life, death and resurrection brought a totally new world order. When it is completed, believers will be given a new body—as Jesus was at his resurrection—and take part in the new creation. So Christians believe not only in the survival of the spirit, but also in the resurrection of the body.

● The Old Testament describes the state of death as being darkness, silence, rest, and the absence of thought and memory. No one comes back from the grave, but death does not end existence and God is able to bring men out of the grave.

● The New Testament continues this picture. The dead are asleep, but there is a difference between those who died believing in Jesus, and those who rejected him. Believers are 'with Christ'; the others are 'spirits in prison'.

In 1966, Dr Hemendra Banerjee flew to England from India to investigate the case of the Pollock twins. Had they lived before? Their father believed that they were reincarnations of his previous two daughters, killed in a car crash nine years earlier.

Though it has been suggested that this is the memory of a previous existence there is much evidence to suggest that *déjà vu* is simply a minor brain malfunction. It tends to occur more readily under conditions of fatigue, or in some types of epilepsy. Many doctors think it can be explained as an unsynchronized electrical discharge in a part of the brain associated with memory functions. The phenomenon has sometimes been evoked by electrical stimulation of the brain under surgery.

Returning to previous lives

'Hypnotic regression' stems from the famous case of 'Bridie Murphy' in 1954, in which a young American housewife was hypnotized and began talking as if she were living in nineteenth-century Ireland. Since then 'hypnotherapists' such as Arnall Bloxham have 'regressed' many patients to past lives, and have tape-recorded the results. Although it is often unaccountably difficult to check out the specific details given by the 'regression', many of the stories told have been remarkably accurate and perfectly plausible.

The 'Wheel of Life' represents the Hindu idea of reincarnation. Hindus believe that we are trapped in an endless cycle of lives, fated to experience rebirth after rebirth until we become pure enough to stop returning. At this stage we lose all personal identity and merge with the impersonal Infinite, Brahman.

WHAT IS REGRESSION?

The difficulty with the question of reincarnation is that all the evidence is completely unverifiable. And it can all be read in several different ways.

Tricks of the mind? Some cases of 'hypnotic regression' have proved to be merely 'cryptomnesia'. The mind plays a trick on itself, imagining and describing in detail a fantasy life.

Unconscious memory? We know that the brain can retain information which we have not consciously stored. Could some regression accounts be the release of such information?

Telepathy? We do not know exactly how the brain picks up information. Is the subject of regression picking up information telepathically from the brains of others—perhaps even from some who have died?

Race memory? Some have suggested that there is such a thing as 'race memory' which is inherited from ancestors and released under special conditions. It has also been suggested that walls and rooms can store information traces.

Effects of hypnotism? We do not know just what hypnotism is. For years it was thought to be a kind of sleep; that theory has now been proved wrong. So we cannot know the full effects of hypnotism on our consciousness.

Nor is this all. If I have lived through several lifetimes, which of those personalities is the real me? If the answer is, 'None of them, but a type of "super-self" that presides over them all,' then why am I never conscious of that super-self's existence? How can I prove that it is real?

LIFE AFTER LIFE?

A serious accident. A patient recovers from the critical list. He claims to have seen a future life. Is this fact or fantasy?

Thomas Welch was an engineer's helper for a lumber company in Oregon. One day he was walking along a narrow trestle, suspended 55 ft/ 16 m above a dam, when he slipped and fell into water ten feet deep. His body was not found for almost an hour; and when he was revived, he claimed to have been to hell.

'It's easy to talk about and describe something you have seen,' he stated. 'I know there is a lake of fire because I have seen it. I know Jesus Christ is alive in eternity. I have seen him.'

Out-of-the-body experiences

What had happened? Welch had experienced an 'OBE' ('out-of-the-body experience'). The same thing commonly happens to patients undergoing critical surgery who 'die' for a few minutes on the operating table. When revived, they often claim to have had glimpses of an after-life. Usually they find their experience difficult to communicate in words, but they are never as frightened of dying again.

In the late 1970s a group of doctors arose who styled themselves 'thanatologists'—students of what happens at death. Dr Raymond Moody's book *Life after Life*, detailing hundreds of OBEs, became an international best-seller. Moody, a Methodist, claims that none of his research proves or disproves the existence of a final judgement, hell or heaven (although some resuscitees report a 'city of light' which sounds like heaven); but other writers are less cautious.

Dr Maurice Rawlings, for instance, claims that OBEs prove the truth of Christianity. Unfortunately, some resuscitees testify that the spirit beings tell them otherwise; Rawlings dismisses these experiences as demonic counterfeits. But how can he judge which experiences are true and which false? Some OBEs include meetings with Krishna and other pagan figures; Rawlings assumes the resuscitees have really met Jesus and wrongly identified him. But this seems an unwarranted assumption.

In fact, thanatological experiences 'prove' very little. They afford ground for fascinating speculation, but no more.

OUT-OF-THE-BODY EXPERIENCES

This composite account of what happens after death was compiled by Raymond Moody from the experiences of several resuscitees.

● You are dying. As the pain reaches its climax, you hear the doctor pronounce you dead.

● An uncomfortable buzzing or ringing noise begins, and you feel yourself moving quickly down a long dark tunnel.

● As you emerge, you realize that you are still in the same place—but *outside* your body. You watch as medical staff try to resuscitate the body you once lived in.

● Others appear to help you— including spirits of friends and relatives, and a 'being of light' who projects love and warmth.

● The being of light asks a question to make you assess the worth of your life, and simultaneously you experience an 'instant replay' of your life's major experiences.

● You find yourself approaching a sort of barrier, seemingly the border between earthly life and the next world, but realize you must return; your life is not yet over.

● You resist, but somehow are returned to your earthly body and regain consciousness...

WHAT DOES IT PROVE?

The evidence for thanatology rests on very flimsy grounds. Many of the leading writers are doctors, but most have no medical experience of the cases which they relate.

● Not all OBEs tell the same story; many are contradictory, and Moody's 'pattern' experience (outlined above) is a compilation from different people's accounts—no one person experienced every detail listed.

● What happens in OBEs is impossible to determine. Is the body really 'dead'? There are currently three competing definitions of clinical death; it is hard to tell the exact moment at which someone passes from life to death.

● Is the OBE a real experience, or merely a fantasy conjured up by some region of the patient's brain? There is no way of telling. But it is suspicious that what dying people claim to see often fits their own personal theological beliefs (or fears).

Out-of-the-body experiences, for example after serious accidents, are the source of most of the ideas on 'thanatology', the study of what happens at death. The world's leading thanatologist is

Dr Elisabeth Kubler-Ross. However, her reputation has been somewhat tarnished since it was revealed that she received much of her information from 'spirit guides' at seances.

MEN WHO NEVER DIED

The wandering Jew... The flying Dutchman... History is full of legends of men condemned to live for ever.

In 1228 an Armenian archbishop, visiting London, mentioned that in his country there was a man named Cartaphilus who claimed to have been Pontius Pilate's doorkeeper. As Jesus had staggered past bearing his cross, Cartaphilus had struck him and jeered; at which Christ commented, 'I go, and you will wait till I return.' He had then been incapable of death, doomed to wander the world for ever until Christ's return at the end of time.

When last heard of, Cartaphilus was apparently baptized and living among monks, devoutly hoping for salvation. Perhaps, though, his hopes were disappointed, for in 1542 he introduced himself to Paulus von Eitzen, Lutheran bishop of Schleswig, this time under the name Ahasuerus. A pamphlet bearing the story circulated throughout Europe—its popularity perhaps explained by the anti-Semitism of the period—and sightings of the 'Wandering Jew' were reported widely. His last known port of call was Salt Lake City in 1868.

The story of the Wandering Jew merely reflects the human fascination with the medieval idea of endless life. Although the story has been a stimulus for poetry, art and drama, there is no shred of evidence for its truth. Apart from anything else, since Christ was prepared to forgive his killers as he hung on the cross, it seems monstrously out of character for him to condemn one man eternally for a single blow. The Christ of the legend is more like a testy wizard than the real Jesus.

Count St Germain

A less straightforward, modern version of the legend concerns the mysterious eighteenth-century occultist, Count St Germain, who moved in the highest courtly circles and counted Cagliostro and Mesmer among his occult apprentices. He claimed to be able to transmute base metals into gold, to enlarge and improve diamonds, and to perform astral travel. Less exotically, he was a superb linguist, pianist, inventor and raconteur.

We first hear of him in 1710, when he looked as if he was in his forties—and last in 1820, which would make him at least 150 years old. This may not be true, but he was certainly active for over 90 years, and there are well-witnessed reports of

Reports of Ahasuerus, the Wandering Jew, were circulated widely through Europe in the seventeenth century.

meetings with him after his supposed burial in 1784. Consequently, many occultists believe he never died, and that he still appears sporadically today. More than one mystical group claims to be led directly by him, and occasional claimants come forward professing to be St Germain.

The story is undoubtedly strange, but there is no real evidence that St Germain still lives.

VAMPIRES

Ever since Bram Stoker wrote the novel *Dracula* in 1897, legends about vampires have been well known. The popular ideas include the following elements:

● Vampires are unquiet spirits who leave their tombs nightly to suck the blood of the living.

● Vampires look like other men, but cast no shadow and cause no reflection in mirrors.

● The vampire's spirit can be laid to rest by driving a stake through the exhumed body.

● Garlic and crosses are protection against vampire attack.

These ideas about 'the undead' derive from Slavic superstitions. Slav religion was based on manism (ancestor worship) and bodies were ritually exhumed for various purposes. It came to be believed that those who had died suddenly—unmarried brides-to-be, for instance—were still greedy for the joys of life, and would return to imperil the living. The vampire legends developed from there, and between 1700 and 1740 there was an epidemic of vampire 'attacks' right across Europe. Colin Wilson speculates, 'It could be that vast numbers of people . . . began to brood on the reports of vampires . . . Huge quantities of psychic energy suddenly became available to the flotsam and jetsam of the spirit world.'

In 1785, at the age of 115, Count St Germain (left) still looked in the prime of life. The elaborate reception has been laid on by him for Cagliostro, another occult follower. Today there are still claims that St Germain is alive—now aged over 300.

GHOSTS AND APPARITIONS

Gothic horror stories are guaranteed to make the flesh creep.
But is there truth behind the fiction?

Mrs Pacquet felt strangely depressed. The mood had been upon her since her awakening that dull Chicago morning, and there seemed no real reason. Then, just as she turned from reaching for some tea from the pantry, suddenly she saw her brother Edmund standing a few feet away. He was falling forward with a rope around his legs. 'The vision lasted but a moment . . . but was very distinct. I dropped the tea, clasped my hands to my face, and exclaimed, "My God! Ed is drowned."' Ed had been—only six hours before.

A telepathic message?

It is common for bereaved people to imagine vividly that they have seen the deceased, but Mrs Pacquet's experience was much more than this. However, it was far from unusual. Apparitions like this often appear when the person concerned is undergoing some form of crisis—illness, accident or death. The Society for Psychical Research, who put together a *Census of Hallucinations* in 1889, concluded that such apparitions were unconscious telepathic messages from the crisis victim to his friend or relative.

This seems quite plausible—we know very little about how the mind perceives objects; hypnosis or dreams can change our perceptions remarkably—but probably the 'receiver' mind has more to do with constructing the apparition than the 'sender'. This is because usually (unlike Mrs Pacquet's brother) the apparition looks quite well and normal, giving no clue of the crisis being undergone; and it seems quite solid and three-dimensional, casting a shadow, causing reflections in mirrors, adapting itself completely to its physical surroundings.

What about 'collective' apparitions, seen by more than one person? The SPR had collected no less than 130 of these by 1943. Do these prove that a dead person has actually manifested himself to the living? Not necessarily; there have also been 'collective apparitions' of people who were existing happily somewhere else at the moment when their apparition was seen. It seems more likely that in collective cases one of the viewers is responsible for receiving the apparition telepathically from its source, and that he unconsciously transfers the visual information to the others there with him.

An apparition of someone unknown to the viewer is more difficult to explain. But perhaps in some situations at some times our minds are unusually receptive to messages. Or perhaps someone else we know, who *did* know the source of the apparition, has transmitted the necessary information to our minds.

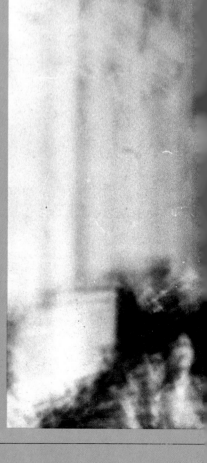

Most alleged pictures of ghosts are rather dubious. But experts who have examined these photographs, taken in Winchester Cathedral, England, say that there is no question of their being fakes. Both pictures show the altar, but when the second one was developed, a group of figures in medieval robes was visible. Witnesses say there was nobody in front of the camera when the picture was taken.

HAUNTINGS

Apparitions are one type of ghost. Hauntings are quite different. Apparitions usually happen only once, look solid, and communicate quite naturally; hauntings are usually repetitive, may look quite unconnected with the surroundings, and pay no attention to onlookers. Over a period of time, haunting ghosts may become fainter and fainter,

like a battery running down. Philosopher H.H. Price suggested that there might be a 'psychic ether' on which mental imprints could be made; thus a haunting would be a playback of a 'recording' made on the ether. Since observing a haunting is often quite like watching a silent film, this suggestion seems plausible.

LIFE AFTER DEATH

There are many possible explanations of apparitions. They certainly show that our visual ability is more complicated than we usually imagine, and is closely linked with our subconscious. But they cannot be taken as evidence to support the idea of life after death.

It is interesting in this context to look at the resurrection of Jesus. The Bible states that on the Sunday after his crucifixion, his dead body had disappeared from its sealed tomb. A handful of his

followers saw Jesus alive that day, and over the next six weeks many hundreds of other people did so, too. But the Bible makes it clear that the risen Jesus was not an apparition. Indeed, he went to some lengths to prove this, by encouraging people to touch him, and by eating food. To his followers, now as then, his physical resurrection was proof that through his death, Jesus had made available a new quality of life which would not end with physical death.

CONTACTING THE DEAD

The pianist John Lill claims to be in contact with Beethoven. Mediums claim to receive messages for the bereaved. Can the living really contact the dead?

This strange conversation was carried out at Borley Rectory, known for a century as the most haunted house in England. As well as apparitions and phantom noises, messages would appear written on the walls. The activity was most intense when Lionel Foyster was rector—his wife Marianne seems to have attracted many of the events (see *Mindforce*).

José Nunes and his friend Mauricio were playing with a gun one day when it went off. The ricocheting bullet killed Mauricio. Although José immediately called the police, he was arrested for murder.

His mother contacted Brazil's top medium, Francisco Xavier, who claims that the dead occasionally control his hand and write messages. He produced a piece of automatic writing which read, 'José was not to blame . . . I was killed as a result of a foolish game.' Impressed, the judge freed José. The writing matched Mauricio's handwriting exactly.

Talking with the dead

Was Mauricio communicating from beyond the grave? Ever since the Fox sisters there have been innumerable attempts to extract messages from the dead, including automatic writing, table rapping, spirit tapes and photographs, and the ouija board or planchette. Mediums in entranced states have produced not only astoundingly correct information (although usually of an utterly trivial nature) but also sometimes 'ectoplasm' (supposedly the substance of which spirits are composed). This material issues from their bodies, sometimes taking shape as a hand or

When in a trance, some mediums apparently exude a substance called ectoplasm which can materialize into recognizable shapes. In 1921 in Warsaw, Franek Kluski materialized a pair of hands, and was able to take this wax impression of them before they dematerialized.

THE LIFE BEYOND?

The Bible's teaching about life after death conflicts profoundly with the information about 'the other side' usually offered by spirits. Witness the report given by a spirit who was allegedly the son of Bishop James Pike.

Pike

'I haven't heard anything personally about Jesus. Nobody around me seems to talk about him. When we come over here, we have a choice, to remain as we are, or to grow in our understanding. Some still seem to be church minded and are waiting for a Judgement Day, but these seem to be the unenlightened ones.'

The Bible

'(In heaven) there shall no more be anything accursed, but the throne of God and of the Lamb (Jesus) shall be in it, and his servants shall worship him; and they shall see his face' (Revelation 22:3–4).

'It is appointed for men to die once and after that comes judgement' (Hebrews 9:27).

INVENTING A SPIRIT

In the early 1970s, members of the Toronto Society for Psychical Research decided to try to 'create' a spirit. They invented a character called Philip, who lived in the days of Oliver Cromwell, and gave him a life story including a real home (Diddington Manor in England). They hoped Philip would 'materialize'; he never did, but instead began to communicate fascinatingly detailed information about himself by table rapping. The information was not self-contradictory, and rarely anachronistic; indeed, 'Philip' corrected the sitters on matters of historical fact. In public demonstrations he made a table rise up a flight of steps on to a platform. 'Philip' has now been 'killed off'. Was he simply a collective fantasy of the group, or did some real but fraudulent spirit power take over the persona which the group had conveniently prepared for it?

SPIRITUALISM

'The scenes of happiness all around us, beautiful white and coloured structures, and the unbelievable colour effects. The placid lagoons, the luscious green meadows and the beautiful colourings of the bird life; and enveloping it all the peaceful, calm and happy atmosphere.' This is not a holiday brochure. It is a description of the 'Other Side' to which Spiritualists say we go after death. And it was given through a medium by a 'departed' spirit.

Spiritualism began in a tiny wooden shack in Hydesville (see *Introducing Mysteries*), and at first its adherents were treated with scorn. But Leah Fox received the message, 'Dear friends, you must proclaim this truth in the world. . . When you do your duty God will protect you and good spirits will watch over you.' Within two years there were 100 mediums in New York City alone. And since then Spiritualism has grown into a massive international religious organization.

Most Spiritualists treat Christ simply as a 'great exemplar', a master psychic, but 'Christian Spiritualists' also recognize him as God. However, none of the varieties of Spiritualism can really be called Christian. The movement contradicts the Bible's teachings crucially: it discounts the teaching that human sin creates a barrier between men and God, and therefore does not believe in a judgement after death. It relies primarily upon dubious spirit data rather than the Bible; where there is a conflict of view, the spirits are trusted and the Bible neglected.

arm; and some mediums claim to have successfully 'materialized' spirits, who will then walk around the seance and shake hands.

How much does all of this prove? First, there is a great deal of deceit in the history of spiritualism. Many 'materialized spirits' have proved to be simply the medium's accomplice; much 'ectoplasm' to be just cheesecloth or muslin. Not one inch of 'ectoplasm' has ever been examined in a laboratory. Second, many astounding feats can be explained as telepathy or group fantasy. The ouija board at a seance in Flushing, Holland, some years ago spelled out the words of an English poem; later it was found that a young boy across the street had been learning the poem, concentrating on each phrase in turn, for his homework. A Canon Douglas received messages at a seance from his dead chauffeur, Réallier, which contained all kinds of accurate detail—but Réallier was still alive at the time. Presumably the medium had picked up information telepathically from a living brain—Douglas's or Réallier's.

FLYING SAUCERS

Little green men in spaceships used to be a subject for jokes. But today scientists are taking the subject rather more seriously.

One day Antonio Villas Boas was out driving his tractor on his Brazilian farm when he saw a strange egg-shaped craft landing near him. He panicked and began to run, but was captured by the craft's occupants—alien beings about 5 ft 4 in/ 1.6 m tall. Taken aboard, he was made to submit to blood letting, scientific examinations, and even an act of sexual intercourse with an alien blonde. Afterwards, they allowed him to go, and returned to the skies. The next day he developed a complaint which looked very like radiation sickness.

Antonio's story is a typical (if dramatic) example of the thousands of Unidentified Flying Object stories which have proliferated since Kenneth Arnold, a Chicago businessman, reported the first modern 'flying saucer' sighting in 1947. Nowadays the Center for UFO Research in Illinois receives about 100 reports each night.

Are we alone?

French astrophysicist Jacques Vallée estimates that if the reports are reliable there may have been as many as 3 million UFO landings in the last 25 years. This poses a problem. Ian Ridpath has calculated in *New Scientist* that even if there are a million other civilizations in our galaxy, all launching one starship annually, we could expect to be visited only once every 10,000 years.

And we do not know that there are any other civilizations. The often-quoted Green Bank Formula, which suggests that there may be many others, depends totally upon guesswork about one vital factor—the length of time during which a civilization could send out interplanetary communications.

Theories about other civilizations depend on the assumption that there are other planets for them to come from; and most stars are too far away for us to be sure. Spotting a planet at such distances is like trying to spot a pea 27,000 miles away.

Our civilization makes noises (televison signals, radio messages, and so on) which can be heard vast distances away across space. We have never heard anything intelligible coming back. As a result, Dr Iosef Shklovskii, who in the sixties claimed that there were millions of inhabited planets, now declares dogmatically, 'We are alone in the universe.'

Some early UFO reports were clearly hoaxes; there were photographs of upturned soup plates and vacuum cleaner canisters, passed off as 'flying saucers'; there was information about conditions on Mars and Venus which we now know to be untrue; there were reports of craft which could never have got off the ground. Other stories are more difficult to explain. Some may be wish fulfilment. Some may be produced by the 'collective unconscious' (see *Glossary*). Others may be spiritual phenomena.

Is this a flying saucer? The photograph was taken by George J. Stock in New Jersey, USA, on 29 July 1952.

Air Marshal Sir Victor Goddard believes that 'the materiality of a UFO is para-physical', and this is borne out by Lynn Catoe's bibliography of UFO literature for the US Library of Congress. She remarks that much of the literature 'is closely linked with mysticism and the metaphysical' and recounts 'alleged incidents that are strikingly similar to demoniac possession and psychic phenomena'. It is entirely possible that some UFO encounters may be occult happenings on a par with materializations and demonic activity.

HOAXES AND IMAGINATION

Imagination has undoubtedly fostered many UFO stories. In the nineteenth century a mysterious 'airship' was sighted flying over many states of America (with its inhabitants on occasion singing *Abide with Me*!) and was described in detail in many newspapers. From the accounts, we can see quite clearly today that no such craft could ever have flown—especially between planets. The descriptions represented what people in a pre-aircraft age imagined a flying ship *might* look like.

A few years ago astronomer Patrick Moore sent a hoax letter to his local newspaper claiming to have sighted a spacecraft—and to his horror over 20 other readers wrote in confirming that they too had seen it!

WHERE COULD THEY COME FROM?

Which planet could UFOs come from?

Venus? The surface is too hot (800°F/425°C) to sustain life as we know it.

Mars? The 1969 Mariner probe seems to have eliminated all hope of discovering life there.

Jupiter, Uranus, Saturn, Neptune? Too cold, with very different gravitational characteristics.

Pluto? Extremely cold and in perpetual darkness.

Mercury? Too close to the sun to support life.

Outside the solar system? The distances are too great to allow extensive contacts.

Another planet on the far side of the moon? Astronomically impossible.

This forces believers to make one of two unprovable assumptions about 'ufonauts'.

● They do not have carbon-based bodies like ours, but are constructed according to a totally unknown principle.

● They can travel at speeds faster than light without disintegration.

CLOSE ENCOUNTERS

The composer Stockhausen claims that his music comes from the star Sirius B. Has a remote African tribe been in touch with the same star?

On a Saturday morning in March 1954, Mr George King of Maida Vale, London, was in his bed-sitter washing dishes. Suddenly a voice boomed, 'Prepare yourself. You are to become the voice of Interplanetary Parliament.' He dropped a plate.

George King had had no previous links with Interplanetary Parliament, but he did have a family history of psychic interests and a spare-time interest in yoga. Now he found himself being controlled by an entity who called himself 'The Master Aetherius', and said he was a Venusian spokesman for the Saturn-based Parliament, which had selected King to alert the world to its cosmic responsibilities as a member of the solar system.

Today the Aetherius Society, still listening to revelations from the skies, has spread world-wide. Messages come now through a variety of contacts, including surprisingly Jesus himself. According to the Aetherius Society, Jesus is living at present on his native planet of Venus, and claims to be 'one of the Great Masters', but not the Son of God.

Encounters today

The Aetherius Society is simply offering the fascinations of spiritualism (see *Contacting The Dead*) in a science fiction guise. But many other people have claimed outer-space contacts. In the fifties, one American woman even sued successfully for divorce on the grounds of her husband's admitted adultery with Miss Aura Rains—a Venusian friend.

The fashion was set in 1953 by George Adamski's claims (in *Flying Saucers have Landed*) to have talked to a long-haired Venusian in ski-pants. Adamski's evidence, and especially his photographs, are now generally regarded as bogus, but he retains a following, and at the time he caused a sensation.

Stories of UFO contacts seem to have little factual evidence to back them up. For example, no one has ever produced an indisputably extra-terrestrial artefact—even a key-ring or Coke can. Stories of contacts probably have one of three origins: wish fulfilment; occult manifestations (see *Flying Saucers*); or apparitions created by

some 'collective unconscious' process, and received by someone psychically gifted or vulnerable (see *Ghosts and Apparitions*).

Encounters in history

Recently it has been claimed that the Dogon tribe in Mali traditionally possess an amazing degree of astronomical knowledge about a small star, Sirius B, which was not even photographed until 1970; and that this proves a landing of extra-terrestrial amphibians in the Persian Gulf area at the dawn of our civilization. The evidence offered is not at all conclusive, although some mystery does remain. It is also claimed that Jonathan Swift must have had 'inside information' when he claimed in *Gulliver's Travels* that Mars has twin moons. Not at all; he was merely echoing a speculation of the astronomer Kepler's, which was certainly not based on close encounters of any kind.

Members of the Aetherius Society believe that through contact with extra-terrestrial beings they are performing invaluable services for world peace and survival. Their leader, George King, has blessed 19 'sacred mountains' in the world and organized projects such as storing up 'prayer power' for use in times of emergency.

TELLING THE TALE

The most famous UFO contact story is that of Betty and Barney Hill, an American couple who under hypnosis gave an outstandingly detailed account of abduction aboard a flying saucer (apparently such a terrifying experience that their conscious minds had subsequently blanked it out). Their stories agreed with one another.

However, it has to be remembered that we are not certain about how hypnotism affects the mind, that there is often a good deal of convincing circumstantial evidence in 'regressions' to 'past lives' and in seances (see *Life After Life* and *Contacting The Dead*), and that one mind may well act as the 'control' in a shared apparition (see *Ghosts and Apparitions*). It is possible that one of the two fantasized the experience and transmitted it telepathically to the other. Psychological factors in the case suggest that the fantasy would have been a subconsciously attractive one; and stranger things have happened.

ARE WE ALONE ON EARTH?

Human beings have always fantasized that there might be a secret race of beings living on earth beside us. Belief in fairies, for instance, has persisted down through history. Scholars nowadays dismiss fairy legends as one of three things:

● A corruption of old superstitions about ancestral spirits.

● Primitive beliefs about the elemental spirits of nature.

● Folk memories of the original inhabitants of the country who were driven into hiding by invaders.

But Air Chief Marshal Lord Dowding, who investigated hundreds of reports, came to accept that there was sufficient evidence for an unbiassed person to believe in fairies. It seems likely, however, that fairy experiences boil down to an amalgam of 'ghost imprintings' on an area (see *Ghosts and Apparitions*), poltergeist activity (see *Mindforce*), and wishful thinking or make-believe.

Modern-day fantasies of unknown races, such as the 'men in black' who sometimes threaten UFO observers, are probably updated versions of the old fairy theme. It is interesting that UFO sightings are nowadays heavily reported in areas where in previous centuries there were tales of fairy contacts.

WAS GOD AN ASTRONAUT?

Scientists have discredited almost all his theories. Yet Erich von Däniken still finds an enormous following for his ideas. Is he a charlatan or a persecuted crusader?

Von Däniken's theories about visits from spacemen are based on scattered evidence from around the world. For example, he claims that this ancient Japanese sculpture is clearly wearing spacemen's goggles.

Erich von Däniken at the site of the ancient Tiahuanaco civilization, which he dates variously as originating in 1000 BC and 600 BC. Radio-carbon dating consistently gives a date of AD 800.

In 1967 a Swiss hotel manager published his first book. Within five years it was a best-seller in 26 languages, had been turned into a successful film, had inspired hosts of imitations, and had made its author very wealthy. Its claim: that the 'gods' of the past were actually astronauts.

Erich von Däniken's book, *Chariots of the Gods?*, was not propounding an original theory; it had been advanced by others before, including Louis Pauwels and Jacques Bergier, and probably originated in a minor work by Maurice Jessup in 1953. But von Däniken was the first to make it popular. He was writing at a time when Westerners were losing their faith, both in traditional religion and also in science's ability to solve the world's problems. A new, scientific

religion, which held out some hope, seemed to be needed. The was-God-an-astronaut theory was ready-made for the purpose.

Stating the exact theory is difficult; von Däniken abruptly changes it, with conflicting claims, from book to book (he has now written six). Basically, he seems to believe that the human race was programmed with intelligence by a race of space visitors (who thus 'created' us 'in their own image' from unintelligent hominoid material); that the Bible and other religious books contain garbled accounts of our contacts with the space visitors; and that the solution to our human problems will be to make contact with our creators once again.

Problems in the theory

The evidence von Däniken presents is contradictory and slipshod. Figures are wildly inaccurate, place-names are misspelled, geographical locations are confused. He claims that our knowledge of history for the last 2,000 years is acceptably accurate; then he dismisses it when talking about South America. In different books he dates the Tiahuanaco ruins at 1000 BC and at 600 BC (the actual date should be AD 800).

He blithely ignores problems for his theory, and relies on several false claims. *Every single statement* in one paragraph about the Great Pyramid, and in another about the New Testament, is absolutely untrue. Four months after publishing *Gold of the Gods*, which contains an account of his tunnel explorations in Ecuador, he admitted that he had never been within a hundred miles of the site.

There seems no evidence for, and much against, his theory. To state just one problem: if *we* could not have evolved to our present state of intelligence, or been created that way, what of the astronauts? Who created them? And who created *their* creators. . .?

'It's true,' he admitted to *Playboy*, 'that I accept what I like and reject what I don't like, but every theologian does the same.'

Obviously von Däniken's theories totally contradict the facts of Christianity. But sadly, this contradiction seems to stem from a total ignorance of what Christianity is. He pictures Christians as devout bewildered people struggling to read ideas into obscure manuscripts. He has no awareness that the message of the Bible is plain, reliable and makes sense as it stands, nor that Christians claim to enjoy a life-giving personal encounter with the real Creator of the human race.

WAS GOD A MUSHROOM?

Another fanciful account of the origin of Hebrew religion which has become popular recently is John Allegro's 'mushroom myth'. Allegro, lecturer in Biblical Studies at Manchester, and an authority on Sumerian languages, claims that by tracing Hebrew words back to their origins it is possible to see that Israelite religion (and original Christianity) was derived from a secret fertility cult. The cult was based on the consumption of the drug *amanita* which comes from a certain mushroom. The New Testament, he says, is full of coded references enshrining the secrets of the cult. However, there are one or two small problems:

● We do not know that the drug ever grew in Palestine.

● The whole theory depends on the idea of a linguistic exchange between Indo-European and Semitic languages, which seems implausible; it also assumes that words *always* retain their original meanings, which is not true.

● Allegro ignores the Old Testament's absolute hostility to fertility cults.

● He offers no explanation of the dynamic life of Christians (unaided by mushrooms) down the centuries and today.

All in all, the theory does not seem to be taken seriously by anyone but John Allegro himself.

Von Däniken claims that the huge statues on Easter Island could only ever have been made by advanced spacemen. But in 1956, the explorer Thor Heyerdahl and seven helpers easily carved a new statue in three days, using only stone tools!

EVIDENCE FOR FAITH?

Miraculous events have often been presented as evidence for faith in God. But do they really prove anything?

The most recent American study suggests that the Turin shroud is in fact a fake. But there are plenty of people who think that this is the face of Christ.

Outside a church in the French town of Arles-sur-Tech is a marble sarcophagus which weeps. There are no apparent reasons. It is not condensation; nor is there a spring in the neighbourhood. Yet it keeps suddenly producing water. Its usual output is up to two pints a day, although in the past it has produced many gallons at a time.

In a chapel by Naples Cathedral lies a reliquary containing the blood of St Januarius, martyred in AD 305. As one would expect, by now it is blackened and solid—except in May, September and December, when at certain religious feasts the contents magically liquefy and look like fresh blood.

Over the high altar in Turin Cathedral, in a silver chest behind two iron grilles, lies a piece of cloth which many people believe to be the actual burial shroud of Jesus Christ. Dr Max Frei, a criminologist, has studied the pollen grains found on the shroud and believes that it must at some stage have really come from Palestine. Upon the cloth are faint imprints showing the outline of a naked Jew's body, as he would have been laid out in death. The wounds in the body are consistent with the wounds Christ suffered on the cross. The mysterious marks do not seem to have been painted on.

But this theory involves incredible assumptions, for the evidence for the resurrection is one of the strongest parts of the Christian church's case for its claim that Jesus is alive today. From the facts we know, it seems impossible that any other theory (for example, that the Romans or Jews removed the body, that grave robbers took it, or that the disciples stole it) could be true. Lord Lyndhurst, one of Britain's greatest ever legal minds, commented, 'I know pretty well what evidence is; and I tell you, such evidence as that for the resurrection has never broken down yet.'

Moreover, there is no good medical evidence to show that the shroud *does* suggest continuing life. If the shroud fails to prove the resurrection, it fails to disprove it, too.

What does it mean?

Is any of this evidence for the truth of Christianity? Probably not— although the shroud has convinced some sceptics (including Ian Wilson, writer of a best-selling book on the shroud) that Jesus was the Son of God. In the case of the French sarcophagus, it seems more likely that there is a natural explanation which as yet we do not understand.

The miracles which Jesus performed were not arbitrary, meaningless party tricks, but were each performed as 'signs' with a definite purpose. In a lesser way, the same seems true of St Januarius' blood; when the faithful are not quite faithful enough, the liquefaction fails to happen, as a warning. This suggests the involvement of extra-sensory powers in the process.

The shroud, if it is a fraud, is impossible to explain. There is striking evidence to support its claim. But serious questions remain unanswered—we do not know much about its history, for one thing. If the early church preserved it, it seems remarkable that they said so little about it. And on the evidence of the shroud, Jesus' body was not washed before burial—which appears to contradict the account in John's Gospel. Ian Wilson has answers for each of these points, but some doubt must remain.

A few years ago 'John Reban', alias 'Hans Naber', a writer of uncertain credentials, claimed that the bloodstains on the shroud proved that the body was not actually dead. After all, corpses do not bleed. Thus, presumably, Christ revived in the tomb and later made his escape. This theory has recently been revived by Rodney Hoare, who believes that the guards placed at the tomb decided to rob it, and that Jesus' followers removed his body and nursed him back to health.

STIGMATA

Clemente Dominguez is a heretic, according to the Roman Catholic Church. But the self-styled 'Pope of Seville'—an ex-insurance clerk who rules his followers from a green corrugated plastic 'Vatican' in Andalusia—has several hundred devoted adherents world-wide, who believe implicitly in the sanctity of their chain-smoking Pope. One of the reasons is that since 1971 he has occasionally experienced 'stigmata'—real wounds, corresponding to the wounds of Christ, which magically appear on his forehead and chest.

Stigmata have appeared sporadically in church history since the thirteenth century, and several cases have been recorded this century. But the Catholic church has always manifested a healthy scepticism; even the most famous stigmatic this century, Therese Neumann of Konnersreuth, was disowned by the church 12 years after first exhibiting the wounds. Auto-suggestion seems the most likely cause of some stigmata, because the wounds often appear where Jesus' wounds were traditionally thought to have been—for example nailprints in the hands—rather than where they would have been—in this case on the wrists. And the possibilities of fraud are vast.

OUR LADY OF FATIMA

On 13 May 1917 a ten-year-old Portuguese peasant girl, Lucia dos Santos, was tending sheep with her cousins Francisco and Jacinta when suddenly a lady appeared to them and announced that she was 'the Lady of the Rosary'. She continued to appear before the children every month thereafter, always on the thirteenth, except in August when she materialized on the nineteenth. The children had been interrogated and threatened by the civil authorities, but their stories had aroused a great deal of curiosity, and in the August vision the Lady promised 'a great miracle' for October.

Consequently, on 13 October there were about 70,000 in the crowd when the Lady appeared once again to the children. This time she announced herself as the Lady of the Rosary and asked for a chapel to be built in her name. Simultaneously, the crowd of adults witnessed 'a miraculous solar phenomenon': the sun seemed momentarily to be falling earthwards.

Although the visions were accepted in 1930 as appearances of the Blessed Virgin Mary by the Roman Catholic authorities, other Christians are sceptical about them. For one thing, the Bible never directs that Mary is to receive worship in her own right, and never suggests that she was in fact specially venerated by early Christians. For another, some of the utterances of the Lady seem to contradict the teachings of the Bible. Finally, the Fatima episode is too vulnerable to other explanations—mass hysteria, collective apparition and so forth—to be intrinsically convincing.

WHAT DOES IT MEAN?

Exotic, extraordinary, fictitious, true? Can anything conclusive be said about the world of mysteries?

Some of the information in this book is almost certainly wrong. Exploring mysteries is a tricky business, and there are many pitfalls for the unwary. Fraudulent claims abound. Sometimes psychics start faking results because of the pressure of success; audiences expect results, and when none are forthcoming, the temptation to maintain one's reputation with a little imposture can be hard to resist.

Fraud, conscious and unconscious

Arthur Ford, one of the leading mediums of this century, had a weakness for alcohol, and is known to have falsified some effects when most under pressure. As a result, it is almost impossible to assess the true worth of his career.

Sometimes faking occurs subconsciously. Medium Eusapia Palladino, who undoubtedly cheated occasionally, asked Professor Lombroso, 'Watch me or I'll cheat; John King makes me do it'—John King being her control spirit. On the other hand, the enemies of paranormalists have sometimes planted evidence to incriminate their psychic investigatees. Even the great Houdini may have 'framed' psychic Margery Crandon.

Confusingly, often those who are duped like it, and go to amazing lengths to convince themselves that the phenomena are real. William Roy was a spiritualist fraud who confessed his crimes in a five-part newspaper series in 1958. Ten years later, he was exposed again, working under the name 'Bill Silver'—and it turned out that some of his followers knew he was Roy, yet trusted him nonetheless.

Unexaminable evidence

Some phenomena are impossible to 'prove' in a scientific sense. Lobsang Rampa, for instance, who claimed to be a Tibetan lama and wrote best-selling books of occult lore based on his biography, was revealed by a Sunday newspaper to be in actuality Cyril Henry Hoskins, an ex-plumber from Weybridge. 'Rampa' immediately claimed to have swapped identities with Hoskins via astral travel. And who can prove he didn't?

But the biggest problem in paraphysical research is 'resistentialism'. This term describes the peculiar habit that psychic phenomena have of resisting examination by researchers. Spectacular PK powers suddenly vanish when the

sensitive goes into a laboratory; UFOs appear at the one moment when there is no film in the camera; ghosts fail to materialize when the ghost hunters set up their equipment. Paranormal phenomena seem to take on a life of their own, rather than following strict scientific laws of cause and effect. As Jacques Vallée confessed about UFOs, 'No matter what approach I take, I can never explain more than half the facts.' It is almost as if a real personality is producing confusing, mischievous results to baffle the researcher.

The magician Harry Houdini waged a campaign to show up fraudulent practices by spiritualists. He claimed to be able to duplicate all their activities merely by conjuring tricks. This picture shows his deliberate faking of a 'spirit photograph' of himself with Abraham Lincoln. However, Houdini himself is thought to have rigged some evidence in his over-zealous attempts to show up other people's forgeries.

Does Loch Ness have a monster? Thousands of people would testify to having seen something in the Scottish loch, but so far the monster, if it is there, has defied conclusive examination. For one thing, the loch is just too vast, deep and dark to be thoroughly searched. But there seem to be other problems, too. One investigator says, 'It's a disturbing fact that hardly any of the original negatives of the better Loch Ness monster photographs since 1933 have survived. Nessie pix are supernaturally accident-prone.'

WHAT DOES IT MEAN?

Is there any way of making sense of the jumbled heap of paranormal claims which confront us? Are we condemned merely to endless speculation, with no sure way of telling the true from the false, the phenomenal from the fraudulent? It is certainly true that simple answers will not suffice. To sweep the whole confused pile under the carpet with explanations such as, 'It's all fraudulent', or 'It's all the work of the devil', or 'It's all tremendous, all a manifestation of the great New Age' would mean ignoring a great deal of the evidence.

Yet it is not impossible to formulate some important principles to guide us in our explorations. These are some of the points which seem to me most crucial.

Unreliable data?

Deceptions take place, and it would be naive to ignore the fact. Serious research into the paranormal must be based upon reliable, tested data—not wild third-hand claims in popular paperbacks, which is unfortunately the source of many people's opinions of the paranormal world. There is not currently enough of this data available to warrant a hundredth of the confident speculations advanced by sensationalist authors.

Christopher Evans has traced how mythical claims of UFO sightings reappear in paperback after paperback—because none of the authors bothers to check with the original source. *Alpha* magazine has researched the famous story of 'Lord Dunsany's ghost', celebrated in hundreds of popular ghost books, only to find that there is no foundation to it whatsoever. It is vital that our opinions should be founded upon established fact, not distortions—whether the distortions are caused by inaccurate reporting, wilful fraud, psychological compensation, or interference by mischievous spirit powers (a possibility which must not be discounted).

Normal laws

Some 'paranormal' phenomena are really 'normal'; we just don't understand the laws governing them. Falls of fish from the sky, spontaneous combustion, ley lines and dowsing—these things *could* be simple manifestations of scientific principles on which we haven't yet stumbled. If so, to condemn them without

investigation would be to fall into the error of the 'conservatives' who attacked Galileo and Copernicus for their genuine scientific explorations.

Not evil—but not safe

Some 'psychic' abilities may not be inherently satanic; but this is no reason for justifying their use. Ena Twigg, the famous medium, cannot

It looks like a conclusive picture of flying saucers, but this picture has a completely natural explanation. The shapes in the sky over a Brazilian town are 'standing clouds'—a rare meteorological phenomenon.

remember a time when she was unable to see the misty shapes of 'spirit people'; she believes she was born that way. Matthew Manning had no occultist past when as a boy he began to experience poltergeist manifestations and became a channel for automatic writing. One Christian theory is that psychic ability is a 'leftover' from before the Fall, the time of man's rebellion against God. Perhaps all men once had these powers, but separation from God has ruined them for most of us.

However, since even the best of psychics now possesses these powers imperfectly, and since they are so vulnerable to demonic counterfeit and misuse, to exploit psychic awareness is to open oneself up to unforeseeable spiritual dangers.

Supernatural deceit

Some phenomena suggest that an underlying intelligence may be playing tricks on us. This is what the Bible suggests. 'We are fighting ... against the wicked spiritual forces in the heavenly world,' it claims, 'the rulers, authorities and cosmic powers of this dark age.' It is easy to become paranoid about demons; but it is only realistic to reflect that if there are *good* supernatural powers there may as easily be *evil* ones. It would be foolish to entrust oneself unreservedly to a force whose origins were unknown.

Beliefs

Many people today are willing to build their deepest beliefs about life around supernatural phenomena they do not fully understand. The Bible, by contrast, invites us into a personal relationship and growing friendship with the God who made both the spirit and the physical worlds.

The proof of genuine spiritual life is not that we are able to perform one or two isolated, bizarre, and usually pointless supernatural stunts. It is that we have made the acquaintance of our Creator by believing in Jesus Christ, and can prove his existence daily in the new purposeful, peaceful life he shapes for us.

We may not know all there is to know about the paranormal. But we can know God, who does. In the security of his friendship we find what years of supernatural experiences will never yield: the true meaning of life itself.

GLOSSARY

Apparition The seeming appearance of someone distant or dead.

Apport Material object which appears to defy natural laws by materializing suddenly or penetrating solid matter.

Asport Opposite of apport; object which disappears from a room and reappears elsewhere.

Astral body Replica of physical body composed of delicate matter, reputedly capable of travelling through space with ease when separated out from physical body.

Astrology Means of assessing the influence of heavenly bodies upon earthly affairs.

Automatism Ability to produce writing, drawings, and music spontaneously, without any conscious effort of one's own.

Cabbala (Kabbalah/Qabalah) Collection of occult Jewish lore, supposed to have been revealed by God to Abraham, but actually nothing whatsoever to do with genuine Judaism. A strong influence on European magicians such as Aleister Crowley.

Clairvoyance The psychic ability to see things or people, past, present or future, which cannot be seen by less gifted individuals.

Collective unconscious Memory traces from former generations of human beings, which may still affect our minds. The phrase comes from the psychologist Jung.

Cryptomnesia Unconscious memory, sometimes released by hypnotism; can be an explanation for unexpected information divulged in trance.

Ectoplasm Strange gelatinous mass exuded from a medium's body while in trance. Opinions vary as to whether or not any such substance really exists.

Extra-sensory perception (ESP) Ability to receive or project information by means other than the generally recognized senses.

Levitation Phenomenon in which objects or persons rise and hover in the air, contrary to the laws of gravity.

Leys Alleged patterns of alignments between megalithic remains and natural features, first observed by Alfred Watkins in 1921.

Magick Attempt to harness miraculous power (as distinct from 'magic', which often refers only to the illusions of stage conjurors).

Mediumship Apparent ability to act as intermediary between the spirit world and the everyday world.

Numerology Attempt to analyse character or foretell the future by the examination of numbers.

Occult Literally 'hidden' or 'secret'. Generally applied to 'secret knowledge' of the supernatural and secret rites and ceremonies.

Ouija board Device for gaining messages from the dead. Letters of the alphabet are placed in a circle around a table, and an upturned glass or other easily-moving device slides about from letter to letter when all 'sitters' place one finger upon it.

Paranormal All phenomena outside usual explanations of cause and effect.

Parapsychology Research and experimental work in areas such as ESP and PK.

Poltergeist Seemingly mischievous ghost, given to causing disarray and noise but using a minimum of energy. Probably produced by human (unconscious) mental processes.

Precognition Knowledge of future events, arrived at in a paranormal way.

Premonition Awareness of impending tragedy.

Psi Term invented by J.B. Rhine to describe psychic abilities such as clairvoyance, precognition, telepathy and psychokinesis.

Psychokinesis (PK) Power of the mind to affect other people and objects.

Scrying Gazing into a mirror, bowl of water, crystal ball, or other object, in order to see and interpret visual images (usually of future events).

Seance Gathering of people to establish contact with the dead.

Stigmata Wounds, marks or spots that bleed, corresponding with the wounds of Christ; perhaps caused by auto-suggestion.

Teleportation Ability of people or objects to transport themselves from one place to another by paraphysical means.

Wicca Name used for the 'religion' of witchcraft by its adherents.